HIGH-MOUNTAIN
TWO-MANNER

HIGH-MOUNTAIN TWO-MANNER

*A Montana smokejumper recalls
hitting the silk and the books
in his college years*

To Bob Moore,

With compliments from Del Kellog, a friend, a college classmate, and a fellow smokejumper.

Enjoy the ride!

— Frank Fowler

9/28/14

Frank Fowler

To order additional copies of this book, contact:
Xlibris Corporation
1-888-795-4274
www.Xlibris.com
Orders@Xlibris.com
31329

CONTENTS

To my mother
who parachuted 28 times.

ACKNOWLEDGMENTS

Purple ribbons go to: Jim Fowler for his numerous readings of the manuscript and his continued encouragement; Ken Marsden for painting the cover picture; and Laura Horst for working her magic on cleaning up old photographs.

Special thanks to those who read the manuscript and made suggestions for improvement: my wife Corky, my sister June, my brother Bill, Ron and Charlene Loge, Alan Weltzien, and Pat Shannon.

My heartfelt thanks to my smokejumper friends who, during the writing of this memoir, shared their memories of that special time when we jumped together.

INTRODUCTION

When my smokejumping days ended in the fall of 1954 my mother encouraged me to write about them. I had written her a detailed account of each jump, which she not only saved, but typed so they could be more easily read, omitting the more personal parts intended only for her. She was certain a good magazine article or two was mixed in there somewhere. For various reasons I was not inclined to respond to her prodding.

I had copies of some letters stashed away, but several years after her death, when her possessions were finally sorted out, my brother sent me a complete set. Reading through them, I was amazed at the detail and how much I had forgotten. It also surprised me that my memory of some events had changed from the written account. It was exciting to revisit those days.

Still, it was several years after retirement before I seriously considered writing a memoir. I began to pull together the remaining artifacts: some newspaper articles, a few pieces of equipment, and my diaries (we were required to keep a daily account of our activities, primarily to keep track of our time, but I often made brief notes on any matter that interested me).

Wanting more, I went to the smokejumper base in Missoula and obtained permission to review the fire log sheets that covered the years I had jumped. Dispatchers routinely record statistics for each fire, such as: the fire name, location, and size; the names of the jumpers and spotter involved; the type of aircraft used; and the time of occurrence of various steps of the operation. Fortunately the historic value of these data has been recognized by succeeding generations of jumpers and the file is carefully preserved. They contain a treasure trove of information.

I took copious notes concerning those fires on which I had participated. In addition, I began to gather information from jumpers with whom I had associated or fought fire.

At first, my objective was to relate only smokejumping experiences, but I soon realized other aspects of those years were intertwined, so the scope was expanded to include college experiences, and jobs not associated with the smokejumping project.

As I progressed, it became apparent that many terms were specific to fire fighting or smokejumping. Definitions have been included for most, but some may have been missed. One term, "two-manner," gave me particular difficulty because of its colloquial nature. Smokejumpers often call a two-man fire a "two-manner," and a four-man fire a "four-manner," but perhaps because "two-manners" were my favorite, I remember the term primarily associated with them.

*   *   *

The letters to my mother included in this memoir have been edited for the sake of clarity and ease of reading. All are italicized so they can be easily recognized for what they are. I tried to maintain their integrity and not taint the spirit of the writing as it appeared 50 years ago.

CHAPTER 1

The Early Years

Washington, D.C.'s residential streets were alive with commercial activity in the 1930s. Many neighborhoods contained blocks with 100 residences, resulting in a concentration of people. The Holmes Bakery delivered bread and pastries right to the door in a horse-drawn wagon emblazoned with a sign reading, "Holmes to Homes." Cheese bread flashes in my memory, partially because we thought the taste of cheese in bread was unique, but also because it was uncut and cylindrical. It was baked with concentric bands around the loaf, like corrugated metal culvert pipe, indicating where it was to be sliced.

The milkman left bottles of milk in the insulated metal box on the front porch, but I rarely saw him since he came so early in the morning. My sister June claims he carried enough milk to make deliveries to several houses before returning to the wagon, and the horse would proceed on its own initiative to the point where the delivery man would pick up more milk.

The alley, however, was the hub where most of the selling took place. Coal was dumped by the ton, soon followed by a knock on the back door by someone trying to hustle a job hauling it from the alley to a basement window in a bushel basket.

The iceman came every other day. From the alley he could see the ice sign at the back door and tell how much was needed that day. The sign was square with a black line from opposite corners making four triangles. One triangle was red with 50 written in the center; one was blue with 25; still another was yellow with 10; and the last one was white with nothing on it.

The sign would be turned so the color representing the desired amount of ice was on top. The iceman could tell by the color what amount was needed, even from a distance. With this system he could split the ice order with his pick and haul it to the house, making just one trip.

The watermelon season could never be missed because we all heard the vendor sing in a loud melodious fashion: "ICE COLD WATERMELON—RED TO THE RIND."

Routinely we would also hear a trash picker bark his presence, "OLD RAG MAN," in a monotonous, sing-song fashion. His call puzzled me because I thought he was saying "Old Rag-man," instead of "Old-rag Man." Without really thinking about it, I figured he was just trying to make folks feel sorry for him so he might possibly get a few more rags.

When the fresh vegetable truck came down the alley the vendor would stop, prop up the sides, and yell, "HERMAN! FRESH VEGETABLES!" A hubbub of activity followed as the neighborhood women took advantage of the fresh farm produce. I didn't recognize Herman as a person's name, but rather as another word for what he was selling. So whenever someone said "Herman," I instantly pictured vegetables. I hadn't realized that this kind of association of a person's name with a product or activity was such a common practice for me until years later when I thought about my introduction to Richard Halliburton.

My mother was an ardent fan of Richard Halliburton who was well known in the 1920s and 1930s. He was born in 1900 and developed an extreme desire to travel and explore—consequently he spent the major part of his life after college doing just that. But he more than traveled; he had a knack for seeing the world in an unusual and daring way. He swam the Panama Canal, crossed the Alps on an elephant, and plunged into the pool at night in the locked garden of the Taj Mahal. He once received a commission to travel anywhere he liked and write about it as he pleased. Some of his exploits appeared periodically in newspaper articles while his travels were in progress, but many were also later published in books.[1]

Halliburton frequently wrote to his parents and recounted his experiences in great detail. In 1939 he attempted to cross the Pacific Ocean in a Chinese junk, but a storm resulted in the loss of the craft and all on board. His parents had his letters published in a book, so even this last trip was shared in detail with his many followers. My mother would read his letters in a way that I was vicariously witnessing his exploits. It was no wonder that I, too, became completely absorbed in his quest for adventure. And once again a name was

---

[1] Some books by Richard Halliburton are *Royal Road to Romance*, 1925, *Seven League Boots*, 1935, and *Second Book of Marvels: the Orient*, 1938.

equated with an activity—Richard Halliburton became synonymous with high adventure. I noticed as she read, Halliburton's letters were frequently signed with the initial "R." I told my mother I would some day write letters to her about my adventures and would sign them with an "R."

"I'm sure you'll have much to write about when you begin to travel, but why not sign them with an 'F' if you don't wish to use your whole name?" my mother logically asked.

"There's no excitement in an 'F,'—everybody knows if you are really having an adventure, you'd have to sign it with an 'R,'" I answered.

"Nonsense. Richard Halliburton is special, but so are you."

"I still like 'R,'" I persisted.

"Well, you can sign your letters anyway you please, but if you use an "R," I will be thinking of something that reminds me of you, not of Richard Halliburton."

"Like what?" I asked, knowing that she was thinking of more than she was telling me.

"Roverboy. It seems to me if Frank doesn't suit you, Roverboy does." It must have satisfied me because I don't remember the discussion continuing—at that time anyway.

And so it seemed, even in those early years, that my mother was preparing me to look for adventure in my life. It was a recurring theme in many of our activities together, but her instructions and lessons were equally centered on religious and moral principles.

My family was a little unusual compared to others in our neighborhood. Twenty-three years separated my oldest brother, Bruce, and me. In between were six siblings, Ella, Earl, Hazel, Dan, Bill, and June, but by the time I entered kindergarten only we youngest three were still in school. Because of problems in two of my sisters' marriages, two of my nephews lived in our household, one four months my junior; the other four years. They became my playmates since the sibling next to me, June, was four-and-a-half years older, and Bill, the brother closest to my age, was almost 11 years older.

My father died at the age of 55 when I was six, so my mother worked outside the home for the first time in her life at age 52. Work was hard to find, expecially for a woman with no business training, so my mother worked at a variety of jobs at rock-bottom wages. She gradually worked her way into a more responsible position in a department store, but her salary was always barely adequate. Still, she maintained a positive outlook and dwelt on the bright side of life.

*   *   *

From my earliest childhood memories, my family visited the various museums and historic spots in and around Washington, D.C. We traveled all over the city and surrounding area on the Capital Transit System, mostly by streetcar. Each week the adults in my family would buy a pass for $1.25 which enabled them to travel to and from work at no additional cost, and also allowed two children free passage on Sunday. Sometimes an adult and two children, other times more, would go sight-seeing on Sunday afternoon.

We never lacked places to go and things to see. I always liked to visit the museums (which are free in Washington). The Smithsonian was particularly intriguing with its magnificent display of high altitude capsules which reached heights of 14 miles suspended by a balloon, or Lindbergh's small single engine airplane, *The Spirit of Saint Louis*. Its interior seemed so archaic with its wooden framing and exposed cables that I didn't even comprehend it had been only a dozen years since his historic non-stop flight from New York to Paris.

These museum trips often left me with the feeling that all the exciting things had been done, and nothing very challenging remained on which I would be able to test my mettle or exercise my adventurous spirit. I didn't fret about these matters, but I did think about them.

*   *   *

I was raised in the Depression years. Everyone felt the effects of tough economic times, but because we were all in the same boat, it seemed normal, particularly for us children. My parents were both deeply involved in religious activities and regularly attended all the functions of Bethany Baptist Church. My father loved baseball and would frequently watch the Senators play at Griffith Stadium on Sunday. However, when he became a deacon in the church, he refused to go to the ball park on Sunday because he felt he would be setting a bad example—after all, going to a ball game wouldn't be keeping the Sabbath Day holy.

My mother faithfully participated in the church's women's activities. I remember in particular going with her when she joined other ladies of the church in a quilting bee. I would play with other tots in the nursery while the women gathered around a huge quilting table and talked and sewed.

She was also involved in the Woman's Christian Temperance Union, at least to the extent that she made certain her children participated in the grade-school subsidiary, Loyal Temperance Legion (LTL). My sister, June, and I attended many of these meetings and memorized essays berating the evils of alcohol and nicotine. We recited them in church before the congregation. I was envious of June because she did so well in her orations, and I did so poorly.

*   *   *

Jack, the nephew four months my junior, and I were inseparable. We were together from our beginnings and frequently dressed alike in our preschool years. My mother often took us for walks, pretending we were explorers. She had a way of making the mundane not only interesting, but exciting.

Once Jack was with us on a hot summer's day hiking in a residential area of the city. We had become thirsty and began to ask for something to drink. We had nothing with us and there didn't appear to be anyplace to easily get a drink. Then we spotted a man with a snow-cone cart. Several folks were in a line waiting their turn while the vendor scraped a perforated metal scoop over a block of ice. When the scoop was full of "snow" he would plop it into a cup and ask, "What flavor would you like?"

Jack asked, "Grandma, can we have a snow cone? Please?"

"It would be nice, wouldn't it," my mother replied, "but I don't have the money."

"We're very thirsty," I pleaded. "And they only cost five cents."

"I'll check my purse, but I'm almost certain I don't have the money."

By this time those who had been waiting had gotten their cones and left. After a thorough search, my mother found three cents in her purse. "Let's see what we can do with this," she announced.

She went to the vendor and said, "Would you please give me three cents worth of ice and distribute it equally in three cups?"

The man didn't say a word, but he took the money and made three snow cones without any flavoring. We walked to a nearby bench and sat down. Then my mother did a strange thing. She said, "I think I'll have blueberry syrup on mine," and pretended like she had a bottle in her hand and poured make-believe flavoring on her snow cone.

"And what flavoring would you boys like?" she asked politely.

"I want raspberry," Jack said excitedly.

"I'll have lime," I joined in.

As we sat on the bench savoring our treat, my mother said, "This is absolutely delicious, but I wonder what yours tastes like. May I have a taste of yours, Frank?"

I offered my cup and she took a small bite. "Mmmmm, very good."

We proceeded to take bites of each other's cones and commented on the various flavors. It was a delightful afternoon.

I have often thought of that day and the lesson learned. It was one my mother taught numerous times during my growing up (and to my siblings as well, I'm sure). It's obvious she was telling us to make the most of what we had. But there was more. She was saying many things in life can't be controlled and we needed to learn to live with them, and to look for ways to turn adversity into something positive.

Pollyanna, you say? Absolutely. Idealistic? That was my mother. She had the power, even in the face of great adversity, to "look for the silver lining." Inevitably she found it, and joyously celebrated it.

Mother loved books and read to us often—*Gulliver's Travels*, *Swiss Family Robinson*, and others, mostly of an adventurous nature. She also loved to read poetry. A quality in her voice held me spellbound even when I didn't understand what was being said. On occasion she had me repeat a poem until I learned it by heart, the way we did with memory verses in Sunday School. She said one was mine. If I wanted it, all I had to do was commit it to memory. I did, and can recite the lines to this day. It was *The Winds of Fate*, by Ella Wheeler Wilcox. I had intended to include it here, but Doubleday denied me permission to print, so I will simply reveal its meaning:

> The first verse tells of two ships at sea being pushed by the same wind, but they travel in opposite directions. This is because the direction of travel is determined by how the sails are set and not by wind direction.

> The second verse makes an analogy between sailing and life, pointing out that our fate is more a matter of attending to our soul rather than what obstacles may be put in our path.

*　　*　　*

It always struck me that my siblings were engaged in unusually exciting jobs. Bruce was an officer in the navy and in charge of communications on a ship in the Atlantic during World War II. Dan, also a naval officer, was a chaplain on an aircraft carrier in the Pacific. Bill, a sergeant in the army, was in the Battle of the Bulge. Earl was also in uniform, but his job in the fire department was deemed essential, so he didn't go to war.

Ella worked for the Navy Department, and Hazel, for the Bureau of Engraving, printing money. June had started college in the fall of 1945, but she got married in January 1946 and left with her husband for the Panama Canal Zone. I thought all their vocations and pursuits were on the leading edge of adventure. I was determined to find a niche where I could pursue my own.

*   *   *

With just my sister, Hazel, her son, Rodney, and my mother and me, our large row house was no longer needed. Coupled with the fact that the neighborhood was rapidly deteriorating, it was decided to move to an apartment in a nicer part of the city.

While making preparations for this move, I was given the opportunity to live with my brother, Earl, and his wife, Willie, and their two children, Jimmy and Susan. They lived in Lanham, Maryland, a rural area slowly moving towards suburbia. At that time the landscape still contained dense stands of trees and generous space between houses.

It must have been a tough decision for my mother to make, and while it was never explained to me, she obviously felt life in Lanham would be better for me. Perhaps she had reasoned that I needed more of a father figure. Whatever the reason, I jumped at the chance to make the move. Earl and Willie had always been good to me, Jimmy and I were close friends even though six years separated our ages, and one-year-old Susan was a joy.

I became very active in school, church, and other community activities. I had joined the Boy Scouts when living in Washington and transferred my membership to Lanham. About the time my interest started to wane, a new scoutmaster took charge. His name was E.J. (Joe) Woolfolk, a man who had worked for the U.S. Forest Service in Montana, but was recently transferred to the Washington headquarters. He made me senior patrol leader, perhaps in an effort to keep my interest. It must have worked because I enjoyed my leadership responsibilities and became more involved. At 16 I was given the role of junior assistant scout master, adding to my leadership duties.

I enjoyed the outdoor experiences scouting provided and steadily worked up through the ranks to Life Scout. I only had a few merit badges left to become an Eagle, but so much of my time was taken up with other activities, my advancement in rank slowed. When the troop went to Camp Theodore Roosevelt for an annual two-week summer retreat, we were frequently without adult leadership. But Mr. Woolfolk had organized the troop so we could effectively function without him or the assistant scoutmaster present. Our *esprit de corps* was high and we were the snappiest marching troop at the camp, sometimes to the frustration of those troops with several supervising adults who couldn't seem to get in front of disciplinary problems.

At the beginning of my senior year of high school Mr. Woolfolk was transferred to Missoula, Montana. My interest in scouting once again subsided, not only because Mr. Woolfolk left, but also because I had become more involved in church and school activities.

I graduated from Bladensburg High School in June of 1950 without a plan for the next step. College was not discussed, and the family financial situation was such that if I went, it would have to be on my own initiative and with my own funds. Even though the University of Maryland was within commuting distance, and would be relatively inexpensive, I was not interested in the prospect. I had experienced the contrast of attending a large high school in Washington, D.C. to a smaller one in Bladensburg, Maryland, and therefore felt an aversion to a large college campus. Besides, Maryland offered no course of study I wished to pursue.

I tried to find work, but in those years the country was in a recession and work was scarce. All I could find were low-paying part time jobs, so that's what I did. I carried the hod for brick layers, carried shingles for roofers, ushered in the evenings at a midget auto race track, dug ditches, built fence, and a myriad of other jobs. It was frustrating wanting to work, but not being able to find anything substantial.

Mr. Woolfolk had come to Washington on a temporary assignment and stopped by our house in Lanham to see me.

"Frank, have you ever thought about a career in forestry?" he asked.

"No, I haven't, but it sounds interesting."

"Well, I know you well enough to believe you are well suited to the field, and if you should happen to decide to pursue it as a course of study, I can assure a summer job working in range research in Montana." His words astounded me. I could scarcely believe that the promise of such good fortune had come my way. In spite of the fact that I really didn't know what foresters did, the prospect of going to school to study it intrigued me, and I certainly was drawn to the opportunity to work summers in Montana. At the conclusion of our conversation I said I would write to several colleges to find out more about forestry schools and let him know my decision.

When my brother, Dan, went to college, he worked his way through. One of his jobs was working in the kitchen on campus. It seemed like a good idea, so I inquired about job possibilities at the same time I requested a catalog. I wrote to every college that contained a school of forestry and studied their requirements and costs.

Montana State University (now the University of Montana) was the only school that gave any encouragement for kitchen work. I was hoping it would be enough to pay for my meals, but the highest paying job paid 90 cents an hour—a far cry from covering meal costs, but it was at least something. The real clincher, however, was that every school except Montana required attendance at a forestry summer camp between the junior and senior years. Not only did the summer camp cost additional money, it also precluded the opportunity to earn money. Montana was therefore the only viable alternative. I decided to try it.

I had been saving all of my income, but now I worked every possible waking hour. In spite of the low wages I was able to work long enough hours to amass funds for my first quarter room, board, and tuition. But then an unexpected windfall came my way. June sent me $90.00.

Bruce had put himself through college by attending night classes at George Washington University in Washington, D.C. It wasn't until Dan was of college age that another sibling went on to higher learning, but Dan had difficulty making financial ends meet and borrowed $50.00 from Bruce. When he later went to pay it back Bruce said to add another $50.00 and hold it until another sibling wanted to go to college. Bill, the next in line, was drafted into WWII shortly after graduating from high school and never exercised a college option. June, however, did. Dan gave her the $100.00 with the understanding that she would later add $50.00 and give $150 to me, providing, of course, that I went to college. Before completion of her first year of school she married and went to the Panama Canal Zone, but she had not used all the money Dan had provided. She worked part-time while in school and added those wages back into the pot. She religiously saved the money and was therefore able to give me $90.

I formally applied for enrollment at Montana State University and was accepted—with a job in the kitchen washing pots and pans.

When Dan was in college he would hitch-hike home to save money. I decided to travel the same way to Montana. I shipped a footlocker to Mr. Woolfolk in Missoula with the intention of hitch-hiking with a suitcase, but several days before I was to leave an opportunity arose to accompany some folks driving to Seattle. All I had to do was furnish a couple of character references and agree to chip in $35.00 of gas money. I decided it was a good investment even though their route passed south of Missoula. I was pleased, however, that I would be hitch-hiking for at least part of the way.

The morning I left, my mother saw me off. After meeting my traveling companions, I put my suitcase in the trunk and spoke briefly with her.

"You know, Ma, it could be I won't be able to return for four years," I said, perhaps a bit melodramatically.

"Yes, I know," she replied. "This will be an excellent time for you to write your 'Love, Roverboy' letters."

We hadn't spoke of Richard Halliburton for years, but she remembered our conversation well. It was so typical of her not to say, "Please write often," but to find a way to put me first.

"You mean, 'Love, R.' letters, don't you?" I chided.

"You sign them the way you wish, and I will read the signature the way I wish," she shot back with a smile.

She then handed me an envelope, gave me a kiss and a hug, and I left for the West.

We drove several miles before I opened the envelope. When I did I found two scraps of paper. One was a magazine clipping:

> We grow great by dreams. All big
> men are dreamers. They see
> things in the soft haze of a spring
> day or in the red fire of a long winter's
> evening. Some of us let these great dreams
> die, but others nourish and protect them,
> nurse them through the bad days till they
> bring them to the sunshine and light which
> come always to those who sincerely hope
> that their dreams will come true.
> —Woodrow Wilson

The second scrap was in my mother's handwritten scrawl, "I love you."

Me, Mother, and Jack

E.J. (Joe) Woolfolk, a special man. My mentor.

CHAPTER 2

Freshman Year

My two driving companions and I left Washington, D.C. at 6:30 a.m. Sunday, September 10, 1950. Margaret, the younger of the two in her early fifties, did all the driving, and her aunt Mary, in her mid-sixties, sat next to her doing most of the talking.

My mother and father had been raised in New England, so our family trips had been confined primarily to the Eastern seaboard from Washington to the Boston area, and before long the scenery was new to me. I had expected our travel to be much faster than it turned out to be; however, I wrote to my mother trying to be enthusiastic:

Sunday, September 10, 1950

Dear Ma,

My trip has been fine up to now. The ladies are pleasant except for the fact that they gab a lot. The scenery so far is very much like Pennsylvania—lots of trees and hilly. In Ohio it's starting to get flatter, but by Tuesday I hope to see some real western country.

Today we traveled across the panhandle of Maryland through Hagerstown and Cumberland, across the southwest corner of Pennsylvania and a little piece of West Virginia at Wheeling before entering Ohio. Margaret decided to stop at Springfield which looks to be about three-fourths of the way across the state. We traveled 450 miles in 12 hours. I guess there is no need to hurry, but there are times when I felt like I should be pushing.

We are spending the night in a nice place in Springfield, Ohio. I was somewhat irritated by the fact that Margaret told the proprietor that I was on my way to college and was on a tight budget, so we were looking for inexpensive lodging. Of course I was, but I think she was also trying to get by as cheaply as possible and was just using me as an excuse. At any rate I appreciated the fact that I slept on a cot that only cost one dollar. And I ate dinner for one dollar, so I have no complaints.

Give everyone my love. Will keep you posted.

Love, R.

Monday, September 11, 1950

Dear Ma,

Today was much the same as yesterday except there is more corn. I have never seen so much of it. I'm getting tired of hearing the ladies gab even though they are friendly.

Prices are low. My breakfast cost 50 cents, lunch 35 cents, and dinner 75 cents. And tonight I again got a dollar room. It really goes for three dollars, but the lady running the place gave me a break. I expect Margaret worked her magic again.

Today we went due West across the middle of Indiana and Illinois, passing through Indianapolis and Peoria. We made it just into Iowa after crossing the Mississippi River. [I had tried to talk Margaret into going through Indiana a little farther north so we could stop in South Bend where my brother Dan was living. It wasn't a good idea because it was in between reasonable stopping distances on our itinerary. I also had hoped she would consider traveling to Seattle on US 10 so we could go through Missoula, but she was adamant about taking a more southern route.]

We have stopped in the outskirts of Burlington, Iowa on a farm that has rooms for rent. It's quite beautiful here and the rural atmosphere is inviting. The ladies are going to town early in the morning and I'm going to sleep in. I hope the landlady lets me do some chores on the farm—just to get some exercise.

We traveled 14 hours today, but we hit a lot of detours and it was slow going. Tomorrow we'll be in Nebraska—what I've been waiting for.

Love, R.

Wednesday, September 13, 1950

Dear Ma,

We only traveled half a day yesterday because the ladies took the car for the 2000 mile check-up—it's brand new, you know. I stayed at the tourist home and worked in the milking parlor [barn], *cleaning it up. I appreciated the exercise because I have been sitting so much lately and I'm not used to it. I got an extra big breakfast out of it (in addition to the reduced room rate), so I felt good about it. The lady running the place was swell. In fact, I'd have to say that all the folks we have met along the way have been very friendly and seem to trust everyone.*

With our short day, all we were able to do was cross Iowa and get a few miles into Nebraska. We stopped in Union, a Podunk on the west side of the Missouri River. The room we stayed in was huge and I had to sleep in it with the yappers (ladies, that is). Boy do they harmonize when they snore! Absolutely no more of that!

[Even though Union was a small town, I remember it better than any other place we stopped. A railroad yard was close by with steam engines working all night and making noise with their chugging, slamming cars together, and tooting whistles. The sounds were hauntingly familiar and brought a lonely feeling that I am not able to explain. Trains at night are like that.]

The first two days it rained off and on, but today and yesterday were clear. I still see a lot of corn, but not as much. There are a few more trees, but no pines. We should see sand today—some anyway. I guess I was wrong about Nebraska, Wyoming is the place I want to see.

Love, R.

Thursday, September 14, 1950

Dear Ma,

So far we have gained three hours: one passing through Central Time, one passing through Mountain Time, and here we are not on Daylight Savings Time.

Today was by far my most enjoyable. Nebraska started out with lots of corn, but by the time we approached its western boundary it was sandy. Wyoming, on the other hand, was all waste land with a few hills. [But Wyoming filled me with awe. Just the names of the cities, like Cheyenne and Laramie, were captivating. They seem to come out of a different world, one I had only seen in western movies. The license plates with the bucking bronc were part of this new scene and it all spoke of the wild West, a contrast to the colonial East I was used to. It all instantly felt very comfortable to me because I had always been drawn to open spaces, the frontier, so to speak, and to a place where people dressed in Levis and more relaxed attire. Early in my trip I had begun to buy decals with the name of a town we went through and placed them on my suitcase. Cheyenne and Laramie were two of my prized ones.]

Early this morning we saw a snow-capped mountain. Only one, but it was something I had never seen and it therefore caught my attention. It's getting colder now and the wind is terrible.

We stopped in Little America when driving through Wyoming. The old Little America burned down and they built this one in its place at a different location. It is completely modern and impressive, perhaps mostly because it is in the middle of nowhere.

We passed a number of army convoys today. Some of them stretched for miles.

We see rainbows every day and frequently they are double. The sunrises and sunsets are glorious. I have a hard time deciding which is prettier, but I don't guess I have to. In the evening the sun always sets in the middle of the road as we are traveling due west. Margaret frequently talks about how hard it is to drive while looking into the sun. I offer to drive, but she is very protective of the car.

When we crossed the border into Utah today I was astounded by its beauty. The mountains were red with clay and red bushes. The road followed the valleys and the hills were high on both sides. I have never seen so many dead rabbits. You see them all over—they must get blinded by headlights at night and get slaughtered by the fast moving vehicles.

We went by Ogden and Brigham City but didn't stop. We skirted Great Salt Lake and found it both beautiful and interesting. The high mountains surrounding this area are majestic and lead me to believe that I wouldn't mind living here.

I'm in Idaho now. Tomorrow I hope to be in Walla Walla, Washington, and the next day in Missoula. That will be Saturday. We have had a number of hold ups—detours and such.

We hit a cow today and put a dent in the fender. The cow didn't seem hurt, but it was quite a scare for us and Margaret is sick about the dent.

Riding with these ladies fourteen hours a day drives me bats at times. I had just about decided to part company with them in Wyoming and head north on a more direct route to Missoula, but Margaret pleaded with me to continue to Walla Walla. She said she needed me to read the maps for her as Mary wasn't able to. When I didn't budge, she said she would charge me five dollars less for the gas if I continued. I agreed even though it will take me longer to get to Missoula.

We stopped for the night at Strewell, Idaho. Tomorrow we turn north through the corner of Oregon and into the southeast corner of Washington. The roads from there to Missoula are bad and I may have to travel north to Spokane before I turn east to Missoula.

Did I mention that the folks out here use silver dollars? I got a few. The West is different. I like it.

Love, R.

Friday, September 15, 1950

Dear Ma,

I said in my last letter that Utah was the best, but Idaho ranks right up there. We went over the highest and widest cantilever bridge in the world. It spanned the Snake River 486 feet below. The river itself is not wide, but time has worn a deep canyon through the rock. The valley is green and sprinkled over it are what looks like Lombardy poplar trees. Way up the canyon we could see Blue Lakes which reportedly have no bottom—at least they can't find it. Doesn't sound reasonable, does it?

We had a 13-hour day, and it was slow because we took time out to wash the car and because Margaret drives so slowly. We traveled 400 miles.

I have gotten used to sagebrush after seeing so much in the past few states. I find it interesting and love its smell.

I've seen the capitals of Wyoming, Idaho, Illinois, and Ohio on this trip, even though I really didn't get to visit any of the buildings.

My legs are stiff. If I run around the block my muscles tighten so much I can hardly walk. I really need to get some exercise.

I'm in La Grande, Oregon now and about to go to sleep. By eight tomorrow morning I'll be in Walla Walla where I'll start hitchhiking. I should easily get to Missoula by evening.

Love, R.

Monday, September 18, 1950

Dear Ma,

It was noon before I left the ladies at Walla Walla on Saturday. I managed to be patient even though the slowpoking irritated me. I was happy to at last be on my way alone. I hitch-hiked from there to Missoula in four rides. It was rough.

[My first ride was in a beat-up Ford pickup truck. The motor knocked terribly and seemed to warn that it would quit running at any moment—which it did after traveling about 30 miles. The driver said he had thrown a rod and it couldn't be fixed short of an overhaul. We weren't far from Dayton, Washington and managed to catch a ride to Lewiston, Idaho, but the guy with the crippled Ford got out at Dayton. Missoula is due east of Lewiston, but since there were no highways in that direction I had to travel north for 100 miles before turning east on US 10.

I caught a ride with a young couple going to Spokane, but as we started up the Lewiston Grade I wondered if I was fortunate or not. The road was a nightmare, full of hairpin turns and steep, treeless slopes. We passed many wrecked vehicles that had failed to negotiate curves—we could easily have suffered a similar fate. Riding wasn't comfortable until we got beyond the steep grade, but even then we were traveling too fast. Our arrival in Spokane was truly a blessing.

It was a long time before a truck stopped and gave me my next ride. Luckily he was going all the way to Missoula. It was disappointing that it was dark most of the way because I had eagerly looked forward to seeing Montana, but had to settle for the joy of reaching Missoula and ending my journey.

It was great to once again see my friends, the Woolfolks. Mr. Woolfolk always signed his name as E. J. Woolfolk, because he preferred his middle name, Joseph—his peers called him Joe. I always addressed him as Mr. Woolfolk, although in writing I would often refer to him as E. J. He and his wife, Yvonne, had two children—Mary Jo, a girl in high school; and Jimmy, a boy in grade school. I had visited them in Maryland many times when Mr. Woolfolk held Boy Scout planning meetings at his home, so I viewed going to their home now as a reunion of friends.]

I arrived at Woolfolk's house at midnight. I hated to arrive so late, but they seemed glad to see me. The journey from Maryland took so long that it felt like I was half way around the world.

I'm writing this letter from my dorm room in Jumbo Hall at the university. I met my roommate, Bob Hansen, when he brought his stuff to our room, but haven't seen him since. He's also a freshman forestry student, so we have a couple of things in common.

I'll be pretty busy taking tests and getting my classes lined up, so it will be a few days before I write again.

Love, R.

Missoula was so different from anyplace in Maryland that I was constantly aware of being in a strange but intriguing environment. It was one of the larger cities in Montana with 23,000 people in 1950, but a Chamber of Commerce estimate put the greater metropolitan area at 36,000. I had always lived close to sea level, but Missoula was 3,223 feet high. Unlike the rolling hills of deciduous trees in the East, western Montana was mountainous and the forests were almost entirely coniferous. Mount Sentinel rose abruptly from the edge of the campus to a height of 6,000 feet but that was low compared to the lofty 9,000 foot peaks a few miles away.

The campus was situated on 100 acres plus the 520-acre face of Mt Sentinel immediately adjacent. I thought it rather special that the campus included a mountain, but its uniqueness didn't end there. It also bordered the Clark Fork River—a trout fishery. So a student could hike up a mountain or fish for a trout without leaving campus.

The town of Missoula was a lake bed formed in early geologic time. With the shifting of the earth's crust eons ago, the lake drained leaving a level area in the midst of the mountains. This explains why Missoula itself is so flat and the mountains abruptly rise up from its edges.

The campus was surrounded by a residential district of modest, attractive homes and streets beautifully lined with hardwood trees, primarily maple. The mile walk to town passed through these neighborhoods and it wasn't difficult to understand why Missoula is called "The Garden City."

When I turned down Higgins Avenue the residential area was left behind. Hellgate High School, the Roxy Theater and other businesses lined the street, but it wasn't the main part of town. As I walked over the bridge across the Clark Fork River, I was impressed by the clearness of the water and the nearness of the main part of town to it. This was a dramatic contrast to the muddy Potomac River in Washington, D.C.

When I reached the intersection of Higgins and Front Streets, I could see the light was about to change and stepped off the curb. I had only taken a step when a policeman's whistle blew. I had anticipated the light change and had started across the street a bit early. Certain I had been caught, I leaped back to the curb. Then I noticed that no one else was near me, much less a policeman. After crossing the street, I stood a few minutes to watch the light change again, and realized the whistle was somehow automatically triggered when the light changed. I checked to see if other lights were similarly equipped, but they were not. This incident stayed with me because I never experienced it elsewhere, and it caused me to wonder what was so unique about that particular intersection to warrant a whistling signal.

Jumbo Hall, a sprawling, two-story temporary building, was erected in 1946 to make room for the influx of discharged servicemen going to college on the G.I. Bill. In 1945 enrollment stood at 1,113, but by 1946 it ballooned to 3,299. Enrollment continued to climb until 1948 when the stream of the returning G.I.s began to subside. By 1950 enrollment had dropped to 2,840, but Jumbo Hall was still needed. All of the other campus structures were attractively designed brick buildings; Jumbo was an eyesore. Sound traveled freely through the thin walls and the heating system was so poorly designed that many rooms were cold. Even so, residents of Jumbo possibly shared a stronger camaraderie than existed in Corbin Hall or South Hall—the other two men's dormitories. If you were on a tight budget, Jumbo Hall was your choice. Looking back, the difference between $40 a quarter at Jumbo and $45 at the permanent dorms seems trivial, but at the time it loomed significant.

Bob Hansen and I were assigned a room together because we were both freshmen studying forestry. Bob struck me as a nice enough guy, but I rarely saw him during orientation week because he was interested in a fraternity and spent a lot of time partying with guys on the fast track—a pursuit for which I hadn't the money, time or interest.

On Monday, freshmen were tested to determine if we were adequately prepared for college. I thought I was, but the results of the exams showed otherwise. I was required to enroll in a no-credit, remedial English class commonly referred to as Bonehead English. Secondly, my chemistry score indicated a need for starting at square one, thus having to take three quarters of chemistry instead of two. I felt adequate in both subjects, but resigned myself to a lengthier path to my diploma. I was somewhat reassured when my advisor said I would still be able to graduate in four years, but would have less opportunity for elective courses. Even so, my ego was wounded, and it didn't help when Bob suffered neither of these indignities.

I immediately began washing pots and pans in the South Hall kitchen for evening meals. In addition to those residing there, all the Jumbo Hall residents ate there as well.

During orientation week several activities were scheduled to acquaint freshmen with one another. The first was whitewashing the "M" located on Mount Sentinel 2,100 feet above the campus. This was a major undertaking as the letter was 125 feet high and 100 feet across. A class several decades earlier had formed a brigade that stretched for a quarter of a mile, relaying buckets of shale to form the "M." Succeeding freshman were responsible for freshening up its appearance each fall. We formed a brigade line and passed up the needed lime and water while a crew on top sloshed the slurry over the shale with brooms. Needless to say, it was a messy job, but a lot of fun since the day was warm and enthusiasm ran high.

Another activity was a Frosh Mixer. I asked an upper classman on the work crew at South Hall what a Frosh Mixer was and he explained it was a mixture of ice, ice cream, and flavoring that had been vigorously whipped in a blender and poured into frosted glasses. The evening of the mixer I asked a few fellows I had met at the dorm if they were going over to the student union for some kind of special milk shake. It didn't take long for them to figure out my mistake, and I got ribbed about it for a long time.

The guys living in Jumbo were a friendly bunch and I soon fell in with a comfortable crowd. Several of them belonged to the Wesley Foundation, a college Methodist youth group, and since I had been active in the Methodist Youth Fellowship during my high school years, this seemed like a logical progression. I wasn't so much seeking some kind of religious orientation as I was looking for friends who didn't see drinking as a necessary part of having fun.

The Forestry Club was also a source for a lot of *esprit de corps* and comradeship. Most of the students in the School of Forestry belonged and enthusiastically participated in meetings replete with boisterous renditions of Paul Bunyan type songs.

An article appeared in the Kaimin, the campus newspaper, concerning the rivalry between the Forestry School and the Law School:

A satiric Example of . . .
MSU's Brotherly Love

A calm campus this fall led many to believe that a lady shyster had married a forester during the summer, and that their example had been followed in a "brotherhood" way by their respective clans.

But the feud between lawyers and foresters that originated in 1905 erupted or rather splashed again Wednesday night.

Each fall when freshmen foresters are initiated into the Forestry Club, they are required to sing "Montana Foresters" in the law school halls. The lawyers were wise this year, and when the foresters entered they were met by a blast from a fire hose. The water fight that ensued could nearly be compared with a Japanese typhoon.

From Okinawa to the Oval . . .

This fall wasn't the first time in recent years that the feud was re-ignited. In 1945 three lawyers threatened to sue to the tune of $300 because of "injury to dignity, false imprisonment, and assault and battery."

That outburst was caused by forestry initiates "borrowing" pictures from the lawyers. Later in the evening the lawyers were caught in the forestry school. After a special meeting the lawyers emerged with "shiny-top" haircuts. A local lawyer, interested in keeping the feud out of court, paid for trim jobs by a downtown barber.

Last year the friendly relationship blossomed again when the lawyers found an outhouse chained to the sign in front of their school. Less than two weeks later the pride of the Forestry School, "Bertha," a giant stuffed moose-head, disappeared and a piece of lavatory equipment was found in her place. Two months later "Bertha" was found under some tar paper in a lawyer's garage.

The issue was temporarily settled for the remainder of the year when the foresters accepted a lawyer challenge and then beat the lawyers on the basketball court.

We Only Go to College Once . . .

We realize that at times "reason" is a nonexistent quality when the lawyer-forester feud is in high gear, yet the spirit, interest, and school pride fostered by the respective factions more than compensates for the occasional examples of poor taste. We don't advocate a wholesale "Hatfield and McCoy" rash of incidents on campus, but we do respect schools with signs of "life."—C.H.

*   *   *

One sunny afternoon coming out of the Student Union building, I overheard three fellows engaged in an animated conversation. The guy doing most of the talking was George Ostrum, telling about his summer experience as a smokejumper. I had never heard of smokejumpers before, but his description of fighting forest fires by parachuting on them gripped me. I paused a short distance away and listened for several minutes as he spun his tales. His stories were so captivating I wanted to spend my summers doing the same thing. I immediately began to gather material on smokejumpers, including instructions about how to apply, and often found my thoughts were pre-occupied with the allure of the exciting possibility.

Wednesday, October 11, 1950

Dear Ma,

    I'm at the point now where I can say I'm settled. That means I've bought my clothes, paid my bills and fees, and am engaged in a routine of classes and working that has brought some order to my life.

    I got some shoes fixed. It cost $3.65 for half soles and heals! I had some pants dry cleaned and that cost 65 cents a pair. Seems a bit expensive to me.

    I thought I had a job as a janitor in Jumbo Hall for Saturdays, but there was a mix-up and I lost out. I did land an intermittent one to clean up after dances at the Student Union on the Friday or Saturday evenings when they occur. It's something I can negotiate with each opportunity—meaning that if I wish to attend the dance instead of working, I can. At best it would only occur a couple of times a month and would pay $3.00 a dance, but what the heck, it beats nothing. The lady at the placement office has begun to feel like a friend, and I think she is really trying to find something for me. However, I think my best opportunity rests with E.J. [Woolfolk]. He recently told me that I can count on working in his office over the Christmas holidays and possibly during the day next quarter if I have two hour blocks of time between classes. What a boost that would be.

    Saturday we have a football game here. I almost hope there isn't an opportunity for me to work some place because I'd like to go.

    I have a couple of friends who live in Butte. One of them, Favre, has a mother who wants to meet me, at least that's what Favre says. She heard that there was a boy from Maryland at the university who thought a Frosh Mixer was a drink. (I think I told you about that incident.) Anyway, she told Favre to invite me up next weekend when he goes home to see a high school football game. It sounds like fun. It will cost two bucks round trip to chip in on gas and another buck for the game. Can't really afford it, but I'm gonna splurge.

    . . . Sorry I didn't get this off sooner. In that Oregon football game we were robbed. We had a couple of touchdowns called back due to penalties, but I thought we played a good game otherwise. Wish we had won.

    The weather is fine here—no sweaters or coats yet.

Love, R.

P.S. Have you ever heard of the smokejumpers?

The trip to Butte was fun. I not only appreciated seeing a bit more of Montana, but it was interesting to talk with Favre's dad, a forester and staffman on the Deerlodge National Forest, about a career with the Forest Service. Saturday night we went to the football game, and I was surprised to see a field without grass—just soft dirt. In spite of the fact that it was an exciting game I can't remember a thing about it, except that at half-time the Butte Marching Band strutted onto the field. I couldn't help but notice the cute drum majorette who led the group and threw her batons high in the air without missing a step. I had no way of knowing at the time that eventually she and I would become lifetime friends.

When classes started I met another life-time friend—Ted Rieger. He, too, was majoring in forestry, so we had several classes together and rapidly became close friends. We were both the youngest of large families—mine of eight was small compared to his of sixteen. Ted's family lived on a ranch in eastern Montana and he received his high school diploma with only five other students. When I asked Ted if he had heard of the smokejumpers, he said that one of his brothers jumped in 1942. Ted was also enthusiastic about trying to become one, so we agreed to apply when recruitment started.

My first quarter expenses included $100 tuition ($50 of which was an out-of-state fee), $40 for room, and $110 for board. In addition I had to pay $15 for books plus a few clothes—mostly several pairs of jeans and plaid, flannel shirts. Of course I also had the cost of personal items and cleaning bills, but I tried to wear clothes that I could wash and iron to cut expenses, and it worked fairly well.

I had some money left, but not enough to pay for the next quarter's cost. I figured my income from washing pots and pans and working at Christmas time would put me in good stead. That meant the spring quarter costs would have to be paid with money made during the winter and spring quarters. My way through it all was unclear—all I could do was take it one quarter at a time and see how it worked out. I lived a Spartan existence, but so did most of my friends, and we always found enough to laugh about. I played intra-mural basketball and volleyball on a team comprised of guys from the Wesley Foundation. We won several games in each sport, but never placed as finalists. We were a little short on height and athleticism, but made up for our deficiency with good team work. Sports were a welcome diversion from study, and we were all better off for the exercise, but I have to admit that my full schedule of classes and work made evening study essential. Consequently, I often found myself burning the midnight oil after playing sports.

Ted lived in Corbin Hall, across the campus from Jumbo. It was equipped with its own dining room, so we neither ate nor slept in the same building. Tom Bray and Chuck Davis had become close friends. They roomed together in Jumbo and both belonged to Wesley. Chuck was a business major from Glendive and a year ahead of me in school. He was a short, slender guy and well coordinated. He did well in sports, especially golf, where he later lettered on the varsity team. He was also a procrastinator, putting off study until crunch time, but he was a night person and always seemed to do well with his course work. Tom was two years ahead of me. After he graduated from Butte High School he worked as a clerk in the F.B.I. office for a year before starting college. He was studious and made straight "As" while pursuing a degree in mathematics.

He had a deep appreciation for music and continued to study the piano while in college. He also had a phonograph and a modest collection of records—some Broadway shows, but mostly classical. Those who appreciated music often stopped by his room and requested a particular piece. I got so I liked them all and found myself humming *Petruschka, Saber Dance,* or tunes from *South Pacific.* I didn't realize how much they meant to me until they were not available. I had learned to like classical music without realizing it.

*   *   *

I wrote to my mother regularly, and have no idea why she saved some letters and not others.

Friday, November 24, 1950

Dear Ma,

Have you found out what a smokejumper is yet? Well, I guess I'd better tell you. As you know, I had dinner at the Woolfolk's at Thanksgiving. I told E.J. about my desire to become a smokejumper and he got all the dope about them for me.

A smokejumper parachutes down from a plane with a bunch of other guys on a fire that would take days to get to by foot. [A rather dramatic exaggeration.] *They put it out and hike out.*

Now I know it sounds dangerous, but if my application is accepted I'll send you a lot of information to show you that it is really harmless. Mr. Woolfolk will also explain it to you if you like. He has made an appointment for me to see the man in charge of the outfit on Thursday. Of course there is a chance that nothing will come of it, but I'm gonna try hard to get in, and I want you to know what's going on. Enclosed is a picture of some smokejumpers. Exciting, huh?

Please don't get all "fested up" [whatever that meant] *over it. I need to tell you that your permission is needed, or I won't be able to do it. You would sign on the dotted line, wouldn't you? I know better than to ask that question—of course you will.*

Love, R.

My mother often wrote to her family and friends. She knew the Woolfolks and apparently corresponded with Mr. Woolfolk about smokejumping.

Friday, December 8, 1950

Dear Mrs. Fowler,

Thank you for your recent letter. It is always good to hear from friends in Lanham. [My mother didn't live in Lanham, though she often visited.] *Now that Frank is with us it seems your letter has special significance.*

I hope you can be happy this Christmas with the thought that Frank is among friends and apparently is reasonably satisfied with his circumstances. He will work for me during vacation and stay at our house while the dormitory is closed.

I sanctioned the smokejumping, Mrs. Fowler, largely because I want Frank to think for himself and live his own life. I can give him summer work but he isn't obligated at all to take it. The smoke jumping is strenuous and it is hazardous. However, the boys are well trained and conditioned before they are allowed to jump and in more than 10 years [since the first fire jump in 1940] *there has never been a casualty from jumping. It pays a little more than other types of summer work. I have asked Frank to be sure that you thoroughly understand what smoke jumping is before he signs on the job. Two years ago some boys lost their lives in a fire and even though jumping had nothing to do with it, their parents became very bitter because they didn't understand. With this stipulation I would approve jumping for my own boy if he wanted it.*

You are experiencing the same things now, Mrs. Fowler, that my mother experienced 22 years ago. She didn't know what forestry was or what the Forest Service stood for. Forestry is an honorable profession and as practiced by the Forest Service is one of the best.

I must close this already too long letter. We have had a good deal of winter already. There is about a foot of snow on the ground here now, the result of several recent storms. Once the temperature dropped to one degree below zero. Usually our most severe weather comes in January and February.

I hope you have a very merry Christmas, Mrs. Fowler, and that the New Year will hold much happiness for you.

Sincerely, E. J. Woolfolk

I don't know that E.J.'s letter of approval was needed for me to gain my mother's support, but it must have been a comfort to her. Without conditions or reservations she wrote back to me saying, "If gender wasn't a problem and I was 40 years younger, I would want to do the same thing, so let's do it."

I would have been satisfied with a reluctant, "You can do it if you promise to be careful," but that wouldn't have been my mother. With decisions regarding her children, if she decided to give support, she gave it 100 percent. There was never a question where she stood.

*　　*　　*

As Christmas break approached, a lot of conversation was about going home. Someone suggested I look into the Railway Fare Fund. A state law passed in 1925 required that any railroad fare for any student in excess of $15 for a round trip between his home and the university be refunded, once each year. The catch, of course, was that it was valid only for those who resided in Montana. Besides, even if the transportation home was paid for, I needed to use the holidays to work.

Fall quarter ended Friday, December 15, but most finals were over by Wednesday. On Thursday I started working full days at the federal building for Merton Reed in Range Research, compiling range field data. This was the division of the Forest Service headed by Mr. Woolfolk. I was hired as a Forestry Aid (Research), GS-3 with a salary of $1.27 per hour—considerably more than the 90 cents an hour for my job in the kitchen. When I returned to the dorm at the end of the day a few folks were still taking finals, but not many. By Friday Jumbo was empty except for me. The feeling of abandonment was overwhelming. Up to this point I had never questioned my decision to study so far from home, but now I longed for the opportunity to be there.

Nevertheless, I hung on at the dorm until I was forced to leave, then I went to stay with the Woolfolks.

* * *

My roommate Bob had not applied himself to his studies and flunked out. He had carried a certain air of superiority because he had done so well on the entrance exams, but I quickly learned that those who studied generally did well; those who didn't fell by the wayside. I easily passed remedial English and got "Bs" in both Zoology and Chemistry. I was shocked at my grade in military science— "D." I didn't particularly like the course, but thought I was doing well enough to easily get a "C." I resolved not to let that happen again and wished for an opportunity to expunge my substandard performance from my transcript.

On the 11 days of Christmas vacation I earned a little over $100. That, plus my income from washing pots and pans, and the money left after paying my bills for the first quarter, was sufficient to cover the winter quarter costs. I felt good about that, but knew spring quarter was likely to be a problem.

Christmas at the Woolfolk's was not like home, but at least it was spent with friends. I had received several offers to go to friends' homes in Butte, but decided the transportation costs and other incidentals was more than I could afford, so I passed them up.

When my friends returned and school resumed, I moved in with Bob Craver, another friend from Wesley who came from Butte. Bob was a short, muscular guy who had an easy going manner that made him generally well-liked. His positive attitude and complete genuineness created a large circle of friends. Stories floated around about what a tiger he was on the grid-iron in high school. He played line backer and was feared because he was so fast and hit so hard. The remarkable thing, though, was his habit of helping the ball carrier up after applying a crushing tackle.

He thumb-tacked a poem over his bed. I copied it down:

A GAME GUY'S PRAYER

Dear God: Help me to be a sport in this little game of life. I don't ask for any place in the lineup; play me where You need me. I only ask for the stuff to give You a hundred per cent of what I've got. If all the hard drives come my way, I thank You for the compliment. Help me to remember that You won't let anything come that You and I together can't handle. And help me to take the bad breaks as part of the game. Help make me thankful for them.

And, God, help me always to play on the square, no matter what the other players do. Help me to come clean. Help me to see that often the best part of the game is helping other guys. Help me to be a "regular fellow" with the other players.

Finally, God, if fate seems to uppercut me with both hands and I'm laid up on the shelf in sickness or old age, help me to take that as part of the game also. Help me not to whimper or squeal that the game was a frame-up or that I had a raw deal. When in the dusk I get the final bell, I ask for no lying, complimentary stones. I'd only like to know that You feel I've been a good guy."

—Chaplain's Digest

We became good friends and engaged in many philosophical discussions, sometimes lasting late into the night. On one such occasion I concluded our conversation by saying, "I have to get some sleep, but I think I'll take a hot shower first."

"Let's take a sauna?" Bob suggested.

"A sauna? In Jumbo Hall?" I answered in disbelief.

"Come on, I'll show you."

The showers were contained in a large room with several shower heads on each wall with no separation between them. Typical of Jumbo, the floor was bare concrete. Except for us, the place was empty, but Bob proceeded to turn on all the shower heads with only hot water. The room quickly steamed so densely that we couldn't see across it. We each adjusted a shower so we wouldn't be scalded and soaked in the pleasure of the soothing warmth.

This was especially appreciated because Jumbo was not a uniformly warm building. The heat source was a hot air duct that ran along the hall ceiling throughout all the wings of the two-story building. Side vents delivered heat to each room, and as a result, the main duct reduced in width. By the time the main duct reached the end of the hall it was very small. Consequently the last room in each hall received little heat, especially when the weather was cold. However, the first few rooms got so much it was necessary for occupants to partially close the vent to keep from roasting. During cold weather the next several rooms also received adequate heat, though their vents had to be left wide open. The last few rooms in a given wing, however, were not so fortunate, and that was our situation.

It wasn't until the coldest part of winter that we learned the students in the room just before ours had inserted a piece of cardboard through their vent into the hall duct, thereby totally diverting the meager supply of heat into their room and leaving us none. We soon found a way to get access into the duct in the hall and inserted all manner of foul material so the smell would be shunted only into their room.

We rolled in laughter at the sound of their moaning when they returned. But, alas, the next day I saw Bob staring at the poem by his bed. He turned to me and said, "I've gotta clean up that mess." I helped him discretely undo what he considered a transgression. I saw his point, but didn't totally agree, so I looked at the window from the outside and noticed it was not pulled tightly shut. I managed to open it, climb inside, and unlocked the door from the inside. After extracting the cardboard from the vent, Bob cut out a hole so all the heat would not be diverted. We then put the cardboard back into place but otherwise left the room undisturbed.

I don't know that we ever resolved our heat problem, but I do remember the joy Bob and I felt at the sound of our neighbors wailing at the odor. After that, if our room was cold, it seemed tolerable.

I rigged our room so we could remotely open and close the heating vent, operate the overhead light switch, and close the window. The window was four feet square and opened out on hinges located on the side of the window, so I could only rig it to close. This was done with a series of cords running through eye hooks. Screwing hooks in the wall would have been forbidden in any other dorm, but nobody cared in Jumbo.

Bob and I both liked the window open at night, unless it was frigid. One evening when we turned out the lights Bob open the window a few inches. During the night the wind began to howl and the temperature dropped. I pulled the appropriate cord hanging over my bed and felt the window move, assuming it was shut. However, snow had already gathered on the sill, preventing it from completely closing. Even a crack was quite a bit considering the window was four feet on a side and three sides were not tight. When we woke up in the morning a snow drift had accumulated across the floor with no sign of dampness from it melting. We were busy for several minutes shoveling it out the window.

My school work was going well even though I was working several hours a week at the federal building and the kitchen. My curriculum called for a switch from zoology to botany, and I began taking English for credit. Chemistry continued. I also had three one credit courses: physical education, military science, and a continuance of an introductory course called Survey of Forestry. The latter was taught by the Dean of the Forestry School and was designed to give freshmen an opportunity to learn more specifically what forestry involved. Instead of bringing interest and excitement about the prospects of a forestry career, his approach was scholarly, and boring. Ironically, with the exception of military science, it was the least interesting subject on my schedule.

*   *   *

Planning for the Foresters' Ball started in the fall quarter, but during January the action picked up in earnest, and in February it intensified. We cut several thousand small trees to decorate the gym. Numerous committees worked various aspects of the task, and the entire Forestry School was at their command when manpower was needed. Each year the entrance to the gym was festooned with trees and some object from the story of Paul Bunyan—a gigantic Babe the Blue Ox, or perhaps Paul himself. The entire wall surface inside the gym was covered with Douglas-fir trees. Handsomely decorative, they emitted the rich aroma of a forest. Dance cards were made of wood and humorously designed with a Paul Bunyan theme. The floors were scattered with sawdust and everyone wore clothes befitting a woodsman. Many of the guys grew beards and mustaches.

The dance was so well attended that it was held for two nights: a huge undertaking, but a richly rewarding one, particularly for those of us involved in putting it on. Because of my working schedule, I could only help on weekends, but even at that, I racked up a lot of hours.

The Wesley Foundation met each Sunday evening for two hours at the First Methodist Church, a mile from campus. We usually began with some sort of group game followed by a light supper. The dormitories only served two meals on Sunday, so a chance for a free meal was a real drawing card.

After eating, the worship chairman led a short devotional service. This was followed by a brief business meeting and then a program of some sort—occasionally a film, but usually a speaker on some mind expanding topic. Our meetings were consistently well attended by 30 to 40 members. Most of us worked willingly on one of several committees.

One of our projects was the organization of deputation teams to visit churches in small towns within 50 miles of Missoula to provide Sunday worship services. We did this in Arlee, Dixon, and St. Ignatius.

The outbreak of the Korean War meant many ministers were called to active duty as chaplains. The Stevensville Methodist Church was one of those affected. Several groups of the First United Methodist Church in Missoula alternated the responsibility for providing services each Sunday. Wesley acted in this capacity four times. Bob Craver was active in these efforts and he recruited me to assist when he gave the sermon.

Winter quarter ended on Friday, March 17, but since most students were through with finals by Wednesday, several of us participated in a four-day spring break retreat. Normally 20 to 30 attended, but other competing events drew from our attendance.

The following is taken from "Cosmos," our local Wesley Foundation year book:

15th Annual Lake Trip

A proper mixture of Christian fellowship, fun, recreation, and constructive thinking was the result of the Wesley Foundation's "Lake Trip," between Winter and Spring Quarters.

An annual event, the trip was held at the Methodist Camp, near Rollins, on the shore of beautiful Flathead Lake. Twelve students attended, as well as our advisor, Mrs. Betty Brody and Rev. and Mrs. Wilcox.

The highlight of the session was a series of six discussions led by Dr. Joseph Pennepacker from Rocky Mountain College in Billings. The general discussion topic was "The Student Seeks Reality in Religion."

The general mood of the whole group was, of course, a very serious one. After the long grind of the Winter Quarter, no one had excess energy to be spent in foolishness. On the first night, Thursday, there was an initiation of new members. As can be imagined, this was quiet, orderly, and uneventful. There were no serious casualties . . .

Our schedule provided ample time to enjoy volley ball, row boating, a treasure hunt, card games, and late night singing and dancing. These activities, however, were balanced with a more intellectual agenda. Dr. Pennepacker began his discussion by saying that as university students we would likely be more open to a questioning of religious dogma than a cross-section of parishioners in a church because some members would consider such questioning heresy. He further pressed his point by saying that as students we routinely tested and explored in our search for truth.

He began to talk about religious things we had been taught since we were children; such as the Virgin Mary, the resurrection, and the miracles. What if it was proven, irrefutably, that none of these things were true? Would it destroy the basis for your religious belief?

Undoubtedly a few folks had surprised looks on their faces. Who would expect a minister to ask such questions? He went on to say that if we were secure in our beliefs, such questions would not be disturbing. He also suggested that those who asked them, and brought them to resolution, were much stronger in their faith as a result.

At some time we all had asked these questions, at least to ourselves, but this was probably the first time most of us had openly explored such thoughts in a meeting led by a minister. It was a cross-roads in my religious growth.

*　　*　　*

My grades for winter quarter were satisfying—"B's" in all my five-credit courses. A "B" in English brought a definite feeling of redemption, and I was also gratified with a "C" in military science.

*　　*　　*

Ted and I both received responses from our application for entrance into the Smokejumper Project. Ted was accepted; I was not. Apparently Ted's Montana ranch background put him in better stead than mine as an Easterner. I was devastated.

As spring quarter progressed, it became evident I wouldn't be able to make financial ends meet. My brother Bruce was a college graduate, married, and had no children. I decided to ask him for a loan of $100.00 with the understanding it would be paid back as soon as I began to earn money in the summer. He willingly accommodated.

Spring quarter rapidly slipped by. Wesley had another weekend trip to Flathead Lake because so many were unable to attend the one at spring break. It was well attended and a much different experience with warmer weather.

I was doing fairly well in my studies, but knew I had to do well on finals in order to earn high marks. I studied hard and was unable to turn off a racing mind when it came time to sleep. For several nights in a row I slept poorly and began to worry that I would be in poor mental shape for the Monday morning finals in English and chemistry.

I went to the infirmary and pleaded for a sleeping pill, convinced a good night's sleep was all I needed. I took the pill Sunday night, but still lay awake late into the night. When I finally dozed off, the alarm was not far behind, and I got up feeling like I had been heavily drugged. I stumbled to my first final, but was unable to take the test with a clear mind. The second test was no better. Fortunately my classwork through the quarter was good enough so I could easily pass with a "C," but I had hoped for better. Two days later I was in better mental shape for my botany final and aced it. I was gratified, but not surprised, because I consistently did well in natural science courses.

Even so, the quarter ended with only average grades.

The vehicles reveal this as a picture taken before my time, but the appearance of Main Hall, Mount Sentinel, and the oval changed little from the time of this picture and the early 1950s when I was there.

CHAPTER 3

Fort Keogh

By the time spring quarter ended on June 8, I had adjusted to not going into smokejumper training and was looking forward to the job Mr. Woolfolk offered me at Fort Keogh in eastern Montana. The fort had long ago ceased to be a military reservation and was used for rangeland and cattle research. I was to live alone in a cabin on the range doing maintenance work and assisting in field studies. It was all a bit vague, but I was anxious to become acquainted with eastern Montana and to learn about management of cattle.

Tuesday, June 3, 1951

Dear Ma,

Mert Reed and I left Missoula yesterday at eight o'clock in the morning in his 1950 Chevrolet car. You remember that Mert is one of the fellows that works in the office for Joe Woolfolk. I did some compilation work for him last winter. He analyzes a lot of the data gathered in the studies carried out at Fort Keogh.

Mert said it would take all day to drive to Miles City since it was 470 miles away. The farthest east I had been was Butte, so most of it was new country to me and I thoroughly enjoyed the trip—especially since we took turns driving. We reached Miles City at 9:00 p.m. and stayed in a motel for the night.

Today we started work—if you can call it that. I really didn't do a thing. Most of the morning was spent talking to Larry Short, the head of the Forest Service part of the station at Fort Keogh. Mr. Woolfolk had that job before he went to Washington, D.C.

The Bureau of Animal Industry (BAI) has a much bigger presence at Fort Keogh than the Forest Service, so most of the fellows I met worked for that agency. I met a few of them and became fairly well acquainted with the headquarters.

Larry and Mert decided to give me the government pickup truck for the summer. It's a brand-new 1950 Dodge with 800 miles on it. It's a deep green color, like all Forest Service vehicles, and has a Forest Service logo emblazoned on the door. I could hardly believe that a truck was assigned to me for my use, much less a beautiful new one.

The station [headquarters] is located a little over two miles west of Miles [Miles City]. The Hogback, where I'm staying, is six miles from the station with nothing but open range land between me and the nearest person. Today at Hogback (called so because of a close by ridge that looks like one) I saw an antelope. He was only about 200 feet away. Larry says he hangs around the cabin a lot. There's a cottontail that lives under the cabin, so I'm not without a friend. The one thing that kind of worries me are the rattlesnakes. I haven't seen one, but I'm always listening for a rattle. I have a snakebite kit that I put in my pickup for emergency use.

This afternoon I went to town with Larry and bought some food. He set me up with a charge account so I can pay my grocery bill by the month. I like that arrangement.

The mosquitoes are horrific here. I have never seen so many. They literally cover you when you walk in tall grass. Larry says they die down after a dry spell—and I guess there's plenty of those.

I don't know just what kind of work I'll be doing. Larry and Mert gave me all of tomorrow to clean up the cabin here at Hogback. When I get that done I'll drive to the station and do something for my pay. There will be days when I won't go near the station, especially if it's wet. There are several portions of the road that turn to gumbo after a rain. I guess it gets so slick you can't drive over it.

Mr. Short showed me how to measure the rainfall here. There's a rain gauge near the cabin and each day I must record the precipitation on a form designed for that purpose. Of course, most days there will be nothing to measure.

Sometimes I will have to stop the windmill so the water won't continually overflow in the watering troth. Also, during windless weather, I'll have to start the gasoline motor so it can do the pumping. These are only incidental jobs.

The pastures at Hogback are configured like a giant wagon wheel, only not as symmetrical. There are six pastures averaging 140 acres in size, although they range from a low of 90 acres to high of 195 acres. Two of these pastures are lightly grazed, two moderately, and two heavily. The objective of the work by the Forest

Service at Hogback is to measure the effects of these different intensities of grazing on the land and on the cattle.

In addition to the six pastures there is a "trap." It's a small wedge of land between two of the pastures that accommodates road access to the cabin and well.

I'll tell you more about all this when I become more familiar with it myself.

Did you read the book I sent to you? In case you didn't notice, the Hogback is on Page 4.

[The book I sent to my mother was published by the U.S. Department of Agriculture, Forest Service and was entitled "The Northern Great Plains Research Center—Its Work and Aims." It defined the research center as extending from Canada to Wyoming and west from the Dakotas to a line which crosses Montana west of Billings and east of Havre. The work area included over 40 million acres in 22 eastern Montana counties with headquarters at the U.S. Range Livestock Experiment Station two-and-a-half miles west of Miles City, Montana.

The booklet also contained information on the history of the experiment station:

> "The Range Livestock Experiment Station occupies the site of old Fort Keogh, by whose side Miles City, one of the earliest settlements in eastern Montana, developed. The Fort, established in 1876 near the junction of the Tongue and Yellowstone Rivers, followed shortly after the massacre of General Custer and his Seventh Cavalry by the Sioux in the Battle of the Little Big Horn. The original buildings constructed of cottonwood logs from along the rivers stood near the present site of the Range Riders' Museum. In 1877, buildings were constructed on the present site, part of the brick and building material being shipped from St. Louis by wood-burning river boats at high-water time in the spring. Some of the buildings constructed as officers' quarters in 1877 and 1878 still serve as residences on the Station.
>
> "Fort Keogh was maintained as a military base until 1901 when the Army converted the Fort into a remount station and operated it as such until 1923.
>
> "The Range Livestock Experiment Station came into being in 1924, when by Congressional action the military reservation was made available to the U.S. Department of Agriculture as a livestock experiment station. Originally 10 miles square [64,000 acres], the area since has been reduced to about 56,000 acres.

"The administration of the Station is by the Bureau of Animal Industry (BAI) which in conjunction with Montana Agricultural Experiment Station has conducted research in livestock breeding and management of wide recognition. Their program, at present, is limited to beef cattle and swine, although previously it included sheep, horses, and turkeys.

"Range studies on the Station have been carried out by the Forest Service in cooperation with the above agencies."]

I'm tired and I have a lot to do. I haven't received any mail here yet; I hope it comes through alright. Ask me some questions and I'll try to answer them.

I'll write again soon,

Love, R.

I didn't sleep well my first night at the Hogback Cabin because of many strange, unfamiliar noises—they would take some getting used to. Nevertheless, I liked my new home and was determined to make it comfortable. When it was thoroughly dusted and washed I made a list of the things needed: paint, pans, another blanket, and replacement mantels for the white gas lantern. The evening before, when lighting it, I had allowed liquid fuel to drip, forming a puddle at the base of the lantern. When I struck a match, a flame engulfed the lantern. Fortunately, with the help of a broom handle, I was able to extricate the lantern with its ball of flame before the place burned down. The experience was impressive, and I thereafter lighted it properly by using a match to pre-heat the generator before opening the fuel flow. As a result, the fuel was converted to an easily controlled gas when the fuel valve was eventually opened. That first time, however, both of the mantels were destroyed.

As a part of my orientation, I spent several days at the station getting acquainted and learning more precisely what was expected. Larry and I began to make a list of jobs to be done and prioritizing them. When Larry was away on business for a spell, I would post amendments to the Forest Service Manual which was comprised of several three-inch binders. They contained the agency's policies, practices, and procedures and were the primary source of administrative direction to Forest Service employees. As changes or additions were made to the manuals, copies were sent to field offices. Since many did not pertain to Larry's work, he let them accumulate. It would have been a boring job to make these postings except that I appreciated the opportunity to become familiar with the system.

We spent a couple of days traveling the rangeland so I would know my way around. We visited such places as Lone Pine, Sadie Flats, and Custer Flats—35 miles from Hogback. Larry pointed out a small hill resembling the shape of a camel's back; it was aptly named Camel Hump. Mostly, however, we spent our time at Hogback.

Since one of my duties was to periodically place salt blocks in each pasture, I had to know how to reach each distribution point. Larry patiently gave me the tour.

He also showed me how the fence stretcher worked so I could tighten sagging fence wires. After he demonstrated how the block and tackle attached to the barbed wire, I could see it would be easy to use.

With that introduction I was anxious to start work on my own. A crew was scheduled to weigh cattle and take blood samples each month at Hogback, and I would assist in the operation. Mert had also scheduled a couple of trips during the summer to gather plant and soil data. Larry and I would be part of the team, but during the interim, I had my list of jobs.

I began to inspect and maintain nine miles of four-strand barbed wire fence at Hogback. Five of those miles were around the exterior of the pastures— the rim of the wagon wheel, so to speak. The other four miles were comprised of fences between the pastures, or the spokes. They were between ½ and ¾ mile long.

Larry had pointed out what he thought were the worst sections, so I started there. It was slow going because many posts needed replacement, but the work was enjoyable and I attacked the challenge with enthusiasm. It took a couple of days to replace the rotted posts, and I would only lightly tack the staples over the barbed wire so it could move when I pulled out the slack.

Each day a Bureau of Animal Industry (BAI) range rider would meander his way through the pastures at Hogback to make certain the cattle were inside the fenced areas. Although I would usually only see him from a long distance, we always waved. I would have felt guilty if he had found me taking a break, so I seldom did.

When in the truck, the deer and antelope paid little attention to me. For some reason the truck was not a threat, but one step out of it and they would prance off a few yards. The antelope would sneeze and pop up and down like their legs were pogo sticks. The deer would just gracefully waltz away. I couldn't help thinking that when some cowboy first started singing *Home on the Range* he must have been in Montana, particularly when he sang about "where the deer and the antelope play."

At last I was ready to tighten up the wires and made certain the staples were all loose on the ¼ mile of fence. I attached the block and tackle tightener to a braced post to provide a solid anchor, and spread the jaws of the other end so they could be attached to the wire. When I began to pull the wire tightened as the slack was pulled out of it. One more pull and it would be taut. Then I figured another pull would make the job that much better, so I reefed on the block and tackle one more time. Disaster struck. The corner post a ¼ mile away broke at ground line and popped up in the air. I had removed the staples from the wires extending in another direction from the corner, so when the post popped up it sprung down the fence line towards me. All four strands of wire coiled in a mess. I should have realized the corner post was probably the most important one to replace, and I certainly learned that if tight was good, tighter was not necessarily better.

Fortunately, the range rider had already made his rounds and my faux pas went unnoticed. Well, that wasn't exactly true—several stupid cows stood gawking about. I had to repeatedly chase them away from the downed fence because they were eyeing greener pasture. It wouldn't have been difficult with a horse, but on foot it was time consuming.

I replaced the three posts at the corner, braced them and began to untangle the barbed wire. The sun had started to set so I only had time to temporarily attached two wires before I returned to the cabin. It looked great when I finished correcting my error the next day, though admittedly it was a tough way to learn how to properly tighten fence wires.

*   *   *

While learning my job I was also sharpening my domestic skills. There was no reasonable way to obtain refrigeration, so I had to buy canned or dry food. I didn't even try to use the wood burning oven because the heat was unbearable. Instead, I used a Coleman gas stove. Fresh potatoes, onions, and eggs kept well enough; during hot weather the eggs were submerged in the watering tank to keep them cool, along with small cans of evaporated milk. By submerging the cans the contents were cold enough to made them palatable. I combined canned milk with an equal amount of water and mixed in some chocolate to mask the smell. After awhile I drank it straight, and, surprisingly enough, thought it tasted delicious.

Bathing was a tougher problem. At first, I heated water in two dish pans, and stood with a foot in each while I drew water over my body with a wash cloth. It was awkward, but the weather was not so hot that I had to bathe every day. But as the days got hotter, I became more grimy and wasn't getting clean enough.

My next alternative was to drive as close as I could to the Tongue River and take a swim. It was about a mile with the final 200 yards on foot. At first I enjoyed the novelty of it. Larry had pointed out the wide sloping buffalo trails worn through the banks leading to the river. It was intriguing to imagine the huge herds that once inhabited the area.

The swim was refreshing, and I took advantage of the opportunity throughout the summer, but it just wasn't convenient on a daily basis.

I thought about building a shower, but the construction was more complicated than I wanted to tackle, especially if I could figure out something less involved. An old wheel barrow of the type used to haul cement had sides high enough to make an excellent tub. After caulking a few leaks, it worked fine. I would wheel it to the watering tank in the morning, fill it, and then set it where the sun would heat. After work, I could either wheel it into the cabin or park it by the porch for an outdoor bath. I could scoot down in the pan with my shoulders under water and my feet on the handles. The water was warm and relaxing, but most importantly, I felt clean.

One midsummer evening it was too hot to bathe under the blazing sun, so I fixed dinner first. By the time I finished the sun was lower in the sky. I wheeled my tub in front of the cabin and stepped in. After washing my legs, I slid down so my torso was submerged and my feet were on the handles.

My routine included playing the songs I had taught myself on my new harmonica. I didn't know many, and played them equally poorly. I would play *O Susanna*, and then sing a verse. It was refreshing to hear the human voice even if it was mine. But I didn't just sing, I sang with penetrating forte.

If I had been standing and looking to the northwest, a vehicle several miles away creating a plume of dust would have been obvious, but seated in my tub I couldn't see it. No one came to Hogback except on business, usually during the day, so I always felt very much alone in the evening.

I had just played *God Bless America,* and was in the middle of singing a verse in full voice when a car came to a stop 30 feet away. The windows were down and a man with teen age girls were grinning profusely—they had obviously heard my howling. I was so startled the wheel barrow tipped when I tried to get out and I fell to the ground in a splash. Now the grins turned to laughter as I ran for the cabin, naked as a jaybird. From then on, I always positioned the wheel barrow with the approach road in plain view, but it was unnecessary because they were the only sightseers the entire summer.

*   *   *

Strange sounds woke me from a deep sleep, and I would lay in bed trying to figure out what they were. I could easily dispel the frequent bellow of a cow or the lonely howl of the wind because I recognized them as part of my environment. Some others I did not. One was the eerie sound of a squeaking gate. Even after I was certain all doors and gates were tightly shut, this sound would periodically recur. It was unnerving to listen to the piercing sound as it slowly changed pitch.

I happened to be at the watering tank one still day when a gentle breeze came up. The windmill struggled and finally began to turn slowly. Then I heard the sound and noticed that the windmill's shaft passed up and down through a hole in a piece of plywood attached to the tower. When the action was slow, the shaft rubbing against the plywood produced the eerie squeak—a glob of grease took care of that.

The second, the most annoying, woke me instantly. It sounded like a rasp being rubbed against wood in short spurts. It was loud and seemed to be in or near the cabin. I kept thinking it had gone away because several days went by before it reoccurred. Then I saw where something had been gnawing on the wooden frame around a vent to the underside of the cabin. It just happened my resident friend, the rabbit, hopped nearby when I made this discovery. I have no idea why he would be attracted to chomping on wood, but he was. A piece of woven wire over the vent solved this second mystery.

The third was a "bong" best described as the sound of a plucked guitar string. It never happened in the dead of night, but frequently occurred at widely spaced intervals in the early morning hours. Thinking the sound came from directly overhead, I climbed up on the cabin roof and found bird droppings under the guy wires supporting the stove's flue. It seemed obvious that a bird perched on one of these wires and "plucked" it when flying off. Just knowing what caused the sound was enough for me to forget it.

The last sound was a barely audible melodic "ting-ting-ting-ting," like the rapid, faint tapping on a cymbal from a distant place. It would come and go in short spurts. Sometimes it sounded like several cymbals played simultaneously. I couldn't imagine where it was coming from and it took me several weeks to discover its cause.

After dark one evening, I went out to get something from my pickup. When I returned, the beam of my flashlight revealed movement along a strand of barbed wire on the fence a few feet from my cabin. I sat on the porch for several minutes, listening intently. When I heard the mystery sound I turned on my light and saw two mice—one scampering left on the second strand and one scampering right on the third. I would never have thought mice could run on a strand of wire, much less produce a melodic sound.

*　　*　　*

The notion of spending two weeks completely alone intrigued me. I stocked up on groceries and informed Larry I wouldn't be coming to the station the next weekend because I wanted to do some hiking. I also confided my desire to experience isolation for a couple of weeks. He confirmed I wouldn't be needed at the station for a spell, but insisted I make periodic contact with a range rider. I appreciated his concern for my safety and assured him I would be within waving distance at least every second or third day.

I had already gone three days without outside contact, so I didn't think it would be difficult. My pickup was not equipped with a radio and I purposefully didn't make arrangements for one in the cabin, so I had no source of human sound. I wondered how many people had gone through a day, much less two weeks, without speaking to another person or hearing a human voice.

I continued to maintain fence and chip away at other chores on my work list. One day I took a couple of hours to stack the boards thrown haphazardly in a pile next to the cabin. It was easy enough to do and I enjoyed the diversion; however, when I started to pull one of the boards I heard the buzz of a rattlesnake. Even though I had never heard one before, I knew instantly what it was and jumped back in fear. I moved the board again with a shovel, and each time the buzz returned, almost like pushing a switch. Although the snake wasn't visible, he either saw me, or was aware of my presence. I quickly decided mending fence was a higher priority job, but even approached that job with caution because snakes weighed heavily on my mind.

The next morning a rattlesnake was coiled in front of the outhouse. If I was at all groggy, the buzz quickly sharpened my senses. I ran back to the shed and got a shovel, thinking I would thump him with it, but the snake attacked the blade in anger. Somehow the handle didn't seem quite long enough, so I decided to lob rocks from several feet away. I killed him, but only with considerable apprehension. I soon realized the prodigious mouse population around the buildings attracted snakes, making them much more likely to be found there than on the open prairie.

Over the next several days I pulled a few boards out of the pile by the cabin and neatly stacked them, but never saw a snake. One might think I had become "snake smart," but it took one more encounter.

Entering the shed one day, I hesitated in the entrance. To my left was a bench almost shoulder height. I was looking for something and glanced in the direction of the bench only to find I was staring into the eyes of a snake. Its tongue was rapidly flicking in and out, only a few inches away. I didn't faint, but melted away.

It was a huge, non-poisonous bull snake, but knowing it could just as well have been a rattlesnake, I never again entered a building without an intensive visual inspection before stepping inside. My experiences resulted in a thorough understanding of the statement, "when a man knows he's in snake country, he walks like he's in snake country." It became second nature to consistently take a course of action that minimized the risk of a snake bite. After awhile, the fear of being bitten subsided.

During this time I painted the cabin's interior with surplus paint Larry provided and called it the rainbow room because so many colors were used. As a part of the job, the cabin was carefully checked so it was both mouse and snake proof—neither ever became my roommates. The mice could enter my pickup by coming through the hole made by the gas pedal in the floorboard. They had a heyday with some food inadvertently left on the floorboard. It took a while to figure out how they got in, but upon discovery I promptly fashioned a piece of tin so it blocked the hole. A few days later a putrid smell became so bad I had to drive with the windows open. When it didn't subside everything was emptied out, but it wasn't until the seat was removed that I found a dead mouse. Evidently some tools had shifted and squashed the critter.

At times the wind was so strong at Hogback I had to "cage" the windmill (i.e., prevent it from rotating). A long period of calm came after several weeks, and I made the linkage adjustments to convert from wind to gasoline power. I pulled on the starter rope several times before the engine fired and came to life. No sooner did this happen than mice started jumping out of the engine; some getting caught in the drive belt and the pulley. Chunks of mouse splattered all over, including on me. I quickly turned off the engine and saw a nest built by mice in spaces between the engine parts. I felt dumb for not seeing it before starting the engine, but was grateful for the discovery before the engine heated and started a fire.

I began to make traps of various types to reduce the mice population near the cabin. Most effective were "gang planks" placed over the edge of a large tub with a few inches of water in the bottom. Bait was strategically placed at the end of the stick so when a mouse ventured beyond the balance point, it and the stick would fall into the water. The mouse would swim to exhaustion and then drown. At times I set as many as five "gang planks" on the same tub, but never got more than three mice at a setting.

I thought isolation would be more difficult than it turned out to be. It did, however, cause changes in my behavior. I had always spoken to animals, both wild and domestic, but in my isolation I became much more focused, and was convinced we developed a greater level of understanding. Other aspects of my environment also became more intimate—such as the wind, cloud formations, and stars. You might think talking to myself would follow, but it didn't. The closest to that was singing, which I did whenever the need to hear a voice seemed urgent. I sang a lot.

My most bizarre behavior took place on Sunday. I had decided to hike to the south along a fence that more or less paralleled the Tongue River. Because of the river's meandering, the distance to it varied between 3/4 and one-and-a-half miles. My hike was to a butte a couple of miles away that was in line with the fence part of the way. As I looked at that "hill far away" it seemed like an "old rugged cross" belonged on top of it, so I proceeded to fashion one by notching heavy timbers. It wasn't difficult. I spiked them together, put my shoulder under the "X" and trudged off with the base of the cross dragging on the ground. After a few steps the weight began to dig into my shoulder. A few more steps and it hurt so badly I had to stop.

The ridiculousness of my actions began to register, and I got a mental image of me carrying that cross. I thought to myself, "All I need is a crown of thorns." I laughed so hard and felt so nutty I found myself looking around to be certain no one observed this ludicrous scene. Then I took the cross apart and carried it in back to the lumber pile by the cabin.

I was still determined to hike to the butte. Half way there I looked out over the sloping ground to the Tongue River and saw a herd of 15 deer ambling along a half-mile away. From their perspective I was easily seen walking against the skyline; they stopped and stood staring in my direction. Then one of them broke away from the herd and started to trot toward me. It traveled at a steady, moderate pace without varying from a beeline to my position. The herd just stood staring, as if frozen in time. I had little experience observing deer, but it struck me this was odd behavior, and, frankly, I began to wonder what he was up to. When he was 30 yards away I nervously half shouted, "What are your intentions?"

The deer stopped, looked at me momentarily, and then turned and trotted back to the herd. When he rejoined them they turned in unison and ambled across the prairie. I stood in awe, knowing that what I had witnessed had been permanently seared into my memory as a unique wildlife encounter.

I viewed my summer as an adventure, and was determined to enjoy it all, but after my experiment with extended isolation, I decided to spend the remaining weekends socially.

Tuesday, July 3, 1951

Dear Ma,

Have you gotten the Round Robin yet? Where is it? [The Round Robin was a packet of letters continuously circulated among my mother and her eight children. Upon receipt of the packet, the old letter would be removed and a new one inserted. Then it would be forwarded on its never ending way. It is still alive today and although only three original siblings remain, nephews and nieces have joined the circle.]

I bought a couple of harmonica books the last time I was in town. Since I don't read music, I have to get this special kind that codes each note with a number and a "B" or "D." The harmonica's slots are numbered and correspond to those in the book. The "B" is for blow and the "D" for draw. Since I don't have a chromatic harmonica I can't play songs with sharps or flats, so my choices are limited, but I enjoy trying to play. I bought another song book without the special codings, thinking I could figure out the numbering system, but I didn't have much luck.

Monday it rained quite hard and I was "mudded" in. I tried to drive to the station to finish some painting Larry had put on my work list, but I got stuck and had to walk back to the cabin.

I wrote six letters and one is on the way to Hazel. [She was my middle sister, 17 years my senior. She and her son lived with my mother in an apartment.] *I received her package today—yummie! Tell her it arrived in good shape, please.*

Today I tried to get the truck out of the muck, but couldn't. Finally the rider who was making his rounds came by and helped me put on chains. It was a messy job because we had to jack up each rear wheel and the weight pushed the jack down into the mud. But we prevailed and after slipping and sliding over a very slick surface, I arrived at the station at noon. It dried up considerably during the day and I was able to return without chains. Weird stuff, this gumbo. Tomorrow, or course, is a holiday. I think I'll go into town.

From this window I can see the sun's reflection off the big Miles City water tank seven miles away. It stands just above the trees that grow by the Tongue

River. The river comes within a half-mile of here, so I can see plenty of trees at a distance. Closer than that, there is only a single tree about 100 yards from my cabin. There are times when it makes me a little lonely to look at it.

Sometimes I can see smoke from the city, or hear a train whistle, but only if the wind is not restless. All around are peaks and ridges that hide something to see. Whenever I have the chance I hike to one and just look. I'm always amazed at the variety of the landscape, perhaps because I first thought it rather boring and unchanging. I sure didn't have that right.

There's one hill I call "Identification Point." No matter where I'm working in the area, I can tell exactly where I am when I see it. I'm sure the reason I've memorized it shape so exactingly is because the sun sets behind it, and I watch the spectacle routinely. You haven't seen a sunset until you've been out West.

Last Sunday while out for a hike on Hogback Ridge, I almost stepped on a skunk. He was behind a clump of sage and startled me, but thankfully he didn't appear disturbed at all. I saw the hole in the ground where he lives and marked the location so I can go back and study it some time. I have never seen one up close before.

The cactus [prickly pear] *is only four or five inches tall here, but there's plenty of it.*

You asked if there are birds here. Yes, and what beauties they are! One with a red head, black body, and white tipped wings. Another is brown with a bright yellow breast. There's a wide variety and if they weren't singing and chattering I think I'd go bats in the silence. [I'm not certain of the names of these birds, but the brown one was likely a Western Kingbird. I later spent many hours studying ornithology and could name them all.]

I'm glad Jack [my nephew] *decided against going into the service. Four years is a long time. I hope he decides to give college a try. Does he ever talk about it?*

You asked for a copy of the livestock magazine that I cut the pictures out of and sent to you. It had been in the cabin since 1947, so I can't buy another; however, there are some others here and I will be happy to send them to you. I didn't realize you would take to the pictures so much.

I guess with the Capital Transit System on strike in Washington, D.C. you are as bad off as I was Monday and Tuesday.

It's beginning to get dark so I turned on my lantern. You know, the mantle in this thing makes it just like daylight. When the room is dark, and I look out the window, I see a search light many miles away. First it's white and as it revolves and the other end comes around, it's green. It continually alternates in this fashion. I can also see a tower from a police radio station on a hill that is lit up in red lights. During daylight hours I can see the road leading to this tower. It's just a narrow, winding, dirt road climbing up the hill. The way it snakes precipitously upward reminds me of a Walt Disney cartoon. Surely the road must lead to a castle.

As you can see, I'm babbling on. I think being alone so much emphasizes a need for me to share some of what I see and feel—and I know you are a willing listener.

Oh, you said you'd like to spend a month here. Well, come on! If you could get here somehow it would cost you nothing to eat and sleep. I could get another bed, mattress, pillow and plenty of blankets. I pay nothing for room, so that's not a consideration. It wouldn't cost much more for two than it does for just me, so I can handle the food cost. The only thing you'd have to do would be to cook and rest, and rest, and hike, and talk with me, and enjoy yourself. I'll even get you to church on Sunday.

I realize I shouldn't be talking about all this because it's quite impossible for you to get here, but you spoke of it first. And it's fun to imagine things even if they all can't come true.

The way I'm writing you'd think I had nothing else to do—ha!

Have a nice vacation.

Love, R.

Shortly after arriving at Fort Keogh, I met Bob Quesenberry, an engineering student attending Montana State College in Bozeman, and the son of the man who was in charge of the BAI at the station. Since Bob had graduated from high school in Miles City he had friends in the area, and he introduced me to many of them.

I frequently drove to the station and Bob and I would go to town in his car. He had a vintage car made in the 1920s that he sometimes drove for the fun of it. Going to swim at the city park one Saturday, we came to the long, steep stretch of highway fairly close to town. We were traveling at a pretty fast clip when he said, "If you want to see this beauty sail, watch when I pull out this knob." He put in the clutch and pulled out a knob that had the words "free wheeling" printed on it. It must have been an early version of overdrive and when engaged, it gave me the feeling we'd fly if we had wings. The car was too light for that much speed and when he let up on the gas it felt like there was no compression. My exclamation was much more out of fear than elation because I seriously wondered if he'd be able to bring it to a stop. But he did.

On those later occasions when we drove in the jalopy he never used free wheeling again.

Swimming at the park was a frequent weekend pastime for us. The pool was actually a swimming hole fed by a creek, but with safety markers, a diving board, and a lifeguard. The water was brownish, but that didn't diminish our enthusiasm for a cool dip in the summer heat. It was also a good opportunity to meet with friends.

The town had developed a teen center called "Harmony Hangout." It was a small building that provided a place to dance, and no one seemed to mind music from a jukebox. It wasn't long before I felt part of a circle of friends and was able to join in other weekend activities.

One weekend a bunch of us went to a rodeo—my first. We had a great time, but what I remember most was Gene Autry singing, of all things, "Rudolph the Red Nose Reindeer." The crowd loved him, but we thought the song was dumb. Rudolph? In the middle of summer?

We also went on several wienie roasts, and occasionally met at the movie theater, but mostly we danced and whooped it up at the hangout.

Sunday, July 29, 1951

Dear Ma,
The Shorts have left on their vacation and I have made myself quite at home in their house. I get a lot of enjoyment out of their phonograph.
Every evening I have to irrigate their garden and water their lawn. Bob's family is also leaving on a vacation, so I take care of their lawn, too.
I had planned to go to Glendive next weekend to see Chuck, but I was offered a part in a community play and decided (under pressure) to accept. It's a small part so it doesn't matter that there's only a week left in which to practice. The "Barn Players" put on several plays just for the fun of it, and any one can try out for a part. They try to take in enough money to pay for royalties and to cover costs, but that's all. They perform in an old barn and it's appropriately called the Barn Theater. Every evening for the coming week someone will pick me up and bring me back. How could I refuse to participate?
Isn't it amazing how we sometimes bump into people we knew in the past? Today, while attending services at the Baptist church with Mr. and Mrs. Hamil [he was a range rider working for the BAI at Fort Keogh] *the substituting layman who was conducting the service asked the new minister to give the prayer. He was sitting in the same row as we were, only his two kids and wife were*

between him and me. Anyhow, the layman said "Will the Rev. Heath lead us in prayer?" I was astounded. [He was a friend of my brother Dan during the war years when Dan was a chaplain in the Navy. Art (Rev. Heath) was also in the Navy and rented a room from my sister, Ella, in Washington, D.C.] *After the service, I handed Rev. Heath a picture of Dan from my wallet. When he recognized the picture he kept smiling and shaking my hand. The whole congregation was held up with us talking until his wife interceded. I'm going to see him sometime in the coming week while at play practice.*

My teeth are fixed, but Dr. Gualtieri said he would like to replace one of my old fillings with gold. He said I could get along without it in the short run, but it would be better to do it now.

"Besides," he said, "with another appointment we will have the opportunity to continue our discussion. And it won't cost you a thing." Can you imagine that? He has cleaned my teeth, put in four fillings and charged me practically nothing. We do enjoy our conversations, but this seems beyond reason. He has invited me to his home several times and I intend to go before long. He's coming out here while I'm staying at Short's house to get some vegetables from the garden sometime soon. He is continually offering to lend me his brand new Ford to use on a date. He's so casual about the whole thing that it's tempting, but I feel it's a little too generous.

You know how impressed I am with the beauty of this country, but I don't think I'm exaggerating when I say the kindness of the people is more attractive than the scenery. I certainly don't feel like a stranger in the community.

I went on a wienie roast Friday night. It was up in the pine hills several miles from Miles. The higher elevation is very favorable to the growth of pine trees. It's pleasant, cool and different—compared to the heat of the river bottom. I had a lot of fun—we all did. There were six of us. Near the end of the evening some uninvited fellows pulled up with beer and began to booze it up. They were intrusive and obnoxious. I was a bit angry, but we were ready to leave anyhow, so we did.

You know, I appreciate writing letters to you. I suppose knowing that you like to correspond is part of it, but I think it also helps me to more fully realize how fortunate I am when I tell you about all the good stuff that happens. I expect there are also some "not so good" things as well, but they seem to get drowned out in my eagerness to tell you about my various adventures. I must admit that my time at the Hogback is sometimes a bit lonely, but I'm truly enjoying the experience.

Busy, tan, grateful, and happy!

Love, R.

*   *   *

During the week Larry and his family were away, I spent two days on horseback with a range rider. It almost felt like a vacation, at least until my butt got so sore I had to get off and lead the horse. I certainly got a different perspective of the prairie and thought about how great it would be to have a job requiring more saddle time.

I also spent some time with a BAI mechanic repairing a cattle guard and retrieving a stalled vehicle at Sadie Flat. We rode in a Power Wagon well equipped with tools. The front fenders were perfectly flat on top and provided space sufficient for his dog to stand while riding down the road. The dog had developed sea legs and could withstand some pretty rough terrain, but occasionally when the mechanic would step hard on the brake, the dog would sail out into space. He never seemed to get hurt, but he certainly mastered the art of giving a dirty look.

His snout was scarred and I asked the mechanic about it. He said rattlesnakes had hit him several times. He then showed me a suction hose he devised that hooked onto the vacuum of his windshield wipers. He claimed he had extracted the poison from his dog's snout on two occasions.

Sadie Flat was the site of some imaginative experimentation. The Forest Service had carefully surveyed the gently sloping ground and marked contour lines. A bull dozer built dikes along these markings so rain-water would be trapped. It was hoped this might be a way to retain moisture and thereby grow more grass. The dikes had only recently been constructed, so the soil was still bare where sod had been scalped away.

A recent rain had soaked the raw soil, but there was no standing water. Even though it was the consistency of pudding, from a distance it reflected the sun in much the same way as water. The illusion had obviously confused the ducks as evidenced by the streaks in the mud where their feet first touched down for a landing. At the end of these streaks were holes where they had plopped down with their bodies. There was also evidence of the struggle each made in their effort to get to solid ground. Obviously they communicate poorly because many ducks made the same mistake.

*   *   *

Throughout the summer three incidents involving my pickup stand brightly in my memory. The first involved the gate at the trap, a 29-acre wedge of land between two pastures through which the road to the cabin passed. It was used for cattle only when they were held to be weighed and to have blood samples extracted, even so, the gate was always kept shut.

I became impatient with having to stop at the gate, get out to open it, get back in to drive through, stop, get out to close it, and finally get back in to continue on my way. I reasoned that a lot of wasted motion was involved, and a different procedure was needed. That's when the "trap gate maneuver" began to materialize.

My pickup had four forward gears but the lowest one was normally not used. It was called "compound" and would only be employed in circumstances calling for additional power, such as when starting out with a heavy load or on steep ground. This was the only gear in which the engine would not stall if the accelerator was idle.

I went to a flat section of road, far removed from fences and gates, and stopped, put a mark on the ground by the front bumper, climbed back into the truck, shoved the gear shift into compound, and stepped out again. The truck slowly moved forward, perfectly straight, while I noted the time it took to travel 15 yards. Then, I jumped back into the truck and took control. It was easy, and perfectly safe.

The gate at the trap was made of old, weathered wood. I pulled up to it and paced off 15 yards and measured the time it took to walk that distance and opened it. It was considerably less than the time I had recorded for the truck to travel that far (in compound at idle speed).

Now I was ready. I approached the gate, stopped 15 yards short of it, shoved the gear shift into compound, stepped out of the truck, closed the door, trotted to the gate (just to give me a little edge on the time), opened it, saluted as the truck passed through, closed the gate, and hustled to the still moving truck. It was easy, and so much more efficient than the old way.

I did this many times and got to the point where I didn't trot at all, totally confident in my timing. Sometimes I would open the gate and throw out my arm pretending I was a toreador with a red cape and shout "Ole" as the stupid animal passed withing inches of my body. The truck always traveled true, and I never had any difficulty—except once.

I had been working all day at the station and was returning to Hogback in mid-afternoon. I pulled up to the gate and began the trap gate maneuver. The procedure went fine until I realized someone had used the gate after I went through in the morning and had looped the latch-chain in a manner not easily loosened. I hit the panic button, and should have immediately rushed back to the truck and stopped it, but my reaction was to try all the harder to loosen the chain. In those few moments the truck, like a charging bull, was bearing down on the gate. I leaped out of the way just as the gate exploded from the pressure.

"Shucky-dern!" I exclaimed. And I immediately jumped into the driver's seat and turned off the engine. I assessed the damages. The gate, of course, was no longer a gate, but three blessings became apparent. First, only the bumper was in contact with the gate, so the truck was not damaged. Second, the posts on either side of the gate did not budge, so the fence did not spring. And third, the gate was to be replaced by a metal one temporarily stored near the cabin, so when I replaced it, no one would question the change.

I worked late into the evening cleaning up the mess and setting the new gate across the opening. Early the next morning I resumed the installation and managed to finish before anyone came by. Several days later Larry came to see me and immediately noticed the gate. He gave me high praise for my initiative and good workmanship, and to this day I open all gates the old fashioned way.

*   *   *

One Saturday night after spending the evening in Miles City with Bob and some of our friends, we returned to the station late in the evening. It had rained, but only briefly and not very hard. I didn't give a second thought to trouble with muddy roads, and left immediately for Hogback. The sky had cleared, the stars were out, and the night air was cool and pleasant. I had driven a little over half way home when I first started to feel the rear end fishtail. It amazed me how a little moisture could turn the soil in that country to grease, or, as the natives called it, gumbo.

The road was straight and without ditches on either side. There were no hazardous trees or large boulders beyond the road prism, so I kept up my momentum in hopes I would slide through the slick spots. The strategy worked for awhile, but soon I reached a long slick spot that put me in a spin and brought me to a stop.

By this time I was familiar with the terrain and the fences. I left the pickup and walked due east knowing that my course would intersect the fence bordering the exterior of Pasture A. From there it would be about a half-mile to the cabin. Straying a bit to either my left or right didn't matter because I was certain to run into a fence leading to the watering tank close to my cabin.

Of course, I could have followed the road, but didn't because it was longer by at least a half-mile. I knew the country well and could confidently leave the road, knowing it was in the right direction; nevertheless, I made a celestial check with the big dipper just to be sure. It was farther to the fence than I figured, or maybe it just seemed so in the dark. I would have felt more comfortable with a flashlight and cursed myself for not routinely carrying one.

After crossing the fence, I felt much better because the danger of walking blindly into barbed wire no longer existed, so I picked up the pace. The increased speed wasn't just to get to the cabin quickly, but also to slip past any disturbed rattlesnake before it could coil and strike. The grasshoppers were prolific and would jump and fly around me, and the noise they made sounded much like the buzz of a rattlesnake—at least I thought so, scampering along in the dark.

While crossing a swale I recognized it as a dry creek bed within a quarter-of-a-mile of the cabin. Cattle were all around me, nervously mooing at my presence. I softly told them who I was and slowed down, knowing a fence was nearby. As fate would have it, I was welcomed by the sound of the windmill spinning in the breeze and saw its towering silhouette outlined against the starlit sky.

It was a frustrating way to end the evening, but I was grateful for getting home dry and without greater difficulty.

By mid-morning the next day I walked to the pickup and drove it back to the cabin with no sign of slick roads. After that experience I would always spend the night on a cot at the office rather than venture to Hogback on wet roads after dark, and I always carried a flashlight.

My last incident was a costly one. I had routinely loaded the rotted fence posts into the box of the pickup with the intention of taking them to the station. Larry said he would cut them up for firewood. Although the butts had rotted, the portion above ground had remained sound. The load was mounded in the box of my truck so I decided it was time to unload them at Larry's place. I was driving at a reasonable speed but should have slowed down on a curve just before reaching Camel Hump. On the inside of the curve several cottonwood trees stood majestically in a row, the only ones between Hogback and Camel Hump. The road surface on the curve was wash-boarded and when I hit it the truck vibrated sufficiently to cause several of the fence posts to fall off the load. My reaction was to hit the brake, and that put me into a skid. Somehow I left the road on the inside of the curve and the truck came to a stop, but not before the left rear fender was creased by one of the cottonwoods.

I had obviously screwed-up and confessed as much to Larry expecting the repair cost would be docked from my pay, but it was fixed at government expense. I had died a thousand deaths over the ordeal, but was given a new lease on life, and vowed to be more careful.

*   *   *

When the weather got extremely hot I began to work without a shirt. It wasn't long before short pants also became a part of my standard dress. Not wanting to get a sunburn, however, I gradually made the transition. My patience worked, and I painlessly acquired a deep brown tan, allowing me to work with exposed skin all day without any ill effects.

Each month a crew from the BAI would assist in weighing the cattle and extracting blood samples. The cows were herded into the trap, one pasture at a time, and then into a corral. A long chute led from there to a metal squeeze chute where a cow was immobilized in a vice-like contraption so a blood sample could easily be drawn from the neck. They were also inspected for signs of injury or disease and weighed before being returned to their pasture.

My job during this operation was to keep the cattle moving through the chute. Some cows stubbornly refused to move ahead. I used an eight foot two-by-four to prod them. It usually proved effective, although occasionally a poke got no response.

I developed a very clever swing with the two-by-four. I could adroitly whirl it over my head to pick up speed and then on the second turn place it exactly between the boards of the chute so it would slap hard against the rear end of a cow. She would bellow and bolt ahead, and frequently one of the other workers could be heard to say, "Nice shot, Frank."

I almost hoped a cow would hesitate when I prodded her so I could wield my two-by-four, but most moved along with a jab. Aha, at last, a challenger. I deftly whirled my board and was leveling out for a clean shot when the cow lifted her tail and gushered forth with a stream of green cow-pie delight. I caught the flow with my blow and plastered it against her rear end, from where it splattered with gusto. My face and bare chest were covered with dripping processed prairie grass. I sputtered and ran for a cloth and water as one of the guys shouted, "Nice shot, Frank."

I did enjoy those several days with the BAI guys, but equally looked forward to those times when Mert would return to gather field data. Larry, Mert and I would sometimes work together for a week digging soil samples for later analysis, or measuring plant utilization. One of the ways this was done was to clip all the grass in a given area and weigh it. Then we would clip all the grass in an equal size area within an enclosure where cattle were fenced out. This would also be weighed and the difference between the two represented the weight of grass utilized by cattle.

I particularly enjoyed working with the pantograph. Square meter plots had been permanently established (marked) so the plant cover within the square could be precisely recorded. The pantograph consisted of four light rigid bars joined together so a pointer on one of the bars could be used to "draw" around a clump of grass and the shape would be reproduced by a pencil attached at another location on the pantograph. By adjusting the configuration of the rigid bars, the scale could be changed, i.e., the square meter could be reproduced on a letter sized piece of paper. All of the vegetation would thus be recorded, analyzed, and compared to other years to determine changes in plant composition.

Sometimes our field work would also include gathering plant specimens for herbarium use. Those species with extensive root systems were hard to gather because it involved digging deep into the ground to extract the roots intact. The technique for pressing them was exacting, but not complicated. All plant specimens were sent to the Washington, D.C. office for formal identification by experts in taxonomy.

I quickly learned the scientific and common names for all the grasses and other plants in my environment. At the time there was no way of knowing I would be compiling data from our field work for the next several years as a part of my part-time Forest Service jobs during the school year.

Friday, August 24, 1951

Dear Ma,

Mert is here to do some field work. We brought up the cows from one of the pastures that are confined to a heavily grazed area to see if they were losing too much weight—because of the lack of sufficient food. Some of the riders were here to help herd the cows, so there was a lot of activity at Hogback.

Mert walked into the weigh-house and the contrast of the bright sun outside and the shaded interior of the building was somewhat blinding. He found himself standing 18 inches from a rattler. Boy was he spooked! We both grabbed shovels and killed it. He's the biggest I've seen. I'm enclosing the rattles for your scrap book and hope they are in one piece.

Got my room bill today for the first quarter of school this fall. Tom, Chuck and I are sharing a room in Corbin Hall. It's a much nicer dorm than Jumbo Hall and is a couple of dollars cheaper because we will be three in a room instead of two (as we were in Jumbo). Bob Craver [my roommate in Jumbo] *is thinking about studying for the ministry and will probably be changing schools.*[2]

I must run. Bye for now.

Love, R.

P.S. I'll bet you can't shake the rattle as fast as a snake can.

Sunday, August 26, 1951

Dear Ma,

I'm in Glasgow to attend the wedding of two friends from Wesley—Wendell Maney and Norma Burrus. Dick Milne, the president of the Wesley Foundation, came through Miles from Roundup Saturday morning and picked me up. I hadn't planned to go, but Dick said he had to be back in time for work on Monday, so I would make it back, too. We drove 78 miles to Glendive and picked up Chuck (who will be one of my roommates next quarter). Dick's route to Glasgow via Miles and Glendive was 150 miles out of his way, but he didn't seem to mind.

Even though it was 150 miles from Glendive to Glasgow, the time went fast as we each had lots to relate about our summer experiences. We ate dinner in Glasgow at the bride's house, cafe style.

Many of my friends from the U. are here—at least those belonging to Wesley. The guys are crammed into three rooms in this hotel, The Roosevelt. We're having a great time although I'm afraid we are a bit loud.

Last night we went out on the prairie and built a big campfire and sang around it until quite late. I was surprised how many of the Wesley girls were able to make it.

After church this morning, we ate lunch at Norma's house, then went to see Fort Peck Dam. It's the biggest earth filled dam in the world and quite impressive to see.

The wedding is at eight o'clock tonight. Some of us have to be at work by eight in the morning, so even if we don't stay long after the wedding, it will be a long night.

Love, R.

---

[2] Bob did become a Methodist minister. Late in his career he served a church in Butte, Montana, and we occasionally saw one another. In 1985, when my wife's mother died, he officiated at a memorial service for her.

Saturday, September 1, 1951

Dear Ma,

All week it's been raining, at least in the evenings and nights. We've been working on a grass survey and this rain has been making it grow. It's really messing up the survey.

Last evening I went into Miles to the library to study. Bob came by and said, "The Hangout will be open tonight (last night) instead of tomorrow night (tonight). So, at nine we left for the dance. By now I pretty much know everyone and really appreciate the opportunity to spend an evening whooping it up with them.

Later that night I slept on my cot at the station office to avoid having to drive the muddy road to Hogback. In the morning Mert woke me up and we left for the hills. I put the chains on the truck so we could get through the mud. It's certainly easier to do on firm ground and I have become quite adept at it.

We normally don't work on Saturday but this survey has to be completed before new plant growth is advanced. I don't get paid for weekend work, but I've gotten time off on those occasions when the rain prevented me from leaving my cabin, so I can't complain. Besides, I'm interested in the work, I'm learning a lot, and I want to see the project turn out successfully.

It started raining at 1:00 p.m., so we left before the worst of the storm hit. I guess I'll work Monday, too, even though it's a holiday.

Because of the wet conditions, I was afraid I'd be stuck (pun intended) at Hogback for the weekend—a fate worse than death. Mert invited me to shower in his hotel, and then to eat with him, so here I am at the Hotel Olive. Bob is coming in later and we'll go out.

A friend from the college at Bozeman (who I met through Bob) has invited me to a dance on his ranch 20 miles away next Saturday night. It's for all the college kids here, and their dates. It sounds like it will be an interesting evening and lots of fun.

I should mention that the wedding went well, as did the reception afterwards. We really gave Wendell and Norma a hard time, but they enjoyed it. I came back with Tom (the guy who will be my second roommate) since he had Monday off and Dick could make better time by heading straight for Roundup. Chuck was with us so we went through Glendive. It was two o'clock in the morning when we got there, and since we were so tired, Tom and I slept for three hours before going on to Miles City. I made it back to work just in time.

The Shorts have some company from California and invited Mert, Bob, me and some others to their house for Canasta tomorrow night. It may sound boring, but I enjoy the folks and always have a good time. I feel lucky to work for such nice people. They feel more like friends than bosses.

I head back to Missoula for school about September 25; classes start on October first.

Think of you often.

Love, R.

Off and on during the summer I spent a lot of time at the city library studying, but it wasn't college subjects. As a Boy Scout I gradually worked my way up to the rank of Life Scout. I only needed civics and ornithology merit badges to obtain the rank of Eagle, but never quite finished. I was determined during the summer of 1951 to complete the work to earn them, and I did, but was no longer affiliated with scouting, as I was over the age limit. However, I took a measure of satisfaction rationalizing the work had been completed.

Art Heath, the new preacher at the First Baptist Church, had been after me for some time to give a sermon at an evening service. He must have thought that because my brother was so good at it, I would be, too. He was wrong, but I conceded. I did, however, put him off until it was almost time to return to school, not only to give me more time to prepare, but also so I wouldn't have to face the congregation for an extended period of time if I didn't do well.

My topic was The Thirteenth Disciple, and I delivered my message at 7:30 p.m. on September 16, 1951. That's all I remember about it—except a promise to myself never to do it again.

I left Hogback and Fort Keogh anxious to get back to school, but not without a few misgivings. I had become attached to the prairie but thought a return visit was unlikely.

The wheel barrow wash tub at Hogback Cabin.

Rattlesnake in front of outhouse.

Me and my 1950 Dodge truck.

CHAPTER 4

Sophomore Year

Fall quarter classes started the first day of October, a Monday. I had arrived back on campus the Thursday before to register and get squared away in the dorm. Enrollment had dropped by almost 500 students, but I didn't notice the change except for several friends who had left for the military. Favre joined the Navy because he was afraid he would be drafted in the Army and sent to Korea—a place none of us wanted to go.

Despite the drop in students, campus construction was on the move as evidenced by the completion of a new business administration building. There was also talk about plans to erect four other buildings: music, liberal arts, women's center, and Craig Hall—a men's dorm scheduled to open the next fall (1952).

As planned, Tom, Chuck, and I became roommates in Corbin Hall. We liked the convenience of living in the same location as the dining hall, and, in my case, it was much easier to work in the kitchen. Even though my job washing pots and pans paid a little more than other jobs in the kitchen, I decided to work with Ted washing dishes. It was hot work, loading dish racks and pushing them through an automatic washer in a cloud of steam, but we enjoyed our time kidding together. Working with him more than offset the slight decrease in my hourly wage.

Ted had had an exciting summer smokejumping. I asked many questions and became more determined to become part of the outfit. Hollywood had come to the smokejumper training center to make a movie staring Richard Widmark, and Ted saw some filming production. The movie was "Red Skies of Montana."

Now that we were sophomores we began taking courses in the Forestry School. Dendrology, the study of trees, was a fascination because it seemed to relate directly to what foresters were all about.

In surveying class we practiced our skills by surveying the oval in the middle of the campus. Other students wondered what we were doing because they had seen previous classes doing the same thing. Several exclaimed that the Forestry School should have the oval pretty well surveyed by now. Unless the weather was miserable we appreciated being out of the classroom and working in the "field."

Other forestry courses that year included, soils, mensuration (a math course), and field technology. The soils course was particularly timely because some of the information could be applied to the work I was doing with my part-time job with the Forest Service. Mert wanted me to analyze the soil samples we had dug the previous summer. I had learned how to conduct tests to determine the percent of sand, silt and clay, but knew nothing about how to determine the pH of soil. Mert told me to take whatever time I needed to research various means of accomplishing the job and to show him the alternatives along with a recommendation for what I considered the best method.

It wasn't a difficult task, but the assignment intrigued me and gave me a sense of importance. Mert probably knew something about how to measure pH, but he saw an opportunity to both challenge me and help in my development. When I completed the research and showed him the results, he was complimentary, agreed with my findings, and obtained the needed equipment.

What an ideal job. I could work any time during the day as long as it was in at least a two-hour block. Once lined out on the project, I was left alone to run the laboratory tests. If I was working in the afternoon, a dozen or so researchers would gather in the lab for a few minutes during coffee break They were always interested in what I was doing and I appreciated listening to their discussions on current events. They were always educational and often humorous.

I was truly fortunate to have such an opportunity. My only difficulty was transportation between school and work. The distance was just a mile, but even if I ran, it was difficult to find a two-hour block of time because many of my courses required lenthy lab sessions. I dropped physical education (PE) to allow time to work, but since six quarters of PE were required to graduate, I had to make them up. Since the problem persisted, I later decided to take PE dance classes at night—a decision that allowed me to work, but also interfered with my evening study time.

*   *   *

Life in Corbin Hall with Tom and Chuck was quite a contrast to Jumbo Hall. Even though it was an old building, it was maintained in mint condition. The heat was consistently even and comfortable; the showers were sparkling clean and nicely tiled. Our room was on an upper floor at the north end of the building facing North Hall—the freshman dorm for women. Since they dined in Corbin Hall, we had gotten to know many of the girls and somehow I began calling from the window to four of them who lived together in a room opposite us. We had a signal—"How have you been?" It had to be shouted in order to be heard because the space between the building was not within normal conversation range.

Neither Tom nor Chuck participated in these shenanigans, but I frequently had short conversations with whomever happened to hear the call sign. And even though all of us later moved to different housing, whenever we saw one another on campus there was always the greeting, "How have you been?" Arlene Hoiland, a linguistic major, was one of the girls. She graduated a year behind me, and went to Europe to study while I was a soldier in Germany. While on leave I met her in Norway while she was studying Norwegian, and later in France when she studied French in Dijon.

Living three in a room had its drawbacks. My schedule was tight with work and time-consuming lab courses. Both Tom and Chuck, with only lecture courses, had ample free time during the day for study or relaxation. In the evening after 10:00, I was ready to sleep, but they frequently talked late into the night. On one occasion after asking them to "knock it off" several times, I dressed, left the room, and hiked up to tree line on Mount Sentinel. When I returned I listened at the door and they were still talking even though it was the wee hours of the morning, but when I crawled into bed they were silent.

We remained close friends; however, at the beginning of winter quarter Tom and Chuck each moved into a single room. Tom said he needed increased solitude to work on his masters degree. Chuck just decided to follow suit. I ended up rooming with a guy I barely knew and rarely saw. He was a business major and spent a lot of time in the evenings with activities at the frat house, but we got along well.

*　　*　　*

Shortly after Christmas I began to feel guilt about not getting home to visit my family, particularly my mother. I needed to go right to work in the summer because of my financial situation. Furthermore, it seemed apparent I wouldn't be able to return until after I graduated. I wrote to my brother Dan about my concerns. He wrote back immediately:

February 12, 1952

Dear Frank:

I am answering your letter pronto—which means that it will probably be shorter than otherwise. However, I know your question is a real one which deserves a prompt reply.

First of all, may I say that I went through very much the same feelings as you express.

Secondly, let me remind you that there is a very definite explanation for that type of experience. A psychology professor could probably give you a much better picture than I, but here goes a try.

Now, we had a pretty good bringing up. That is, we never had to worry about the most important thing in growing up—we knew we were loved by our parents. (If you or I felt that our parents or family did not love us, we would never have any qualms about ditching the whole gang and striking out for the wild and wooly west—this would be unhealthy).

Then, regardless of how much our family cared for us, we reached that age where we had to begin to make a place for ourselves in the world. (If you or I were a frustrated individual, tied to our mother's apron strings, we would stick close to home and never make a place for ourselves in the structure of society. We might say our mother needs us or I'm needed at home. Really we would probably be covering up a complex. A person MUST learn to stand on his own two feet.)

Actually, it is necessary for the mother bird to throw the baby bird out of the nest and make it fly. A cat might get it. It might break a leg in the fall. But if that bird is ever to be any good, it must stretch its wings and get away from the nest. That's what we're doing.

Mother understands this. Don't have any guilt feelings (which I know you do—just as I did) about thinking only of yourself. It is the natural process of finding one's own personality.

Guilt is the word that the psychologist would use for your present quandary. It is an honest guilt that rises out of a loving home. It is difficult to reconcile "love" with "distance." So when you get far away, you wonder if you are being ungrateful and hard and cruel about affection for family. If we do not understand that this is natural, we have to express it some way—so we begin to feel a little guilty.

You needn't, Frank. Of course, you would like to get home and let Ma know you are still her boy. But it is right that you should consider the money it would cost, the time you would lose in work, etc.

It is almost impossible for a fellow to go through the process of growing up without feeling some of these guilts. You're doing okay. Mother understands and would let you know if she did not.

If I have not hit the core of the thing you were thinking of, please tell me.

Best wishes, Dan

P.S. A baby in April will likely wreck our plans for the trip west.

Although I already sensed most of what Dan explained in his letter, it helped to have his validation. His perspective allowed me to clearly see my guilt as misplaced. While I continued to think of home (and my mother), those thoughts were never again accompanied by feelings of distress at being so far away for so long.

*   *   *

Field technology was an eight-hour Saturday class that took place in the spring quarter—usually at a sawmill or on the Lubrecht Experimental Forest, 30,000 acres owned by the university east of Missoula on the Blackfoot River. We learned to scale logs (measure the number of board feet in a log) and to cruise timber (determine the volume per area of standing tree). The field work was welcomed by all of us, but we felt the loss of our Saturdays. We depended on catching-up on uncompleted projects during the weekend and Saturday classes tended to make us feel the grind.

I continued my involvement in the Wesley Foundation and at spring break once again attended the retreat at Flathead Lake. The change of environment and activity was refreshing even though the late nights were exhausting. On Saturday several of us were in rowboats and came upon large chunks of free floating ice. We stepped onto the ice sheets and found they would support us. Danny On, an ardent member of Wesley, was on one slab and I was on another—both fairly close together. As our respective chunks began to break up, I said, "Guess we'll have to swim for shore."

"I'll do it if you will," challenged Danny.

Thinking he was kidding, I said, "Okay."

In went Danny, swimming hard so he could cross the 30 yards to shore as quickly as possible. I was dismayed to say the least. Although the rowboaters picked me up, they would not take me to shore, saying I had obligated myself to make the swim. I did, and never swam faster in my life. The cold water was such a shock that I still feel it when thinking about my many Wesley trips to the Flathead.

*   *   *

The sophomore forestry curriculum also required two botany courses, plant physiology and plant ecology. I always enjoyed the professors and the subjects in that department. In the winter, Dr. Chessin taught the physiology class, and an incident occurred that stuck with me through the years.

I was reminded of it in 2001 when I read an article in *The Montana Standard* about four retired professors from the University of Montana who meet each week for a hamburger and a pool game. It was a lengthy article with pictures, and I immediately recognized Dr. Chessin as one of them. The story related their conversation and was sprinkled with wit and humor. It seems the WWII vets were displeased with the hoopla being given to "the greatest generation." They also talked about the pressure put on professors to give high grades, resulting in grade inflation. But the item that caught my eye was the statement, "I don't think the university is as much fun as it used to be."

Chessin said, "It seems to me that there is a lot of emphasis on outside research funding, and that's what seems to drive the school." But I had memories of Chessin's lectures and they all brought an image of a man who thoroughly enjoying teaching, so I decided to write him. Following are portions of that letter:

January 5, 2002

Dear Dr. Chessin,

I read the article about you and the other retired UM professors in the December 23, 2001 edition of "The Montana Standard" with great interest . . .

The comment about the university not being as much fun as it was in the '60s and '70s also caught my eye. Perhaps this topic was approached mostly from the point of view of the professor, but I couldn't help thinking of my time at

Missoula as a student in the early '50s . . . During that time I took a botany class from you—[Plant Physiology in the winter quarter of 1952.] *I would like to relate an experience in one of your lectures that you may remember:*

The lecture portion of your class was taught in the Botany Building in a room that resembled an amphitheater. At ground level there was a large laboratory table behind which you usually lectured. One day prior to the beginning of class you sought out my roommate, Ted Rieger, and me with a request to participate in an exercise to help you explain some terminology . . . Ted and I [had taken] *our usual seats. When you reached a point in your lecture where you used the word "germination," Ted and I both got up and ambled down the tiered rows of seats to floor level. We each stretched out on the lab table—Ted with his head one way, and me with my head the other. All the while you totally ignored us and didn't miss a beat in your lecture. Ted and I both could hear under-the-breath comments from our classmates indicating that they thought we were in for big trouble and that you would not put up with our nonsense. But we remained silent with our eyes shut while you continued. You explained in considerable detail that a seed was a dehydrated, resting embryo with a barely detectable metabolism. This eventually evolved to your explanation of the characteristics of "quiescency" and "dormancy."*

You explained that in the case of quiescency if the seed were hydrated and atmospheric and edaphic conditions were correct—e.g. temperature was suitable and oxygen was present—germination would occur. On the other hand, in the case of dormancy, even though the requirements for water, temperature and oxygen might be met, germination still would not take place because there was some other inhibiting cause.

[You asked a female] *in the class (I'll refer to as Jane) to approach the lab table. Pointing to Ted you said, "This is Dormancy. No matter what Jane does, notice how totally unresponsive Dormancy remains. Please, Jane, try to get some type of response from Dormancy . . ."*

Jane was terribly embarrassed and awkwardly strutted around Ted's end of the lab table, but he remained stone-like.

"Now, Jane, would you please go to the other end of the table and do the same kind of things to Quiescency." By this time Jane was obviously uncomfortable, but she did as she was asked. I don't remember what her inducements were, but when she executed them I leaped off the table and tried to grab her. She screamed and bolted out the door.

I thought you might be interested to know that at least one of your students well remembers the difference between dormancy and quiescency. I appreciated your willingness to have a little fun with your classes while teaching, and I have often wondered if you used this charade in subsequent classes through the years . . .

Many good wishes for continued success in the pool room.

Most sincerely,
Frank Fowler

In a few days came the following reply:

Dear Frank—

I received your most welcome letter of 5 Jan and I'll say at the outset that I remember you very well (you were one of my top students) even your appearance. Were you from Maryland—and did you mention that you detected a hint of my Eastern U.S. upbringing in my voice? (A most perceptive observation.) [I was amazed he remembered so much detail after 50 years!]

I'm glad you remember the demonstration on seed germination—your involvement seems logical . . .

My recollection of the details is essentially like yours, although if your account is correct, I should also be embarrassed at some stage of the embellishments!

I don't think the demo was repeated—just didn't have the right cast!

I'd very much like to hear further from you (and Ted) about your former professional lives (I assume you're retired now).

All the best!
Sincerely, Mike Chessin

As it turned out we did meet in Missoula in April, 2002. We talked for a couple of hours and then went to a string concert at the music school on campus—he and his wife, and me and mine. I wonder how many thousands of students he has taught since that incident 50 years ago. I still marvel at his memory. It was a remarkable day.

*   *   *

My winter quarter roommate decided to live in his fraternity house spring quarter. As it happened, Ted also lost his roommate, so he and I moved into a room and stuck together for our remaining years in college.

One of my spring quarter courses was plant ecology taught by Dr. Joseph Kramer. He was fondly known as Smoky Joe—a small man with dark olive skin and a receding hairline of white, wiry hair. He loved to teach and quickly gained the respect of the entire class. His objective was to be certain that you learned. He started out with the formal definition of ecology—something like "the reciprocal relationship of plants and their environment." But he immediately followed up with a less formal one, "the painful elaboration of the obvious."

Dr. Kramer's classes were educational and fun. Several times he took us to the open hills surrounding Missoula and taught us to identify grasses and forbs in the field. If he asked someone to name a plant and they couldn't, he would tell them. Later he was certain to ask the same person to again identify the plant. His persistent and encouraging approach rapidly brought us all to a high proficiency in plant identification.

[A decade later when I was the forest ranger at Powell Ranger Station 60 miles from Missoula, Smoky Joe used to occasionally visit my district. He had retired and sometimes felt the need to poke around in the woods, so we usually strolled along on a nearby back road. He never tired of asking about the people he once taught, and I always felt honored by his presence.]

*   *   *

When I was turned down for a job with the smokejumper project the year before, I was left with the impression from Mr. Woolfolk that a year's experience with the Forest Service would make me a viable candidate, provided, of course, that I received a satisfactory performance rating. I knew that Woolfolk considered me a desirable employee and would convey that opinion to any potential employer, so when the time came to apply again I listed him, Merton Reed, and Larry Short as references.

It was not a great surprise when the notification letter came accepting me for training as a smokejumper, but I was ecstatic nonetheless. Ted would be returning as well, so I eagerly looked forward to summer.

However, while playing basketball I jumped for a rebound and came down on someone else's foot, turning my right ankle. The resulting sprain was severe and swelling and soreness remained for a long time. Even after the passage of several weeks, if I took a wrong step with that foot, I could feel tenderness. It concerned me that it might interfere with my fitness to jump from an airplane.

*　　*　　*

I ended up once again having to borrow money from Bruce to make it through spring quarter, but it was only a few dollars and could easily be covered by my first paycheck in the summer.

My grade point average (GPA) for spring quarter was a little better than 3.0, but for the year it was somewhat less, in fact, quite similar to that in my freshman year. I knew I could do better.

Above: Danny On in Flathead Lake; me diving.
Below: Danny and I congratulating each other for a successful swim.

CHAPTER 5

Smokejumper Training

It was Sunday, June 15, 1952 when Mr. Woolfolk dropped me off at the federal building in downtown Missoula to catch the ride to the smokejumper training center.

I had eagerly awaited that day. Anticipating training filled me with such elation that I saw everything with a kind of surreal quality. It's difficult to explain, but if you have ever intensely wanted something for a long time, and finally found it within your grasp, you will understand.

The training site, located 27 miles northwest of Missoula near the Ninemile Ranger Station, was a secluded spot in a forest setting isolated from the public. The buildings were single story barracks sided with brown-stained lumber that had weathered so they looked like they had always been there. There were no concrete sidewalks—just paths of gravel covered with pine needles. The structures were left from Camp Menard, a CCC (Civilian Conservation Corps) facility abandoned shortly after World War II began.

I was assigned a bunk in one of the barracks and began meeting recruits. Some I knew from the university and a few of them were in my forestry school class. Those who had jumped in previous years were referred to as "old men" (nothing to do with age). They were not a part of our training program because they were only required to take a one-week refresher course. Our training would last a month and we were referred to as "new men."

Monday was an easy day. We received some general orientation and listened to several lectures on safety and fire equipment. We also signed our contracts and were issued hard hats, for use when working in the woods. Mine was number 138, which I dutifully recorded in my diary.

On the second day the training camp atmosphere was unmistakable. The first half hour was calisthenics, so rigorous I was exhausted. This was somewhat surprising because I was in pretty good shape, but obviously wasn't used to this regimen. Everyone had difficulty, and several couldn't do all the repetitions. Perhaps this was to be expected at this stage of training.

Fortunately the remainder of the morning was spent inside listening to lectures and watching training films. Just before lunch we were issued jump suits, a welcomed event because it further confirmed that we were smokejumpers—or soon would be. Training in them was several days away, but before we actually needed the suits it was necessary to be certain they fit and were properly adjusted. It didn't take long to select a jacket, although I had to find one a bit large in the chest in order to accommodate my long arms. It was made of heavy canvas with padding sewn right into the fabric to protect the elbows. The collar was always to be worn in an upright position. The back extended to the middle of the head while the front came to my chin. This unique design prevented branches from piercing under the helmet if a smokejumper landed in a tree.

The pants were also made of canvas and contained padding in the knees, shins, and seat, making them considerably heavier and bulkier than the jacket. Each pant leg had a zipper that could be extended beyond the matched teeth. When this was done, it caused the zipper to "unravel," allowing the entire pant leg to quickly open. To put them on, we simply put our arms through suspenders, engaged the zippers, and zipped up the sides of both pant legs.

The pants had two more unusual features. First, a heavy web strap extended from the arch of one foot, up the inseam to the crotch, then down the inseam of the other leg and under the arch of the other foot. The strap ended on the outside of each foot at a buckle. Its adjustment allowed the pant leg to ride low or be hoisted high. This might at first seem ridiculous until you realize the strap's function was to prevent the parachute harness from pulling up against the groin. The buckles were cinched up so the strap crossed the crotch three or four inches short of the groin. Thus, when the parachute opened and the opening shock pulled hard against the harness, all the jumper felt was a little pressure on the bottom of his feet. Loose buckle adjustment could subject a jumper to a world of hurt.

Second, a large pocket sewn on the outside of the right pant leg carried a hundred-foot length of five-eighths-inch cotton rope. This was used when a jumper hung-up in a tree and needed rope to rappel to the ground.

The last two pieces of equipment were equally significant: one obvious, one not. In those days football helmets were made of leather and differed from the ones used on the grid-iron by the addition of a heavy wire face-mask hinged from the brow of the helmet. A chin pad attached to the mask prevented the wire mesh from injuring the skin.

The other item, a girdle, provided stomach muscle support and was intended to prevent strain from the exertion of jumping. It was worn over our denim pants and secured in place by several buckles on elastic straps. It probably served the same purpose as the belt worn by weight lifters to avoid hernias. The back of the girdle also provided some protection for the tail bone should an unfortunate jumper roll over a rock when landing. As time went by, many judged the apparatus unnecessary, but I accepted it as part of my garb.

The weight and bulk of all this equipment made walking difficult. Since it was worn over our regular clothing, it made us hot, especially on a warm summer day.

The afternoon was full of physical activity, beginning with instructions on how to climb a tree using climbing irons. The uncomplicated irons were easily strapped to each leg in two places: at the ankles and just below each knee. They each extended down the inside of the lower leg and bent at a right angle under the arch of the foot, so we actually stood on them. Located at the instep was a sharp spur protruding at an angle that could easily penetrate tree bark.

It looked fairly simple to scramble right up a tree—at least when watching an experienced climber do it. But all of us were new at this and lacked the confidence required to feel safe in such a precarious situation.

We wore a thick leather climbing belt. "D" rings were located on each side close to the user's hips. A second belt with snap hooks on each end was draped from one of the D-rings. Before beginning a climb, one end of the belt would be unsnapped and extended around the tree and snapped into place on the free D-ring. This prevented a climber from falling backwards, and gave considerable confidence to a novice.

It took awhile before it was second nature to wear the belt low on our hips instead of around the small of our backs. In the latter position it didn't take long to become exhausted. Even when the belt was correctly positioned our movements were tentative, reflecting our apprehension. To establish a secure hold, we tended to jab the spurs into the bark when taking an upward step, but this led to greater difficulty because they would stick and become difficult to extract. We were also inclined to hug the tree trunk, but when this was done the knees were also drawn closer to the trunk putting the spurs at an improper angle. In fact, if the knees were drawn to the trunk, the spurs would likely lose their grip and the climber would slide down the tree—at least to the extent allowed by his safety belt.

The first day on climbing irons or "spurs," as we commonly called them, was a bit scary even if I didn't get very high off the ground. It amazed me how quickly my legs would begin to shake. It wasn't so much a result of fear as it was from using improper technique, resulting in fatigued muscles. Later we would learn how to improvise a climbing belt since they were never dropped to us on a fire.

The purpose of this training was to prepare us for parachute retrieval should we (or cargo) happen to land in a tree. We all had a healthy respect for the hazards associated with climbing, and while most of us got used to it, we usually tried to avoid a tree landing because it was so much easier to retrieve a parachute in open ground. Of course, if there were ground hazards such as rocks or numerous fallen trees, we welcomed a tree landing.

The rest of the afternoon was spent learning how to fell a tree with a crosscut saw (often referred to as a "misery whip"). We trained almost exclusively on snags (dead trees) so there would be no wasted wood. We were also introduced to the Pulaski,[3] and taught how to safely chop branches and trees. By day's end we were all beat.

That night I wrote home describing these details, adding:

"The food is terrific—all you can eat, family style. Plenty of milk, a big variety of food and seconds on dessert. The fellows are swell. Some from New Jersey, New York, Maryland—just all over. All of them have worked summers for the Forest Service.

The camp is beautiful. It's in the middle of the woods. There is a ball diamond, volley ball court, basketball court, two horse shoe pits, a Ping-Pong table, a pool table, etc. It's really nice. I guess they figure we'll spend our evenings playing and getting in shape.

I like it very much.

There are about 60 of us new fellows in training. All together there's about 140 jumpers in Montana."

The morning of the third day was devoted to a lecture on smokejumper behavior. For example, jump gear would be packed and "hot to go." That is, our names would be on the gear sack and would be stored where easily accessible in the loft. Our personal gear sacks would be equipped with extra socks, toothbrush, shirt—whatever we deemed essential. The sack was large enough

---

[3] A single-bit ax with an adz-shaped hoe extending from the back, invented by Ranger Pulaski following the great fires of 1910.

to hold only the bare essentials. We were told logger type boots with composition soles were mandatory, and a small note pad and pencil would be carried at all times to serve as a diary. It hardly seemed necessary to be told, but it was made clear that a hard hat was a mandatory part of our equipment.

The lecture continued with detailed protocol for every aspect of smokejumper behavior. It established a skeleton of knowledge upon which later discussions, films, and hands-on training would build to "flesh out" a complete picture of a smokejumper's job. The training was beginning to make us feel we were finally on our way into the ranks.

In the afternoon we were shown how to dig fire line, but since there was no fire it was called "cold line." We also worked at timber management, i.e. thinning and pruning trees so the forest would be more productive. This served a dual purpose: getting physical exercise and learning the proper use of tools.

After morning exercise on Thursday we split into four groups and rotated through four different activities. First we chopped wood and bucked logs with a crosscut saw. It was surprising how quickly most of us became quite adept at using the saw efficiently, although it took practice to learn to work together smoothly, allowing the saw to do most of the work.

Then we spent more time climbing with tree spurs. I was not alone in feeling that this was one of the more difficult tasks to master, and only through continued climbing did the fear begin to subside. It was a great sense of satisfaction for me to begin to feel proficient.

Next we built more cold line and I began to appreciate the versatility of the Pulaski. It was easy to twist the handle 180 degrees so the grubbing side was replaced by the axe side and I could switch from scraping to chopping without missing a stroke. We finished the day with more timber management improvement activities.

I knew several fellows from school, but by this time many of our crew felt like old friends. I seem to hit it off particularly well with Dave Lodzinski. He was attending a university in Utah, majoring in range management. We decided that when our training was complete we would try to go on "project" together. Project consisted of a temporary assignment to do some type of field work, usually on a ranger district, until we were needed to fight fire.

Friday was a milestone: the first week of training was over. We watched a film about cargo handling and dropping to a fire. Then, we once again went to the woods to improve our tree climbing skills. I climbed several times and felt like I was getting the knack of it when I was able to go up 60 feet. The rest of the day we felled snags. These were big lunkers with diameters at breast height of two feet or greater. We not only improved our crosscut sawing skills, but we also learned how to size up a tree to avoid pinching the saw blade or dropping it in the wrong direction.

I wrote to my mother the following Monday:

Monday, June 23, 1952

Dear Ma,

Well, here it is the second week of training. Saturday I went to Missoula to make a dental appointment for next Saturday. Since it rained both Saturday and Sunday I spent most of the weekend at camp reading and playing Ping-Pong, pool, and cards.

Today, after exercising, we split into four groups. My group started at the "let-down" site. We put on all our jump gear including the harness. I don't believe I have told you about that yet. It's a rather simple get-up made of inch-and-a-half cotton webbing equipped with clips on the shoulders so a parachute can be attached. [Clips are also located in the front for the emergency parachute.] *What fascinated me was the mechanism located on the chest called a single-point-release box. The strap over the left shoulder is permanently fixed to the box, but the strap over the right shoulder and the ones around each leg are snapped into it. By pulling a pin from the box, rotating a plate, and then smacking it with the heal of the hand, the single-point-release box allows the harness to pop free.*

In order to practice let-downs, an apparatus comprised of a heavy cable strung across two poles is used. Attached to the cable are several pulleys that provided the means to hoist several jumpers in the air—simulating their position in a tree landing. Today we only went up a few feet, so if we did something wrong we wouldn't fall very far. It was actually sort of fun. You have to reach down to your right leg to get the let-down rope in the leg pocket and then "weave" it in a prescribed manner through some "D" rings at your waist and up to the ends of the parachute—being careful that the rope is fed under the harness—otherwise it will not spring free when the single-point-release box is smacked. A rather crucial step is remembering to undo the bayonet strap[4] and unthread it from the harness. It's purpose is to prevent the jumper from separating from the harness should his single-point-release box somehow happen to release. This strap would prevent a

---

[4] I queried several smokejumpers, including overhead, about the derivation of the name "bayonet strap." Some didn't even recall its function; many remembered its function, but not its name; a few knew both the name and function; but nobody knew why it was called a bayonet strap.

free fall to the ground. It would also prevent a jumper from separating from his harness when making a let-down if he failed to uncouple it.

There's more to weaving the let-down than I am able to explain, but let me assure you that when done properly it allows a controlled, gradual descent down the rope.

We then simulated parachuting from an airplane by jumping off a tower with our harness attached to a heavy nylon rope that stretched so much that I was surprised when I reached the end of it. I thought it would jar me silly, but I felt like I had reached the end of a rubber band.

This was our first day to run the obstacle course. It's designed to be physically demanding, but we are in pretty good shape now and enjoy the challenge. Thank goodness we were allowed to take off the jump gear before starting, otherwise it would have been a killer. The course included a platform several feet high from which we would jump and roll on the ground. This is intended to teach us how to land after our parachute descent.

The mock-up was the last of the four units we trained on today. It was supposed to be the fuselage of an airplane, although it didn't look like one at all— just sort of a rectangular box affair. We would get inside and go through the motions like we will when we actually jump. The spotter would pretend to give directions to the pilot, give the signal to cut the engines, and give the slap on the shoulder, the signal to jump. We were suited-up, of course. It certainly didn't feel like we were flying, but we got the idea of the procedure well enough.

In the afternoon we were given muscular tests to see how we ranked with each other. In future years they intend to set up physical exercise standards for recruits, and if they can't meet them, they will be dropped. Supervisory personnel feel that if a fellow can't make the grade in the physical tests, he's more injury-prone.

Many of us were given physicals today.

We jump a week from this Thursday.

Love, R.

In this letter I didn't tell my mother about the difficulty caused by my amblyopic left eye—a condition commonly referred to as a "lazy eye." The condition was discovered early in my childhood and resulted in blurry sight in one eye. It had never bothered me even though I could only read the top line or two of the eye chart with my right eye closed, resulting in a score of 20/200 for my left eye. The doctor was from the Department of Agriculture in Washington, D.C., and although I passed the depth perception test, it was difficult, and it concerned him. The test required looking through a stereoscope at several different shaped objects and identifying the one appearing closest. In a natural setting I have no difficulty seeing in depth, but in a test situation where the view to each eye is isolated, I do. First, I closed my right eye (the one with 20/20 vision) and forced my left to function. Then, when the right eye was opened, I could see stereoscopically. The process was a little slow and the doctor, aware of the poor vision in my left eye, decided I was a poor risk. I was devastated, and knew I hadn't heard the last of it.

[Interestingly enough, 43 years later when we had a smokejumper reunion in Missoula the fellow who had been behind me when we took the physical remembered the incident clearly—which reflects the impact a dismissal threat of anyone had on the group at large.]

The next day the training supervisor, Fred Brauer, called me aside. He began by saying Joe Woolfolk would probably give me a job if I wanted to go back and work for him instead of smokejumping. I was beside myself. It looked like it was over for me, but I reacted with determination to continue with the jumpers. It wasn't until later that I realized he was testing the depth of my commitment.

He concluded, "Well, we'll do the best we can to keep you, but even if you're able to stay, there's no guarantees about next year. This doctor could get some minimum requirements established that could keep you from qualifying."

"Are you saying I'm okay for this year?" I pleaded.

"No. The doctor wants to interview you this afternoon. A lot depends on how he feels after the interview," Fred cautioned.

I was utterly devastated. I may have felt differently had there been difficulty standing up to the physical demands of the training, or if I was unable to get the knack of executing a proper roll when hitting the ground, or if I was unable to master tree climbing. I knew I was doing as well as most—perhaps better than some. The dream so long pursued was now slipping away.

In the afternoon I was singled out for a consultation with Dr. Johnson. Fred was there along with two other supervisory personnel. The doctor asked me several questions about the history of my amblyopia and how it affects my every day activities.

"I'm not aware my eyesight causes difficulty in any situation," I said.

"Well, how about sports—say basketball, or Ping-Pong. Do you sometimes find a compromised depth perception hinders your playing?" he pressed.

"No, not at all. I frequently shoot the long shot in basketball and make a fair percentage. And I play Ping-Pong most every day here in camp and I'd say I win more than I lose," I answered honestly.

"Well, let me get to what bothers me the most. I realize you haven't made your first jump from an airplane yet, but when you do I can't see how anyone could say that you are not at greater risk than someone without vision difficulties. Are you the least bit concerned that when you are approaching a landing and the ground comes rushing up, that you might incorrectly anticipate contact with the earth and pull your legs up prematurely, subjecting yourself to a very hard landing and possibly injury?"

"No . . ." I started to reply, but Dr. Johnson cut me off and said, "Please think carefully about your reply for a moment . . . and try to answer as truthfully as you possibly can."

I thought for a moment and then replied, "We're taught in training that this is a risk that all jumpers—even those with perfect vision—are faced with. So, in order to minimize the danger, we're instructed to watch the horizon when we are getting close to the ground so we won't prematurely anticipate ground contact. We're taught to let our legs tell us when we reach the ground, not our eyes."

I glanced at Fred's face as I finished this explanation and could detect an ever-so-slight wry smile on his face. One of the other overhead[5] seated in a position where Dr. Johnson could not see him gave me a "thumbs up" while grinning from ear-to-ear.

That ended the consultation. I was told a final decision would come later, but my training would continue in the meantime. It was a relief not to be terminated on the spot, but I would carry a burden of dread until Brauer gave me a green light.

The rest of the week we continued to train in groups on the four units, i.e., the let-down, towers, obstacle course, and mock-up. We also spent time in first aid training and radio use.

Saturday, June 28, 1952

Dear Ma,

I'm hanging around camp this weekend because I'm broke and don't wish to go in debt. I washed a few clothes and went over to the obstacle course to watch a few fellows who are having a hard time with their rolls. The instructors have stressed the importance of a good roll when you hit the ground, so those who are

---

[5]   The hierarchy at the Smokejumper Project level consisted of two administrative assistants (Fred Brauer and Jim Waite), seven foreman, and 16 squad leaders. This group of 25 was considered overhead.

having a difficult time practice on the weekend. Four or five fellows left in the middle of last week because of poor physical fitness or inability to perform well. I know some were deeply disappointed, and I couldn't help but empathize with them, but I expect it is for the best. A lot of emphasis is put on avoiding our first jumping fatality, so you either measure up or you're out. Nevertheless, we all bleed a little.

Last week we were having our second four-hour period of first aid. As we got close to the end of the session, one of the overhead said someone wanted to see me in the office. I rose slowly (afterwards the fellows said I was as white as a sheet—I believe it, too) and went thinking of only one thing . . . the doc . . . my physical . . . the boot. But to my delight, Mr. Woolfolk was there. He had spent the day at a Ninemile Ranger Station, two miles below our training camp, and had come up to say "Hi."

He asked if I needed anything and said he had made a dental appointment for me on July 5. He also said he'd be on a trip that weekend and I could have the Ford the following week. It's a 1937 model that he mainly uses for fishing. Just how fortunate can a guy get? If he'd just bawl me out once in a while, he'd almost feel like a father.

In fact Mrs. Woolfolk had cracked down on me the last time I was in Missoula. I was out with a friend and a couple of girls and when we drove up to the house (Woolfolk's) we made an unnecessary amount of racket and started the dogs to barking. When I came to the foot of the stairs Mrs. Woolfolk was at the top. She said, "See what you've done." I said, "I'm sorry." Then she sharply said, "You should be," and stomped off to bed. Yep, really feels like home. She wasn't mad in the morning, though.

I know you realize that the first week of training was confined to conditioning, tool training, and fire fighting, but do you realize that we receive only seven days of actual parachuting training before we jump? We worked on it all this past week and we will have two days next week, then . . . Geronimo! We are to the point now where we train all morning every day in our jump suits. They are so hot that it's sickening at times. It's a relief when we can get them off. Friday we put on both the regular and emergency parachutes and did some practicing. That's not something a guy will ever get used to because it is so cumbersome and the suits and parachutes are so heavy.

We jump next Wednesday and Thursday and every day the following week—seven jumps in all. It really feels close to home now and I get butterflies just thinking about it. There are many things I'd like to tell you, but it took me two weeks to learn it and I could hardly put it on paper now.

Oh, I want to mention that we had two training exercises that were very interesting last week. The first was how to set up and operate a radio in case one is dropped on a fire. They always drop one if a jumper is injured so that the extent of the injury can be communicated to the spotter in the airplane. The second was training with a special gurney made for smokejumper use. It's somewhat like a stretcher only fashioned more like a basket, but what really makes it different is the airplane wheel that it rides on. We trained with harnesses that allow those stationed at either end to carry the weight on their shoulders rather than arms. If a jumper is hurt and needs to be transported to a road or airfield, a ten-man crew jumps to perform the task. So much for that.

Saturdays and Sundays we only get two meals, one at 9:00 a.m. and one at 4:00 p.m. It's now 7:00 p.m. and I'm starved!

My muscles are becoming used to exercise and hard work, thank goodness.

Love, R.

*   *   *

On Monday we exercised and went to the units to train for the last time. We had trained there so much that it had become routine, and we felt ready for the real thing. In the afternoon we received training in map reading followed by an explanation of the development of the parachute.

The first parachutes were made of silk, but grasshoppers would occasionally eat holes in them. The material of choice quickly moved to nylon. Parachute design also changed rapidly. When they first started in 1940, jumpers used Eagle parachutes, but the opening shock was extreme, often resulting in bruises on the shoulders.

Our chutes were designed with much more steering capability than the Eagle and were packed so the shroud lines deployed first and then the canopy blossomed in a manner that substantially reduced opening shock. Our main parachute was 28 feet in diameter and the reserve 24 feet. [In later years the diameter was increased to 32 feet, thus slowing the rate of descent.]

Parachute training was not on the Tuesday agenda—that was all behind us. We spent the day learning how to read a compass and measure the area of an extinguished fire. We practiced pacing to measure distance and learned several formulas to calculate the area so we could accurately make out a fire report. Though it was interesting, and important, we were somewhat preoccupied thinking about the next day and our first jump. It was surprising how many of us had never flown before.

We usually played softball in the evening though it was strictly voluntary. Several of the crew had sustained injuries from playing sports, and I always taped my ankle because I didn't want to risk spraining it again. We played that evening, but our numbers were a bit fewer than usual, and we quit early because we were scheduled to get up before dawn the next day.

Wednesday, July 2, 1952

Dear Ma,

Last night as I lay in bed I must have jumped umpteen times. On most of them I had a line-over, that is, a cord that should have run from the canopy of the chute to a riser, but which instead crosses over the canopy and causes a bulged chute. Because of its appearance we commonly refer to it as a Mae West. Regardless of what you call it, if you have one, your descent is hastened. Then some of the time I imagined I had a streamer, which is a fully collapsed chute, and, of course, I had to use my emergency. When landing I broke every bone in my body on one jump or another. Between a rotten cold I have and my wandering mind, I was a long time getting to sleep. When I finally got there I awoke with a cramp in my foot, probably because my feet were wet most of yesterday.

At 4:00 a.m. I heard the dinging of the camp wake-up bell. It wasn't the usual "ring-a-ding-a-ding-a-ding . . . ." of a metal bar ricocheting its way around the inside of an iron triangle; instead, it was a slow pounding on one side of the triangle in the cadence of a funeral march. The cook was obviously trying to spook us.

They got us up early to take advantage of the high density air and the low temperature. Both low density air and high temperature are conducive to a higher rate of descent.

I ate a light breakfast because I didn't know how airplane riding would affect my stomach—or vice versa. Also, my nervousness might have helped to upset things. By 5:00 a.m. I had my ankle taped (I twisted it again about a week ago but refrained from telling you for obvious reasons. It wasn't bad and it didn't even swell, but I always get it taped when I feel the activity calls for it.)

I was hiking the mile-and-a-half to the airstrip with my jump gear and my cohorts while we joked about making our first jump. Even though we all kidded about it, I knew that inside they felt as scared as I did. We took a few exercises when we reached the airstrip and waited for the planes to arrive from Missoula. Finally they came: two Travelairs which hold three jumpers, two pilots, and a spotter (he tells you when and where to jump); and one Ford Trimotor which carries eight jumpers, two pilots, and a spotter. The Travelairs jump one man at a pass while the Ford jumps two. I was slated to go up with the second load in the Ford.

[Anyone living in Missoula would frequently see a Ford Trimotor flying over the city, so it was familiar to me. It is indeed a strange looking aircraft with a skin of corrugated metal, a feature borrowed from the German Junker. Its design was a combination of the Junker and the Fokker, so it looked more German than American. The distinctly American control wheel was actually a wooden Model T Ford steering wheel.

The Ford was without flaps and many of the control cables were located outside the airplane, a tell-tale sign of an early design. Henry Ford began building successful Tri-motor airplanes in 1928 and when he quit in 1933 he had made 199 of them. When commercial airlines started replacing them with more advanced aircraft, Ford Trimotors became affordable to bush pilots. They came to be regarded as perfect back country airplanes and were well-known for their ability to carry heavy loads and land on short airstrips. Their wings were three feet thick where they joined to the fuselage and their wingspan was 78 feet. A Ford Trimotor could carry eight jumpers and their cargo. It was slow flying, with a cruising speed close to 100 miles an hour, but could slow down to 65—a desirable feature for jumpers since the wind blast would be less at slow speed.

The official name was Ford Trimotor. Its nick name was the Tin Goose, but most of us simply referred to it as the Ford.]

The planes took-off with their first load, made their drops, and returned for more jumpers. We were suited up and ready to go. I was so excited about flying that I forgot about jumping for awhile. The ten of us sat on the floor and could hardly see out; in fact, we could just see the tops of the mountains. We kept climbing until we reached an altitude of 2800 feet (above ground, not sea level), leveled off and made a pass over the jump spot. The spotter threw out a drift shoot to determine the wind direction. It only drifted slightly, so wind was not a concern.

The doors have been removed on all smokejumper aircraft, so when we refer to the "door" we are talking about the space once occupied by a door. Because of this the temperature in the plane is not much warmer than that outside, and since we've had very little warm weather lately, it was quite cool. Maybe that was a blessing. Anyway, we circled around again and it simply amazed me to think there was nothing but air between us and the ground. The first two jumpers got in position and at the given signal they jumped. We circled and the second two got ready. *When the man in the door was given the signal to go he just turned and looked at the spotter. I thought he had "chickened out," and I instantly began to wonder if I'd have guts enough to do it. Evidently he didn't think he had been given the signal and when he realized he had, he went. Of course he was past the jump spot, but he was able to steer back pretty well.*

I slid over by the door as I was next to go. I could see everything clearly. I watched the guys who had just jumped descend all the way to the ground. The spotter hooked up my static line, and the guy's behind me, and then it struck me—I was the next to go. I looked out the plane and saw the barracks, and I couldn't help but wish I were there. Then I saw the airstrip and little ants that were men waiting their turn to go airborne. Just to think that I was there a few minutes ago wishing I was up here made me sick. Then I saw the jump spots off in the distance—two of them in the meadow marked clearly by orange crepe paper in the form of an "X." I was to guide to the one on the right and the man behind me to the one on the left.

The spotter called for positions, so I put my right foot out the door and into the step as I had done many times before in the mock plane, only I had never before experienced the strong wind blowing my leg to the right. I didn't let the unexpected blast keep me from forcing my foot into the step, and I sat back on my left heel. The fellow who was to follow was hunched over close behind, and I couldn't help but wonder if he would be able to hit the step when he left in a hurry. Hitting the step was necessary in order to drop low enough to avoid hitting the top of the door, a tricky maneuver at best, and I was glad I was the first man.

Those next few seconds seemed like an eternity. "I wonder if the static line is hooked up okay? Is the safety secure on my single-point-release—one push with the safety "off" and the harness could fly off except for one dinky little safety strap that might hold you and your chute together? Would the chute open okay? Does the spotter know what he's doing? Do I know what I'm doing?" Then I remembered what someone said in training, "Once you leave that door no one can help you. If you don't know what to do if something bad happens, it won't take long before it's all over." At the time it seemed trivial, and as a matter of fact, jumping didn't seem difficult, but at this time it really seemed like it takes a lot to leave the door. Out of the corner of my eye I watched the spotter immediately to my left with his head out the window. I saw him wave one way and then the other to give the pilot directions. Actually this was only a few seconds, but . . . well, you know.

He waved his arm up and down, I straightened my kneeling position (still one foot in the step out of the door), gripped the lower part of the door firmly, and looked at the horizon to keep my head erect and eyes forward. This was pounded into our heads with every jump from the tower in training. The waving motion was a signal to cut the engines. I don't know if all three of them are cut or not, but I felt the sudden release of power, and the relative quietness brought by the engines at rest. We were gliding and the wind gently whistled in the door, but only momentarily. With the slap on the back I rose on my right foot and brought my left one through the door and jumped. I tried to yell "Geronimo" as we all did when jumping from the tower, but I couldn't. I folded my arms across my chest emergency parachute and brought my feet together. Oh, my stomach. Some fellows got no sensation of falling, but I did—or maybe it was just butterflies. I felt the welcome jerk from my chute when it opened and then heard the plane pick up its engines and drone away. I checked my canopy and found I had no line-overs and that I had a white chute with no tails. I had hoped for a candy stripe, that is, a red and white one.

One of the overhead on the ground began to speak to us over the megaphone with directions. "Pull on your right guide line. Plane. Plane more," referring to the maneuver of pulling down on the front risers so the chute tips forward and spills air out the back, thus giving you more horizontal speed. It was really nice hanging up there. We were told that this would probably be the highest we would ever jump. It didn't seem like I was falling at all, in fact, it didn't even give me the sensation of being precariously perched. I felt a hundred times worse 50 feet up a tree with spurs on. It's so peaceful up there I didn't want to come down, but I guided for my spot and missed it by 50 feet. Before I hit I reached for my risers and put my feet together and then the ground really came at me. I didn't realize I was falling so fast (18 feet per second they tell us), but I rolled okay. The ground was wet and soft, so the risks of getting hurt were minimal. I got a "VG" (very good) on the handling of my chute and a "VG" on my roll. Few men received grades above a "G" and only three of us had a "VG" on both. Normally, it probably doesn't mean all that much, but because of my scare with being washed out, I was grateful for high marks attesting to my capability.

Did you realize that we can steer a chute? All of ours have slots in them which give us a four mile an hour horizontal speed (with no wind). Slots are just two slits about seven feet long in the back portion of the chutes. By pulling a guide line you close one slit and the air coming out the other causes you to turn. Tails are like a small awning in the rear of the chute through which air funnels out, thus propelling you about five miles per hour. So you see, you can really move about horizontally quite a bit. You can even buck a wind if it's not too great.

We jump again tomorrow and I promise I won't talk it up like I did this one, but I had to tell you about my first airplane ride.
I'll be at Woolfolk's over the weekend.

Love, R.

P.S. Wonder what it's like to land in a plane?

We were back in the classroom that afternoon—a little anticlimactic after spending the morning in a weird combination of fright and aerobatic ecstasy. Nevertheless, we buckled down and studied the theory of wild land fire fighting, knowing that it was important to the accomplishment of our mission. "It only takes a couple of minutes to parachute to a fire, but it takes many hours of hard work to put a fire out. Always remember that a parachute is just a way to get there, fire fighting is your primary job," admonished our trainers many times over.

*　　*　　*

The next day we jumped again and I was assigned to the Travelair, whose black and orange colors always reminded me of Halloween. Its official name was Curtis Travelair, but no one called it that. Travelair was enough. It was a single engine plane whose high wings had a span of 48½ feet. The wings and fuselage were fabric-covered. The maximum speed was 120 miles per hour, but it cruised at 102 and landed at 55. Although it could carry four jumpers when making practice jumps, it usually only carried two when going to a fire because of the added cargo weight.

I was slated to jump first. I was glad because that meant avoidance of having to fly around in circles watching the other three fellows jump before my turn came.

When it came time to jump I scooted to the door in a crouched position and put my right foot on the outside step. It was an awkward maneuver in cramped quarters—no wonder it was common practice to jump one at a time from this plane. I found myself momentarily wondering why the Travelair was provided with such a wide step compared to the Ford's narrower one. I concluded there was no reason, it just happened to be the way it was. When I got the slapping signal to go, I rose up and hopped into space. I managed to get a little yell out, but not the confident, robust bellow I was trying for. Once again I was graded with two VGs, and began to wonder if somebody liked me, or if perhaps I was being graded in a fashion that would cover the overheads' butts if any question were ever raised about my eyesight problem, or if I really did that well. I concluded the latter: it made me feel good to think I had done well. Nevertheless, I still wondered when Brauer would give me the green light.

Monday, July 7, 1952

Dear Ma,

We received our first paycheck several days ago, so with the three-day Fourth of July weekend coming up most of the fellows decided to do something different.

What an enjoyable weekend I spent. Thursday after my jump, the second one, I went to Missoula. I stayed at E.J.'s [Woolfolk's] thinking I had a dental appointment Saturday morning, but no such luck. I wish I had known earlier and I would have gone to Glacier National Park. Mr. Woolfolk said I could use the car as I wished, so I struck out for Placid Lake some 50 miles away. Dick Kreitzberg, one of my smokejumper friends, has a cabin on the lake and he had invited me to come up. Another jumper, Dave Lodzinski, was there, too.

We went boating, fishing, and swimming. We also took a motorboat up a creek that was bordered on either side by overlapping willows. We came to one of many turns in the creek and a little doe was just ahead of us. She just stood and watched us until we were right up on top of her. Osprey were continually diving for fish and muskrats kept swimming by. I caught two trout, but the other guys caught more. I stayed there that night and while eating dinner, a large deer came up to a salt lick just outside the window. Just how can you stand not living amidst the beauties of the West?

I came back Saturday evening, and Sunday I went fishing with E.J. I caught two more trout. Boy, are they good eating. E.J. is leaving town this week, so I have the car up here. I'm really awful for taking it, but I think he appreciates helping me. I should be so lucky.

We didn't jump today, but we will the rest of this week and next Monday. Fires broke out over the weekend and the first jumpers went out.

I was sitting outside under a tree this afternoon listening to a fire behavior lecture when Fred Brauer came and sat next to me. He said, "How would you like to work for Mr. Woolfolk this summer?" I said I wouldn't and got red in the ears—the way they do when I am embarrassed or angry. He said the doc wanted to let me go. Then he said I could stay and that he was kidding about working for

Woolfolk, but he did make it clear that the doc didn't think I should stay in the program. Fred said he'd take the responsibility and that I was doing as well, if not better, than the rest of the fellows. He also said if more stringent requirements were instituted next year, I might not be able to come back. Although I am capable of jumping with the best, a line might be drawn that leaves me on the wrong side, meaning, of course, that I would be out of the program.

I guess I'll have to live with that.

Love, R.

P.S. We jump again tomorrow. I'm going to try very hard to yell. The first time I opened my mouth, but the sound just wouldn't come out. The second time I only managed a squeak, but tomorrow I'm going to get "Geronimo" out all the way. Geronimo, that's Indian for who-in-the-hell-pushed-me.

*　　*　　*

After the conversation with Brauer, I felt great. I remember my relief even to this day. I have always been grateful that Brauer and the other overhead went to bat for me. It struck me then, as it does now, that the easy way out would have been to drop me from the program. As I was writing this memoir, I called Fred in Missoula, where he resides. He couldn't quite place me although he remembered my last name. I told him I wanted to thank him for going to bat for me back in 1952 when a government doctor wanted to wash me out. "Oh, that was Dr. Johnson from the Department of Agriculture back in Washington, D.C. I had requested that he come to Missoula to teach the overhead how to administer Demerol shots in case a jumper was hurt in a remote area and needed a strong pain killer," he quipped, revealing that his age hadn't diminished his memory.

I told him my tour as a smokejumper had always meant a lot to me, and I wanted to thank him personally because I believed his leadership had significantly enhanced the experience.

"It pleases me that you feel that way, Fowler." He went on, "You know back then the outfit wasn't as encumbered with red tape as it is today, and I really wasn't looking so much at whether a guy's eyes were perfect as much as I was trying to find boys with a good work ethic—that's what was really important to me—and you must have had some good references or you wouldn't have been there. I think the vast majority of the boys did work hard and it was reflected in the *esprit de corps* of the outfit. I am still proud to have been associated with that bunch of guys because . . . well, because what we became was a band of brothers. You had to know that the other guy would be there to save your neck if it came to that. And you knew he would be, and you for him. I have often thought that there is no harder job in the world than fighting wild fire. Many times our boys had to go 24 hours without stopping—working hard, too. It takes the right attitude to be able to do that."

This brought a thought to mind that supported what he was saying. Two years ago I signed up for a week long wilderness trail maintenance project manned solely by ex-smokejumpers. Even though Ted was the only guy I remembered from my jumper days, I immediately felt I was with a group of exceptional fellows—the same feeling I had as an active jumper. I was grateful for that special work experience 50 years ago, and was surprised that it reappeared when I worked with that trail crew. We were all committed to doing a good job and everyone worked hard. I shared these thoughts with Fred and was concluding with, ". . . but it was more than that . . ."

"A band of brothers," Fred broke in, "I know what you mean."

We talked for a long time. Fred said he would be 87 in August. I asked him when he joined the jumpers, and he said 1941. The first fire jump was made in 1940 and the next year they started jumping on a project basis. It amazes me that so many of those pioneer smokejumpers are still here today.

*   *   *

We rejoiced that the fire season was in progress and were anxious to be part of it. When we returned we had expected to make another practice jump, but it was back to training on the units in the morning and then to the classroom in the afternoon for more instruction on fire behavior. Perhaps the planes were busy, or maybe it was deemed prudent to allow a day of recuperation after the long weekend. At any rate our training was extended a day.

The next jump was made more challenging by the selection of a site in Patty Canyon that contained numerous stumps. The intent was obvious—to avoid a hazardous landing by precision steering of the chute. The stumps were not so dense that they couldn't be avoided but you had to pay close attention to what you were doing. Again I was assigned to the Travelair, only this time I was scheduled to be the second man out of the door.

I was more relaxed on this jump and closely followed the first jumper. Even though I managed to hit the step on my exit, I wasn't able to come up straight; instead, I started into a dive. My poor position didn't seem to cause any difficulty because my parachute blossomed out just fine. I immediately grabbed my risers and tilted my head back to check the canopy for a line over.

No problems. I had a green camouflaged chute without tails. For some reason it responded sluggishly when I pulled a guide line to initiate a turn. I was heading away from the landing spot and needed to turn quickly or I would lose any possibility of gliding into the spot. When I finally got turned in the right direction I was well over the trees, so I grabbed my front risers and pulled them down as far as possible. My back risers continued to carry a lot of my weight, but my arms were still carrying a heavy load. In the quiet of the descent every grunt seems loud, a striking contrast to the din while riding in the plane.

I barely glided over the timber. Not that it would have been hazardous to land in the trees, but the objective of the exercise was to land in the opening. The lines on my chute caught in a small tree in the clearing, but didn't affect my landing. I received a grade of "Good" for the handling of my chute, and a "Fair" for my roll. This jump confirmed that the assigned grades were the evaluator's best judgement and had nothing to do with the imagined criteria I had earlier entertained. I blamed the chute for my difficulty in steering, but didn't have a clue why my roll wasn't better.

In the afternoon we discussed plans for fighting a fire that would be ignited after our training jump the next day. It wasn't more theory on fire behavior or alternative approaches to dealing with a theoretical wild fire; it was the real thing. Many of us had no experience fighting wild fire, so we were attentive, challenged, and somewhat intimidated.

*　　*　　*

Until now our jumps were on level ground, but our fourth jump would change that. I was jumping second in a two-man "stick" out of the Ford—a stick refers to those who jump together on the same pass. It turned out to be an easier jump than I had anticipated and the slope of the land presented no problem. I got a "G" on my handling of the chute and a "VG" on my roll. However, I noticed that my left buttock was sore. I speculated that I was hitting the ground a lot harder than I realized and because all of my rolls had been to the left, the accumulated effect of slamming against the earth was beginning to tell. I smiled when I had thoughts about "breaking my butt" for the outfit. That afternoon we fought the fire that had been started for our benefit. We split into two crews and worked from the bottom—one crew going to the left, and the other going to the right. We spread out with 15 feet between us and began to clear away the organic topsoil to reach mineral soil. When one of us had completed his 15 feet and reached the fire line that had been built by the person on his right, he quickly scooted over his line until he caught up with him, and said, "Bump one." This meant that he was to immediately stop constructing line at that location and move on to the next man, relaying the "bump one" message. Of course, if two men had completed their assigned length and were moving up the line, the message would be "bump two." This eliminated the necessity of the lowest man in the line having to make his way to the top of the line and avoided the hazard of passing a man swinging a Pulaski.

In spite of our commitment to work at break-neck speed, the fire got away from us—at least for awhile. It proved to be more of a workout than any of us expected, but we finally prevailed even though it required working four hours extra. A couple of those hours were spent in mopping up, that is, extinguishing hot spots by mixing them with dirt or exposing roots to the air by digging them out. Anything judged cold was thrown out of the burned area.

I came upon a small tree about 12 feet tall that had been badly scorched but was now completely out. Since it was inside the fire line, I chopped it down with my Pulaski. I misjudged the direction it would fall and suddenly realized it might hit two overhead standing near by. One was a squad leader named Marv Amundson, an ex-Marine who had fought in the South Pacific during WWII. He was a quiet fellow and a little difficult for me to read.

I shouted a mild warning, commensurate with the size of the tree, conversationally saying, "Timber!" Marv turned just in time to reach up and grab the top of the sapling, but it still brushed his hard hat, knocking it to the ground. I felt rather dumb and apologized for my indiscretion, but he just sort of grunted with no expression that let me know whether my apology was accepted.

I told several friends about the incident and they suggested I might be in for big trouble, but I just laughed with them and let it pass. The next day, however, as we were gathered at the airstrip suiting up and putting on parachutes, Marv came up to me and asked if I was on the jump list to go first out of the Doug—that's what we called the DC-3 since it was made by Douglas Aircraft Company. The nomenclature is also a bit confusing because the passenger version of the DC-3 is labeled a C-47, and while these names were sometimes used interchangeably, DC-3 was the correct nomenclature for the jumper planes. Anyway, I confirmed what Marv already knew, "Yes, I'm to jump first out of the Doug."

He said, "Well, I have a special chute for you, so please use it instead of the one you have."

"Sure," I answered, "it doesn't make any difference to me, but why do you want me to use this one?"

"We just want to observe it while it is in descent, so use the guidelines as much as you can," he requested.

After thinking about it several more questions came to mind, but he had sauntered off and it was not convenient to waddle after him in my jump gear. The guys close to me had overheard the conversation, and knowing I had inadvertently knocked off Marv's hard hat the day before, they began to kid me about what was packed in the chute.

"When you go to check your canopy I wouldn't be surprised if you didn't see a sky full of dirty laundry," one friend said. I laughed with everybody else and shrugged it off; at least I thought I had. Aside from this development I was already apprehensive about this jump, and I didn't know exactly why. Perhaps I was just beginning to know enough about parachuting to fully realize how dangerous it was, or could be. It was particularly disconcerting because I had assumed that with each jump I would become less apprehensive, not more. I was more apprehensive about this jump than any previous ones.

I remember reading about some general from WWII talking about courage and fear. He claimed courage didn't exist in the absence of fear. As I thought about it, I could see his point because if a person was totally relaxed in a hazardous situation, it would not be difficult to function. But when filled with fear, it would take an equal amount of courage to proceed. With that in mind, I'd have to say we were a courageous lot. On this particular jump I was my most courageous, and I had enough on my mind without thinking about dirty laundry.

The Doug was different from the Travelair and the Ford in many ways, but I was most impressed by its size, speed, and high door opening, allowing us to exit from a standing position. Standing in the door, I thought about the rushing air sucking me prematurely out of the plane, but this was not true of any of the aircraft we used. The spotter was lying on the floor with his head out the corner of the door while giving hand signals to the pilot.

When conditions were right the engines were cut and the spotter slapped my ankle—and I left with two buddies close behind. The static line for the Doug was several feet longer than the ones used in the Ford and Travelair, allowing a few feet more drop before the chute opened, thereby avoiding any possibility of it hitting the tail. I thought the added time it took for my chute to open was detectable, but that's unlikely. The prop blast was extremely strong in comparison to my jumps out of the other planes. When I checked the canopy it was normal and green, like the camouflaged one I had on my third jump, and it responded much the same way when I tried to make it turn. I wondered if it was the same chute. Marv was watching and could see that it was turning, but much too slowly.

This jump location was selected so that we would have to land in trees, and I did. They were not mature monarchs with a lot of height, but much shorter second growth, and provided what was commonly referred to as a feather bed landing. I broke through the branches and hung up, but I didn't have to make a let-down because my feet just reached the ground.

After popping my harness and shedding the jump gear I felt a sublime elation. Perhaps it's normal to have a greater "high" after a jump if you had a greater fear before it. I regarded this jump as a rite of passage, and having passed through it, I had reached a higher level of acceptance into the world of smokejumping.

I began to sack my jump gear and had just started to "chain" the shroud lines of my parachute when Marv Amundson walked up to me. Chaining is very similar to crocheting except that the hand is used in place of a needle and instead of a single thread all the parachute lines are treated as a single line. The result is that the lines are bound together so they will not tangle when sacked.

"What did you think of that parachute, Fowler?"

"I never thought I'd be glad to see another green one, but compared to dirty laundry it looked pretty good," I quipped.

"What are you talking about?" Marv asked, but the way he said it I knew he really didn't want to know.

I decided to pass it off and stick to business. "It handled pretty much like the green camouflage one I had on a previous jump, sluggish when trying to turn."

"That's what I thought observing your descent. I want to put a note in with the chute so the riggers can identify it when it gets back to the loft. We may not use this one if we don't have to."

That afternoon we returned to the site of our practice fire and finished mopping it up.

[Twenty-six years later I worked with Marv on the Beaverhead National Forest. He had been the ranger on the Dillon Ranger District, but we both came to work in the supervisor's office in the planning section. When I had come to know him well I asked if he remembered our encounter at Ninemile. He didn't even remember me much less the incident. I thought it interesting that two people could experience the same event, but because of their different perspectives could be affected in radically different ways—or, in Marv's case, not affected at all.]

* * *

One of the guys had a line-over, or, as we called it, a Mae West. It results when a line runs over the top of the parachute causing it to bulge. As instructed, he grabbed the front risers and shook them vigorously. Fortunately, the line slipped off. If it hadn't, the next step would have been to remove the knife attached to the top of his reserve chute and attempt to cut the line that was out of place. Several lines could be cut without affecting the proper functioning of the chute. If that didn't work, then the two options were: ride it out, hoping you weren't coming in too fast, or deploy the reserve chute. It was risky to ride two chutes to the ground because they could become tangled, but it was seen as a the better option, and we were taught how to open the reserve to minimize the chances of entanglement. While the cause of a Mae West was not known, it was thought that poor positioning when leaving the aircraft was a likely contributor. The possibility of it being true led most of us to try and jump as instructed.

The next day we made our sixth jump. I missed the step leaving the Ford in the second man position, but it didn't adversely effect my opening and I felt comfortable with the whole event. A smoke pot was used to mark the landing point. I came within 10 feet of it, but was disappointed that I still hadn't gotten a candy striped chute or one with tails.

We got the afternoon off to compensate for working extra time on the practice fire so I went to Missoula for the weekend.

Sunday, July 13, 1952

Dear Ma,

Well, I've jumped six times now. Two of those times I was second man and went out head first—perhaps not straight up and down, but I was headed that way. There's such a short time-span between leaving the plane and the chute opening, that you could hardly go over, but even if you did, in most cases it would be okay.

My ankle hasn't bothered me a bit. In fact, every landing has been soft for me. I've been jolted a lot worse jumping from the five foot training ramp. Five guys have suffered sprained ankles jumping, and none of them had trouble with their ankles before. It looks like there's no guessing who will get hurt.

Tomorrow we jump into a little opening in the timber. After we jump, we put out signals to the plane to indicate we are okay (or otherwise), just like we would do on a fire. Then we assemble in the same manner as we would on an actual fire jump.

The guys that jumped on a fire last week in Yellowstone National Park all got air sick going to the fire. I guess most guys do, even if they've flown a lot. It seems that the planes make many sudden rises and drops in the mountain air currents when flying low in warm air. Also the hot jump suits and the lack of fresh air (especially in the Doug) are conducive to a good heave. We heard that one guy got to the door and threw up with his mask on. It sounds horrible. Some vomit went on the floor, and when the second man went to jump he stepped in it and slid right out the door.

By the way I write and the things I tell you, you must think it's simply awful, but really it's fun and I enjoy it to the hilt.

I guess Tuesday or Wednesday we'll leave for "project," so I won't be here much longer.

It's really hot here now.

Love, R.

*   *   *

Wednesday, July 16, 1952

Dear Ma,

I never seem to be able to remember when I last wrote. Regardless of how much time goes by there's always lots to tell.

You said something to me in a recent letter about guys getting pushed out of planes. It was in response to something I had written to you. If a fellow isn't in the door ready to go out, he won't be pushed. In other words, they don't haul you to the door and throw you out. It's only when you are in the door and hesitate that you get "helped." If a jumper gets ready to jump on a fire and he thinks the jump spot looks too wicked, he can decline to jump. I suppose it would depend on the conditions how that decision might affect his standing.

Let me tell you about our final practice jump. I was assigned to jump again from the Doug—the last man in a three-man stick. Of course the plane was full of jumpers who were assigned to other sticks. The Doug can carry 16 jumpers and it cruises at 160 miles an hour.

I was pleased that this seventh jump hardly bothered me at all: in fact, I was anxious to leap. However when I left the door a strange but interesting thing happened to me. I've always thought my eyes were open when I jumped, but I never remember seeing anything until this last jump. I'm talking about the lapsed time between when I leave the plane until the chute opens. On this last jump I saw the horizon go sideways before I got the opening shock from the chute. Surely my eyes haven't been closed on the previous six jumps. But I wonder.

On the last two jumps the landing spots have been designated by smoke. I've hit within ten feet of the smoke both times, and even though trees were close by I managed not to hang-up in them. Lots of fellows did, and that's okay, too. It's encouraging to think that we can steer our chutes accurately enough to land in a very small opening within a dense forest.

The red and white chutes are only different from the others by their color, although some guys say they are newer and handle better. In any case, they're so beautiful I just have to get one sometime. I did get tails on this last jump, and I was thankful for the experience before I make an actual fire jump.

After the jump, they dropped cargo to familiarize us with what it will be like on an actual fire. Then we ate the "C" rations that come in our fire packs. They aren't bad even though the variety is limited.

In the afternoon they called out the names of those judged as needing additional fire training. Some have been on seven or eight forest fires, but had to take more, and then some guys like me [who hadn't had any previous training] were judged okay. I hope they know what they are doing.

Next they read off a long list of "project work" with the names of the jumpers assigned to them. I mentioned to you earlier that when the smokejumpers started they were funded by raking off funds that would otherwise have gone to ranger districts to fight fire. This precedent continued, but theoretically the districts were compensated by the availability of smokejumpers to fight remote fires at no cost to the district. Also, when the fire season was at a lull, smokejumpers were made available to work on district projects with the smokejumper organization paying the salaries and the districts paying only for meals. This was an economical way for districts to get good help at a cheap price, and it was good for the jumpers, too, because after training they would have to start paying for meals eaten in Missoula, and going on project provided an opportunity to avoid that cost.

Love, R.

Thus, our training came to an end on July 14. The fire season had begun and we all exhorted Zap, the god of lightning, to visit our mountains soon, and in his wake leave an aftermath of many small fires. To a man, we ached to make our maiden fire jump, but for many of us that wouldn't happen until well into August.

*   *   *

I knew the likelihood of going on project with my college friend, Ted Rieger, was highly unlikely, so I wasn't too disappointed. This year Ted was an old man. He had finished his one week refresher course three weeks ago, and was already out on project. As it was, I felt fortunate that Dave Lodzinski and I were assigned to the same project.

On Tuesday Dave, Frank Orosy and I rode with Jack Burrows in a Forest Service sedan to Priest River Experiment Station in Idaho. Jack was in charge of the fire laboratory in Missoula and was making a field inspection of some fire research projects in Priest River. Len Gavin and Bob Chrismere were assigned to the same project, and, since one of them had a car, they rode together.

We left after lunch and arrived at the experiment station at dinner time. We all welcomed the folksy atmosphere of the chow hall and relished the food. Several non-jumping seasonal employees had been working there prior to our arrival, and unlike us would stay there for the summer. Our boss, George Fonstock, was a non-jumper with a college degree and a permanent appointment with the Forest Service. The town of Priest River, population 1500, was not far away, but the station was otherwise isolated. Most of the buildings were rustic in design and nestled in a dense forest of tall trees. It was very inviting if you liked a forest setting, and we all did.

We worked on a study to determine the characteristics of slash burning for several species of trees. In an open area several large squares, about 30 feet by 30 feet, were staked out. An individual square was to be covered by slash of a single tree species, but it wasn't to be piled in a helter-skelter manner. Instead, the slash was carefully weighed and systematically laid within the square, so when the job was done they would all have the same tonnage and be configured in the same way. Our job was to fell mature hemlock trees with a crosscut saw and lop off the branches. The non-jumper crew hauled off the slash, weighed it, and placed it in the proper square. Presumably, after the slash had cured in the fall, it would be ignited and various data recorded so the burning characteristics of each species could be measured and recorded for comparative study.

Before we arrived at the experiment station the non-jumper seasonal workers had been able to wrangle some non-traditional work hours. Our schedule was five hours in the morning and three in the afternoon. It made the morning a bit long, but we all enjoyed a little free time in the afternoon so we could go swimming in Priest River before the evening meal.

Unfortunately, by the second day I began to feel ill. I had been singled out to paint the weather station, consisting of several fence posts and small hutches containing weather instruments. Despite not feeling well, I easily completed the chore by lunch time, so I went back to work with Dave, Frank O., Len, and Bob sawing and splitting wood in the afternoon. But before long, sickness prevented me from doing anything. I neither swam nor ate dinner.

Along with three other guys I periodically threw up throughout the night. I spent the next morning in bed after eating some dry toast. By noon I felt well enough to move about, so I went to work, but in low gear. Fortunately I was able to join the guys weighing slash because it wasn't physically demanding. By evening I not only felt well enough to eat, but also well enough to go to the Friday night square dance in Priest River.

The food continued to taste great, but I still thought that four of us had contracted food poisoning through the kitchen. Thank goodness it wasn't a recurring problem.

We all felt fortunate that Len and Bob had traveled by personal car because the four of us frequently went places together. On Saturday we poked around at Sandpoint, 37 miles away, and on Sunday we drove 50 miles north to Priest Lake: beautiful country, covered with stands of big timber. The lake was so picturesque that we concluded we'd like to work there, or perhaps someday jump on a fire in the vicinity.

*   *   *

You might think that with all the heavy sawing we would be using chain saws. Certainly by 1952 chain saws were in use, but they were not as prevalent in the Forest Service as they were with loggers. They were heavy, temperamental, cumbersome, expensive, and seemed to be viewed by the Forest Service as a specialty item. They could only be purchased with special permission, and there didn't seem to be a big rush to modernize.

Crosscut saws were a part of Forest Service culture and field personnel were experienced in their use. Unlike today, skilled filers were readily available, and they routinely sharpened the saws so they were efficient tools. Many field-going Forest Service trucks were fitted with pipe side rails on which saw boxes were mounted, so a crosscut would be available in the event a tree had fallen across the road in some remote area. Even after chain saws became more common, it was well into the sixties before crosscuts were a thing of the past.

Of course they persist in areas where chain saws are not permitted, such as Congressionally-proclaimed wilderness areas.

*   *   *

In our daily routine we bucked up logs and split the blocks into firewood. Because we were doing this work constantly, we raised our proficiency level another notch. It was satisfying to be a part of a saw team that worked so tirelessly and so smoothly. We became efficient sawyers and learned to get the most out of each stroke. Between sawing and splitting, the latter was the harder job, so we took turns. It may have been different had the wood been dry instead of green.

Only once did I spend the entire day with the splitting maul, and my back was killing me by day's end. We went to the movie in Priest River that evening and I could hardly sit there with my discomfort.

Wednesday was a special day because a professor from the Forestry School, Dr. Waters, visited the station in some sort of official capacity. I had taken a dendrology course (study of trees) from him the previous quarter and we spent some time that evening discussing the forest environment. He was my favorite teacher and we remained friends for years after college.

On the same day, Dave Lodzinsky received his draft notice and would have to leave August 7. We had become good friends and I hated to see him go. It seemed rather unfair that he would not be able to experience a fire jump before leaving.

He worked with us the next day on our sawing and splitting project, but when we were directed to spread poison on some invasive goatweed plants on Friday, Dave left for Missoula to see about the draft. Although Dave and I corresponded for a short time after he was inducted into the Army, I did not see him until 15 years later when we attended a month-long administrative leadership training course at the University of Montana. He was working for the Bureau of Land Management and I was still with the Forest Service. He looked much the same, and although we enjoyed talking over old times our friendship remained distant.

That evening Frank Orosy left in his car for the weekend in Coeur d'Alene. It was lucky for the rest of us that his leaving stranded us at the station for the weekend. A fire call came at 9:00 a.m. There should have been five of us, but Dave's departure and Orosy's weekend sojourn left only three. We weren't to be transported until 10:45, so when I had my personal gear packed in my duffle, I decided to drop a note to my mother.

Saturday, July 26, 1952

Dear Ma,

Just a hasty note. It's Saturday and we just got notice to leave for Missoula right away. I don't know if we'll fly or go by car, but at any rate we're leaving— yee-howww!

One fellow went to Coeur d'Alene for the week end, poor guy.

If you don't hear from me for a short period, you'll know why. On the other hand we might be on stand-by for a few days waiting for a fire. I'll write when I can.

I'm excited.

Love, R.

We were a happy trio when we piled into a Forest Service truck and headed for the airport at Sandpoint. We met 18 jumpers called in from nearby projects, and the 21 of us eagerly took off in a DC-3 for Missoula. It was only an hour flight, but what a ride. The turbulence was terrible because the day was hot and we were flying low over mountainous terrain. Although bench seats were on both sides of the plane, many of us were sitting on the pack sacks of personal gear or directly on the floor. I was seated at the tail end and could see everyone for the entire length of the plane. Periodically the plane would drop so rapidly that everything, men and baggage, would be momentarily suspended in air two feet off the floor. One poor fellow heaved; I suspected that the others felt as I did, and would have been much more comfortable with a parachute strapped to their backs.

When we landed on the dirt strip at Hale Field in Missoula we learned that we were to be part of a group of 50 that would jump on a large fire. However, the situation had taken a turn for the better and the order for re-enforcement was canceled. We would have welcomed the jump, but comforted ourselves with the hope that our call would be the quintessential two-manner, high in the mountains, far removed from civilization.

The camp at Ninemile was too far from Missoula to be a billet for jumpers during the fire season; Fort Missoula served that purpose. It was a large military reservation used by cavalry in the early part of the century. Several large buildings were located in the center of expansive fields; one providing smokejumper housing and mess hall facilities.

We were given a kapok[6] sleeping bag and told to select a cot in a large bay with space for 30 or more jumpers. Looking back, it wasn't very accommodating, but we accepted it as home, except for two things. First, we would have to pay for our meals; and second, a buzzer was used for a wake up call that sounded like the signal a submarine used when making an emergency dive. It was such an in-your-face sound that even the soundest sleeper bolted upright on his cot. It made reveille sound like a ballad, and none of us ever got used to it.

Two jumpers went out the next day. My name was so far down on the jump list that I knew it would take a big fire, or a lot of small ones, to put me close to any action, so on Monday I willingly accepted an assignment to Bonita Ranger Station, 24 miles distant.

Wednesday, July 30

Dear Ma,

Thunder storms are predicted for tonight, so maybe we'll go out tomorrow—I hope.

A fire was reported 30 miles from here that a ground crew went to last night. Two of us went up there today in a truck (it was right between the road and the river) to put a hose to it. We had a gasoline powered water pump and made fast work of it. It was evident that a careless fisherman left a campfire.

Love, R.

The work at Bonita was pleasant and varied. We spent a couple of days trimming trees, cleaning up messes, and grooming the grounds at the ranger station. We finished the week by hauling rock for a new septic system, planting posts for a corral, and stacking firewood. Missoula was so close we went there for the weekend hoping the need for jumpers might escalate. The fire danger was up, but without lightning there was no fire activity, so we started a second week at Bonita.

I was assigned to work with the road grader up Rock Creek. I walked behind the grader with a rock rake, a tool shaped like a pitchfork only its tines were more numerous, shorter (about 8 inches long), and stouter. After the

---

6   Kapok is a light, soft fiber that is harvested from the seedpods of the kapok tree (genus Ceiba). Because of its insulating qualities and resistance to water absorption it was commonly used as a filler in sleeping bags.

grader dressed the road surface, some rocks occasionally remained on the surface. I would pitch them over the shoulder of the road.

That night lightning was predicted and we did a little dance exhorting Zap to look favorably upon us. The next day I was hauling sand for the septic system when Missoula called at 11:00 a.m. Eighteen men had jumped. Since I was number 10 on the jump list, it was obvious that several jumpers were more readily available than I was. We scurried to the dispatcher's office located in the loft at Hale Field. It also housed the parachute riggers' long tables and the tower where parachutes hung for repacking. I was put to work packing fire equipment.

Saturday, August 9

Dear Ma,

I'm a real jumper at last.

Wednesday morning Missoula called Bonita and alerted us for fire. At 11:30 we were called in, but there was a mess of guys ahead of me on the jump list. Just before quitting time I heard my name called. I suited up and crawled into the Travelair for a two-man fire with Bill Demmons, a second year man. We took-off and went over the university and E. J.'s [Joe Woolfolk] house. After flying in a NW direction for a few minutes we came to Placid Lake and I saw the cottage where I spent the fourth—and I could also see the stream that we had gone up in the boat.

Next we flew over the town of Seeley Lake and over the divide between the Swan River drainage and the South Fork of the Flathead River drainage. Snow on the mountain tops was still plentiful, but it was still plenty hot in the plane. We kept tipping and dropping, but it didn't make me sick. Because we were flying so low we could see many elk foraging in the openings. The terrain below was speckled with lakes, high mountain cirques, and streams coiled around like snakes. The land became a big rug of trees, just as far as the eye could see. No farms, no roads, no air fields—just a few lookout towers on mountain tops and trees. Out on the struts of the wings it looked like ants crawling across and falling off—it had started to rain and the wind played tricks with the water droplets. Also, the wind rocked the Travelair so much that I wondered if I would get air sick.

As we flew down the South Fork I was amazed at its vastness, and the only topographical feature that I was able to make mental note of for later identification was Big Salmon Lake. It was almost a half-mile wide and four miles long. Finally we saw a little curl of smoke coming out of a gorge in the side of a mountain near Beaver Creek and Deer Creek. We made several passes over it and each time our spotter, Lee Gorsuch, threw out a drift chute the wind blew it a half-mile horizontally. Since it was so windy, Lee and Bill decided to land at Spotted Bear airstrip, ten miles west of the smoke, and wait for the wind to die.

I landed for the second time and found that the small wheels on a rough gravel strip made such a noise it was disconcerting. A little later we took off again only to find that it was still too windy to jump. When the pilot reported back to the dispatcher we were reassigned to a fire on Count Peak, 40 miles to the south back towards Missoula. We found it. It was a fallen, burning snag in the middle of a box canyon at about 8,000 feet of elevation. When a drift chute indicated only a slight wind Lee instructed Bill to get ready to go on the next pass. Just after the Travelair cleared a ridge, Lee gave the signal and Bill went. The wind carried him over some snags, so he headed for a live tree and hung up. We made another pass and I jumped. I was hardly scared and even managed to yell. I saw my feet come to the ridge—I was falling on my back. When my chute opened (thank God) I checked my canopy and reefed on a guideline so I immediately turned into the wind. I was bucking the wind pretty well and felt I was heading for the spot. I shot over a few trees and heard Bill yell, "Put your feet together." I did, and landed okay.

We then remembered that we had jumped on a different fire than originally planned and consequently had the wrong map. Quickly we wrote "M-A-P" on the ground with our orange streamers [crepe paper]. *After the cargo and crosscut saw was dropped, Lee dropped the correct map and we made an "L-L" on the ground to indicate we were both okay.* [Every jumper carried a card showing appropriate ground-to-air signals. "L" meant that a jumper was okay. "L-L" meant a crew was okay.]

By this time it was 8:00 p.m., and we hustled to the close-by fire. Luckily water was so close that we could use it to fill the canvas sack of our hand pump. We immediately extinguished the flames. It wasn't a big fire and we easily got a line around it and had it looking pretty sick. There was a snowbank close by and we shoveled some of it on the fire, not so much because we needed it, but because we thought it would be rather clever to be able to say to our cohorts that we fought our fire that way. Bill decided at midnight that we had progressed to the point that all night work was not necessary. I was easily able to retrieve my parachute to make my bedding more comfortable, but since Bill had hung-up in a tree, he had to settle for one of the cargo chutes. We stuffed them into our paper sleeping bags which made the difference between a cold, uncomfortable night and a toasty, comfortable one.

It rained a little during the night, but not enough to bother. I've never seen country as pretty as this. I've studied similar vegetation in school, but this was the first time I actually experienced it. At this elevation the landscape is not heavy with brush, and the trees are so symmetrical that they seem almost unreal. The ground is covered with low growing vegetation that appears carpet-like. It was beautiful. We were on the Flathead National Forest in the Primitive Area. That means no roads for miles and miles. [In 1964 when Congress created the Wilderness Act it became the Bob Marshall Wilderness].

We ran our bare hands over every inch of the fire and Bill declared it out at 10:00 a.m. the next morning. We were trained to stay with the fire until after the burning period (late afternoon) of the day following the one it was declared out. Bill didn't think this fire was "usual." Even so, he wasn't prepared to leave yet, however, he did think it was fine to start hauling our gear cross-country for two miles to the nearest trail. What a haul! We made two trips and by two o'clock we were ready to leave. The trail was terrible. Windfalls frequently made it impossible to follow and heavily grown grass and brush often made it impossible to see. We frequently lost it, but we knew from the map that it closely followed the stream, so we followed the water course until it showed up. We carried our manties (pieces of canvas), our paper sleeping bags, our flashlights, and some grub because we knew we might have to spend the night on the trail.

We hiked without the use of our lights as long as we could to conserve them. We passed within 50 feet of a grizzly and I almost went up a tree, but he headed out of the way. Every time I heard or saw a porcupine I thought it was a bear. The elk were crashing through the timber and making all kinds of racket. We were trying to make it to a cabin, but had to give up when we crossed a large stream and were faced with multiple game trails radiating from the far side. We were unable to tell which one was the trail. It was 10:00 p.m. and we were beat. We crawled into our sleeping bags without the benefit of parachutes to augment their comfort, but still we slept. I woke up in the morning to the sound of elk bugling— a new experience for me.

In the daylight we easily found the trail and made it to Hahn Creek Cabin which had a grounded telephone mounted outside. [A grounded telephone was comprised of number nine galvanized bare wire strung through insulators attached to trees 10 to 20 feet up the trunk. Wires connected to a crank telephone that had two large batteries to power the ring when the phone was cranked. This caused every telephone on the system to ring, so in order to provide a means to direct a call, a code was assigned to each location. The code was comprised of a short ring, a long ring, or a combination of short and long rings. For example, one location might be coded a long and a short; another, a long, two shorts, and a long. Before radio this was the only means of communication in the back country.] *We couldn't get the telephone to work* and so we proceeded on our journey towards Big Prairie. At 11:00 a.m. we met the packer with two horses and three mules on his way to pick up our gear. We told him it was well marked along the trail, but that the trail was difficult to follow. It didn't seem to phase him a bit. It was 2:00 p.m. when we made it to Big Prairie Ranger Station. There're no roads to it, but there is a small airstrip. We had covered a good 30 miles plus the back-tracking and looking for the trail. I was beat. My legs ached and my ankles were swollen. I don't think Bill was any better off.

We flew out at 3:30 p.m. and arrived at Fort Missoula in time for dinner. We logged 20 hours of overtime and I felt like I had just experienced an ideal jumper fire—a high-mountain two-manner.

It's Saturday now and I'm at the loft. It looks like I'll go out again.

Love, R.

P.S. I'm a real smokejumper!

Above: Smokejumper trainees practicing let-downs.
Below: A gathering at the Smokejumper Training Camp,
Camp Menard, Ninemile, Montana.

Learning proper positioning on a tower jump.

Me at the base of a jumping tower.
A tight harness prevents an upright posture.

Photo Credit: U.S. Forest Service, Phil Stanley Photo #431789

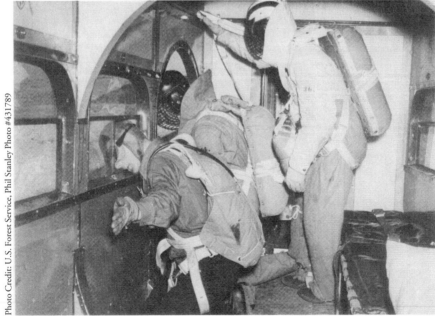

Above: Ford Trimotor loading up for training jumps.
Below: Spotter Bill Wood is giving hand signals to the pilot of
a Ford Trimotor as they approach the jump spot.

A smokejumper parachute with slots and tails. The tails are the awning-like protrusion on the back of the chute that add horizontal propulsion. Only one of the two slots can be seen. They are slits in the chute used for steering.

Above: The DC-3, the largest plane used in smokejumping.
Below: Travelairs were our only single engine jumping aircraft.
Here are two loading up for a practice jump.

Two candy stripe (red and white) chutes coming in for tree landings.

A risky hang-up.

Chuck Dysart after a successful practice jump. Notice the sheathed knife attached to the top of his emergency parachute.

CHAPTER 6

Rookie Fire Season

Since my name was near the top of the jump list and the probability of a fire request was high, I hung around the loft on Saturday. A call came in for a 10-man rescue team to retrieve a trail maintenance worker who was suffering with appendicitis, but my 5' 11" height was deemed "too tall" compared to the rest of the crew and I was passed over.

True, it was easier to hold the stretcher level if all members of the crew were close to the same height, but I wasn't taller than all the others. Apparently someone in a commanding position had erroneously concluded that my bean-pole stature meant I was taller than I actually was. There was no opportunity for debate, but it was a bitter pill to swallow.

Later in the day the dispatcher received a request for two jumpers, and it was great to catch another "two-manner" rather than the rescue, but my satisfaction didn't last long because it turned out to be a dry run. In flight we looked diligently for the fire but could not find any smoke, so we returned to base.

Sunday it rained, so Monday rolled around with no fire activity. The work at the loft was caught up and it appeared there would be no fires. Those of us high on the jump list were sent to the Ninemile Ranger District on a work detail so it wouldn't take long to return to Hale Field if something did come up.

Jumpers who already had two or three fire jumps were being sent to Idaho on project since it would be a long time before they could work their way to the top of the jump list again. When several of us left for Ninemile the guys going to Idaho were waiting at the depot for a train.

At 4:15 p.m. those of us at Ninemile were called for a fire and left immediately for Hale Field. As we approached Missoula we saw two Dougs (DC-3s) take off with 32 men—the guys who had been waiting for the train. Another disappointment. I was now third on the jump list.

I worked at the loft the next day straightening jump gear and watched as the jumper on the top of the new man jump list suited up and left for a fire, moving me to the number two spot. Waiting was tough, but my time to go seemed imminent.

The next day, August 13, while rigging crosscut saws for parachute drops, two men came off project who hadn't jumped yet. They went to the top of the list. Though understandable, it was frustrating, and, adding insult to injury, the jumping activity ended for the day.

Work at the loft was not physically demanding, so in order to provide some exercise it was the policy to take a break at 10:30 in the morning and 2:30 in the afternoon to play volleyball on an outside court. We all welcomed this opportunity, but it was still difficult to hang around the loft all day trying to keep busy. I found myself considering the advantages of going out again on project.

Friday, August 15, 1952

Dear Ma,
This has been a poor (or good, depending on how you look at it) fire season. Last year fellows got five, six, or seven jumps. This year a guy will be darn lucky to get two or three. They tell us that if rain comes as forecasted, the season could be over.

Yesterday at 5:00 p.m. we (ten of us) went on a rescue jump. A ranger, Doug Morrison, was on a game survey with several other men when something spooked his horse. The horse reared up and backed into a stump and went over backwards, breaking Morrison's leg.

[Later I heard rumors Ranger Morrison was leading a public relations "show me trip" comprised of several business men from the Helena area.]

Flying in the plane en route to the site of the accident I began to sweat like mad under my girdle—as I always do. My feet were a little uncomfortable too, because the crotch strap puts pressure on my arches (I told you how that happens when I explained the jump pants during training). Bob Johnson piloted our Ford Trimotor for an hour before we were over the Danaher.

[It was hard to imagine that in the early 1900s Thomas Danaher applied for a homestead near the location we were to jump. There never was a road, so the only access was by 30 miles of trail from Ovando, Montana. All tools, equipment and building supplies were packed in by mule train. That meant disassembling farm machinery and packing it in pieces. He did the same thing with a piano for his musically inclined wife. They raised two daughters in this remote setting, and on August 15, 1907 a land patent was awarded for the 160 acres they had "proved up" on. The adventure was short lived, however, as it was too difficult to trail cattle. Some evidence of the settlement still remains, i.e., a mowing machine, dump rake, an irrigation ditch, and the foundation to their home. In the late 1940s John Toole, Sr. bought the land and sold it to the government for $1.00 so it could be put back into wilderness. If for no other reason, the Danaher name will likely be remembered because of the geologic features named for him on the Forest Service map of the area: Danaher Meadows, Danaher Mountain, and Danaher Creek.]

Looking down at the Danaher we could see a big pile of white canvas by a tree and the injured ranger. I was to jump in the first-man position on the third stick. Fred Brauer, the spotter, dropped drift chutes on two passes, and their descent confirmed that we couldn't miss the big meadow that was to be our jump spot.

Our foreman, Len Krout, went on the next pass with another man. The next round two more men went; I was to be next with Mac McDonald. I stepped into the door and Mac tried to get behind me, but because the Stokes litter (stretcher) was situated there, he had to stand on it. This stretcher is probably different from any you have ever seen. Including the long handles on either end, it's all of 12 feet long. It's built of aluminum and is basket-like.

Well, anyway, Mac asked me if he could go first because he figured he'd have a hard time getting off the stretcher and scooting down low enough to get below the top of the door. [Mac was six-foot-one and weighed 185 pounds.] *I agreed, not only because he was taller than I, but also because I had come to like the second man position. Mac got the slap on the shoulder and left; I followed clumsily. Even I had a hard time getting off that stretcher, but I managed and lunged for the step outside the plane. To my surprise I hit it, but my poor position turned me to the right and put me on my back. I know this because I saw the horizon and the tail of the plane go by. As always, I felt that welcomed jerk from my chute opening. I yelled to Mac so we wouldn't collide and we were doing fine. I picked a spot on which to land, but it became obvious I couldn't get there, so I picked a second. For a while I thought I'd hang-up, so I was working the chute pretty hard. The fellows said I looked like a chicken with his head cut off, the way I was flipping around up there, and because I was steering the chute right to the ground, those who had already landed said they thought I would never prepare to land.*

I hit the meadow and went backward so hard that I rapped my head. Boy, if I didn't have on a helmet, I bet I'd have been knocked cold. As it was, I was okay except for a star or two, so I sacked my gear and carried it the 100 feet to the gear pile near the injured man.

[From the summer of 1952 it was 52 years before I again spoke with Mac. He conveyed the same gentle nature I remembered—it was like talking with an old friend. He recalled the rescue well. One of his most vivid memories was a member of the riding party rushing up to him before he could even get out of his jump gear and offering him a drink. Mac supposed that after watching us leap from the Ford and parachute to the ground, the observer thought the thing we needed most was a stiff drink. I either got missed or retained different memory detail than Mac—not surprising after the passage of so many years.]

Morrison was lying under a tree and Krout was administering first aid. There were six or seven other horsemen he had been traveling with who were also gathered around the tree. They had two bottles of gin and two bottles of some kind of whiskey, not that they had been drinking, but Morrison was obviously feeling no pain. Krout was going to give him a Demoral shot, but figured it would be too much for his system with the alcohol.

After the rest of the crew jumped and the stretcher was dropped, we readied it for use. The stretcher was actually a Stokes litter, a wire mesh affair fashioned with sides so a patient couldn't roll off. Also, the contraption was equipped with a 12 inch airplane wheel in the middle so that when traveling over smooth ground most of the weight could be supported by it. Morrison was secured by straps and we were ready to go.

The equipment included a large Hershey bar and a can of fruit for each man—high energy food that we could eat on the run. It was eight miles to the airstrip at Basin Creek and we were going to try to make it before dark, so we took off right away—almost at a trot.

I need to explain how the ten of us worked together to carry this rig. It was standard procedure that we learned in our training school. The handles on either end extended two-and-a-half to three feet beyond the Stokes litter. Men were stationed fore and aft with a special harness that allowed the handles to be totally supported without lifting with the arms. Of course, the hands gripped the handles but when held correctly, the shoulders carried the weight.

Four men were stationed on the sides, two on the right and two on the left, close to the point where the handles joined the Stokes litter so they were well out of the way of the men on the ends with the harnesses. This accounts for six of the crew. Two of the remaining four were each equipped with a harness and were immediately before and after those carrying the load. The other two guys were in the "rest" position and stationed at the extreme front and rear of the crew. The side men would help lift when necessary to keep the wheel from bumping a rock or log in the trail. They would also help steady the load when necessary, but it was particularly tough for them because the trail was often not wide enough and the footing off the trail was frequently precarious. At one time when I was on the uphill side I was walking with my hand against the hill. Often the downhill man would go sprawling with no alternative except to fall behind on the trail.

We stopped briefly a couple of times when Morrison heaved, and once when Krout figured the alcohol had worn off enough so it was safe to give him a shot of Demerol, but other than that we pressed on to keep a four mile-an-hour pace. Every ten or fifteen minutes Krout would shout, "ACQUAINT YOURSELF WITH YOUR POSITION," meaning we were about to rotate stations around the litter and to be alert. "SIDE MEN CARRY." Which meant the side men would be in complete control of the litter. "CHANGE." The men fore and aft who had been carrying the litter slipped out and those equipped with the harnesses replaced them. Everyone shifted to a predetermined new position so that we each periodically had a turn at all positions. We never even slowed up, not even when we plunged through two shin-deep streams.

When we finally came to the airstrip it was black as the ace of spades and I was soaked with sweat. The stars were out, but we could still make out the horizon.

We put Morrison in the plane and were informed that four of us would spend the night at Basin Creek in order to reduce the weight for take-off. They would be picked up in the morning by another plane. Since a rescue jump does not affect your position on the jump list, I was still second. I couldn't see staying and possibly missing a fire jump, so I didn't volunteer, but four did, and the rest of us climbed aboard.

[From the vantage point of 52 years later it seems rather absurd that the question posed to us was, "Who will volunteer to *stay*?" rather than, "Who will volunteer to go?" This was an infrequently used airstrip, it was pitch black except for stars and the outline of mountain tops in the distance, we were wet, there was no heat in the plane and the door was open. Why would it be presumed that we would want to make such a flight?

I expect we all felt particularly confident because Bob Johnson was the pilot. He was an early pioneer in mountain flying and provided all the aircraft for the Missoula smokejumping operation. He was no young man, but he still continued to fly routinely even though he had other well-qualified mountain pilots. This Ford Trimotor was a model 5-AT-C, numbered NC 8419, with three 420 horsepower engines. It was the biggest Ford Johnson owned. This same plane crashed seven years later at Moose Creek, an airstrip in the Selway-Bitterroot Primitive Area.

The copilot with Johnson, John Dillon, was killed a year later when a smaller Ford he was flying (model 4-AT-E) hit a cable while he was working on a forest spraying operation near Helena. He tried to land the plane in a nearby field, but the whipping cable wrapped around a pole and he crashed.

Both men were excellent mountain pilots, had landed on the airstrip at Basin Creek shortly after we had jumped at Danaher, and were able to assess, in the daylight, the problems of a take-off in the dark.]

Johnson's landing lights allowed him to see well enough to taxi down the field to the very extreme end and turn around. Those staying behind had built two fires at the far end of the strip and waved their flashlights. Johnson had cocked the plane at an angle because it was difficult to see forward when the tail is not elevated. I stuck my head out of the side window and shone my flashlight ahead.

"My God, he's headed for the timber," I thought in a flash of panic. I was going to yell when he lined up on the fires, still preparing for his dash down the field. The blackness was overwhelming. Then he revved up the motors so hard that I thought surely we would go straight up. When he released the brakes we started moving fast—much faster than I had ever experienced. The Ford is noted for its wing design that produces tremendous lift, even at slow speeds. The night air also resulted in denser air, and Johnson had further tipped the scale towards a quicker lift-off by reducing the weight (by four men) and "maxing" the RPMs. As a result, we used very little runway before we were airborne and when we passed between the signal fires we were high in the sky. We climbed with a strain for several minutes before leveling off. The motors on either wing spewed blue flame from the rear, a sight I had not witnessed in my daylight flights. Every once in a while they'd squirt a stream of sparks, and from sitting on the floor it looked like lightning because I couldn't see the sparks, just the light they gave. It was thrilling. I got up and looked down and saw a river, but only vaguely. Then it got too dark to see anything, except an occasional light in the far distance.

I sat back down and tried to rest, but my feet felt like icebergs and my sweaty clothes were so cold that I shivered with goose bumps. I couldn't get warm. I laid down for 30 or 40 minutes and then looked out again. I could see car lights plowing through the darkness and then up ahead I saw a glow like a shell. Missoula. No lights were in sight in the distance, except for an occasional beacon.

It took a long time to get there. We went over Bonner Lumber Mill (five miles from Missoula) and I saw the incinerator (called a tepee burner) which looked like a huge red hot bullet perched on end. When we finally came over Missoula it was simply beautiful. It looked like a Christmas Tree flattened out, and the Clark Fork River made a big black streak in the middle of it. The two bridges were identified only by a string of lights across them. The edges of the city were sharply delineated because the lights ended where the steep surrounding mountains abruptly shot up.

We buzzed the field. The field? Gad, where is it? I saw lights by the hangars but no field. Then I saw smudge pots in a row down the field. They didn't light it up at all, just identified it. We circled again over Missoula, quite low this time and the air was much warmer. I could read all the neon signs clearly and was relieved to be home. I sat on the floor and braced myself for the landing. We bumped and hopped up once and landed smoothly at 10:41 p.m. Morrison was immediately loaded in a station wagon and taken to the hospital. The rest of us loaded into a truck and went to the Fort and went to bed. No supper, but we did get six hours of overtime and rested comfortably knowing we had helped Morrison get the medical attention he so desperately needed.

Love, R.

The next day was Friday and those of us near the top on the jump list were kept at the loft in case there was a fire call. But the prospects looked pretty bleak and project began to look pretty good. I decided to surrender my jump list standing on Monday for a sure opportunity to finish the season with work. It made sense, however, to stay readily available over the weekend in case something did develop.

Sunday, August 24, 1952

Dear Ma,

Sunday, a week ago today I was wishing for a jump because the next day I was scheduled to go on project in Idaho. At 2:20 p.m a fire call came in for six men to go to the Kaniksu National Forest (northern Idaho). It was 2:51 p.m. when we left in the Ford for the Lookout Mountain Fire on a slope over looking Priest Lake. Just a month ago I had talked about how nice it would be to jump in the Priest Lake area, isn't that rather remarkable?

[Two of the guys who were on the rescue jump were also in this crew— Mac McDonald and David Clippinger. Bob Walkup was in charge and Bill Hoskinson and Erwin Stafford filled out the crew.]

When we reached the fire we couldn't find any openings for a jump spot, so Paul Dennison, our spotter, decided to jump us in the trees. A long time ago I told myself I'd never hang up, but after flying low over the terrain I changed my mind in one big hurry—there were just too many logs on the ground to risk a ground landing. I jumped in the second stick and was supposed to be the first man, but Mac again wanted to go first, so I obliged. On recent jumps I have consistently ended up on my back, but not this time—my position was classic. I like jumping with Mac because he always tells me what he's doing and keeps away from me while we're in the air. Ever since I watched two guys come together in a practice jump causing one chute to collapse and forcing them to ride a single chute down together, I've been leery of it. Mac is heavier than I and therefore drops a little faster, minimizing the chances of a collision.

While I was descending I looked for a good tree to land in. I found one to my liking and worked toward it, but when I got closer I held a guide line too long and headed straight for the trunks of two side-by-side snags. Reflexively I pulled the opposite guide even though I felt it was probably too late, and prepared myself for a clobber into the snags. I saw them becoming bigger and bigger. Then, when I was about five feet from impact my canopy caught the top of the tree I had been aiming for and I came to a comfortable stop about 30 feet above the ground. Below me were numerous crisscrossed logs. Boy, would I have hated to have landed on them. But the logs were not my greatest surprise. Standing below me were three ground pounders (fire fighters who had walked to the fire). Alas, it was evident we were not needed.

[What happened next was one of the most bizarre sequence of events I ever experienced in a landing. For some reason I chose not to go into the details of it in a letter to my mother, but I remember it well. When I saw the ground pounders below me I must have felt a bit like a shining knight who had come to assist those poor souls staring up at me, but I was due for a rude awakening—I was the Don Quixote of the sky.

"Hi, I didn't expect to see you guys here," I said, trying not to disclose my disappointment.

"Hi. It sure was fun watching you guys jump," one of them replied.

"What's the fire doing, you got a line around it?"

"Not yet, but we got one started. It won't take long with you guys to help," he replied. "How are you going to get down from up there?"

"First, let me warn you about the cargo the plane will be dropping, it can be dangerous, so play heads-up," I warned. "And since we all have hung up in trees, the spotter will be free-falling climbing spurs, and that's really dangerous, so stay close to a tree."

"Okay, thanks, but how are you gonna get down?"

"We're trained for this kind of thing. Nothing to it. I'll show you." I tried to say these words so they didn't sound like they were coming from on high, but I probably was feeling a bit superior and likely my attitude and voice reflected it.]

Despite the repetitive training that emphasized the need for a carefully executed let-down, I screwed up. I took off my helmet, removed my tight fitting deer skin gloves (Mr. Woolfolk had them made from a deer hide he had tanned and the thin, soft leather made it easy for me to feel the guide lines on my chute when I reached up to find them.), and placed them in my helmet. It was my intention to attach the helmet to my jump suit, out of the way, but it slipped from my hand and fell to the ground.

["Hey, was it part of your training to learn to drop your helmet like that?" a voice from below queried. There were a few chuckles.

"No, it slipped," I answered honestly. What else could I say?

"Won't you need your gloves to get down?"

"Well, they would help, but I can manage without them," I said, knowing it was more of a prayer than a fact.]

I removed my emergency chute with the intention of snapping it to the side of my harness so it would be out of the way when I began to prepare for my let-down. In the process it, too, slipped from my hands. I grabbed for it, but only got the handle. Naturally enough the chute opened and fell to the ground in a ball, and I was gawking in disbelief with the handle still in my hand.

[The laughter below was not at all sarcastic, just a genuine response to a continued display of buffoonery. "Will that help break your fall when you come screaming down to the ground?" one of them asked. This remark was obviously meant to gore, and it did.

From the start I had been distracted by the presence of ground pounders, but now I was rattled. I resolved to concentrate on my task and put an end to this charade. I carefully pulled out several feet of the let-down rope leaving the bulk of it secure in its coil in my leg pocket so it, too, wouldn't fall to the ground.

Methodically, I threaded it through the D-rings on my waist being careful to keep the rope under my harness. I then threaded it up over my head through the ring of one riser and across to the other and tied it off. Now the rope was attached to my parachute so when I exited my harness I could slide down the rope to the ground. All I had left to do was extend the rope running between the D-rings until I had a loop long enough to drop under my left foot. This would cause more friction on the rope so I would descend more slowly.

I paused and thought through the procedure to be certain nothing had been overlooked. Satisfied, I grabbed the rope that led to the loop under my foot along with rope of the same loop as it came back up. Squeezing them together formed an effective break. I would not descend, even after exiting my harness, until I gently released my grip on the rope.]

I removed the 100 foot rope from my leg pocket and made the necessary connections for my let-down. After checking it, I popped my release and slid down.

[Technically I hadn't lied in my letter to my mother, but it was far from "the rest of the story." I had failed to undo the bayonet strap and slip it free of the harness. It was this strap that would keep the harness from flying off if the single-point-release was inadvertently activated during a jump, and without slipping it free a let-down was impossible. I pulled the pin from the box on my chest, rotated the lid, and prepared to strike it. I first looked at the three guys below and said, "Well, here goes nothing."

I struck the single-point-release and immediately dropped three or four feet while the slack was pulled out of the rope. This was normal. But because I had failed to extract the bayonet strap it instantly lifted my arms in the air disallowing me to exit my harness.

"You can say that again," the guys on the ground seemed to bellow in unison. The laughter was unrestrained. It must have been a hilariously funny sight—me hanging with my elbows out like a skinned chicken's wings, 30 feet above the ground, with little hope of doing anything except eat crow. Don Quixote had been summarily unseated from his horse.

"Do you want us to find the other jumpers so they can help get you down?" someone asked.

"No, no, they've got enough to do. I can handle it," although I didn't know how I could do anything, but I certainly didn't want to hear the laughter from my peers.

I forced my elbows down to my sides. If I hadn't dropped my emergency chute I could have used the knife attached to the top of the cover to attempt to cut away the bayonet strap. As it was, I had no alternative except to reach up to the risers and pull myself upwards, thereby relieving the pressure on the harness. I tried this, and it worked rather smoothly even though I had to lift considerable weight, but when trying to hold the weight by one arm and uncouple the bayonet strap with the other, I quickly became exhausted and had to rest. After several attempts and several rests, I somehow managed to free the strap, and although I had no gloves to guard against rope burns, I was able to descend slowly enough so it didn't make any difference.]

We put a line around the fire and declared it controlled at 7:45 p.m., so Bob decided the ground crew could take care of it. The next morning we spent several hours retrieving our chutes. I put on the spurs and started up the tree with the foot-long pruning saw. I had to cut many branches so I could squeeze my way up to the top. I had taken the strap containing the D-rings (the one I used in making the let-down) and attached a piece of rope that I could use as a safety belt when I stopped to cut a limb. When I went up as far as I could go I lifted my chute over the top of the tree. There were big holes in it, but the boys in the loft knew well enough how to make repairs—it would sail once again.

[I had become very adept at tree climbing and approached it with the confidence of an expert. It had been a lot of work climbing up through the labyrinth of spruce limbs particularly in the upper portion of the crown where the branches were thickest. I couldn't worm my way up without cutting many of them off, but I proceeded, undaunted. With the certainty of an old hand, I would thread my safety rope around the tree, secure it to the "D" ring on my belt, lean back, and use both hands to cut and discard obstructive limbs. I only needed to remove the limbs on one face of the tree until I got to the top 10 feet, then I had to remove them all in order to be able to lift the parachute free. It was tough because spruce typically dripped with pitch and the needles were stiff and sharp, but I was professional enough to stand up to these obstacles. And after removing my parachute, I justly felt triumphant satisfaction. But as I watched my parachute drift to the ground, my line of sight crossed my safety rope. I was instantly racked with fear, grabbed the tree trunk and hugged it while I shook uncontrollably. Each time I had sawed a limb the teeth had dropped onto the safety rope, cutting it just a little. But this procedure had been repeated so many times the rope had almost been cut in two. It was literally hanging together by a thread. The thought of what could have happened to me was so emotionally draining it took a long time to descend. Upon reaching the ground I said a little prayer of thanks and hoped my Don Quixote days were over.]

We had everything sacked and ready to pack out when we sat down for a breather and one last look at the panoramic view. Upper Priest Lake shone like a jewel four miles to the north. It was connected with Priest Lake by a two mile thoroughfare of water wide enough to allow boats to travel between the lakes. While seated there we looked at the expansive view across Priest Lake (two miles south of Upper Priest Lake) and observed one teensy, weensy, cotton ball cloud, in an otherwise clear sky, drift over Blacktail Mountain. It appeared totally innocuous. Then it happened. One bolt of lightning came from it and hit the ground, and a plume of smoke immediately resulted. Zap, the smokejumper god of lightning, had demonstrated his power to strike even in what may appear to be a cloudless sky. It was a helpless feeling to observe this occurrence and not be able to do a thing about it.

We hiked eight miles to Priest Lake where a motor boat picked us up for an hour-and-a-half ride to a dock near Priest Lake Ranger Station. I wanted very much to observe the countryside, but the drone of the boat motor was intoxicating and in spite of myself, I went to sleep. We stayed at the ranger station that night and in the morning went to Sandpoint in a station wagon to catch the train to Missoula. What a sight we must have been on that train. We had showered, but still looked very much like we just got off a fire—and smelled like it, too. We arrived in Missoula at 4:00 p.m. and went to the Fort for dinner and a night's rest.

The next morning, Wednesday, fellows were leaving in large numbers for project work because there were no fires. I had to wait to get on the project list because all the requests had been filled, so I went to work in the fire warehouse. As fate would have it, after the guys assigned to project had all left, a fire call came in for eight jumpers, and when they left I went to the top of the jump list. That night just before 10:00 p.m., eight of us were told we would be leaving early in the morning to re-enforce the eight-man crew already on the Sheep Creek Fire on the Wisdom Ranger District of the Beaverhead National Forest. We were awakened at 3:30 a.m. and taken downtown to the Oxford for a quick breakfast before heading to Hale Field. At 5:07 a.m. we were in the Tin Goose [a common name for a Ford Trimotor] *headed for our fire.*

[Members of the fire crew were Fred Barnowski, foreman, David Clippinger, Frank Fowler, Bill Hoskinson, Jim Tripp, Jack Dyson, Joe Wilson, and Erwin Stafford. Besides me, the other new men were Erwin, Jack, Joe and Bill. The spotter was Al Hammond.]

The Ford is so slow that it took an hour-and-a-half to fly to the fire. At one time we were flying within 150 feet of the ground and I could see a herd of elk. Fifteen minutes before we got to the fire we could see the smoke because in the cool air it just didn't dissipate.

[When we circled over the fire we could clearly see a man waving frantically. We all thought he was "waving us off," meaning we were not to jump. We had no way of knowing he was a crackpot who had nothing to do with the fire, and only later learned he was a prospector. We returned to Missoula and after straightening out the mix-up, took off again at 8:30 a.m. So much for an early start to the fire. It was 10:00 a.m. before we jumped.]

When we flew over the fire for the second time we strained to locate a clearing close to the fire that would serve as a jump spot, but there were no openings and the trees below were diseased and full of snags and downed timber. It looked like an accident waiting to happen so we scanned the countryside more distant from the fire. About a mile-and-a-half from the fire Al, the spotter, and Fred agreed on a stand of reproduction about ten feet high that looked safe enough, so we jumped.

Mac had gone on project, so I had a new jump partner. He is a year behind me at MSU—Bill is his name. When we got to the door I said, "Bill, there's plenty of room down there [in the patch of reproduction], but if we miss the reproduction, we'll end up in the snags. Let's talk to one another so we can stay out of each other's way and both make it safely to the spot."

He said, "Okay."

I said I'd take the bottom of the spot and he could head for the top of it. Again he said okay. Just before we left the plane I said, "Speak to me, Bill," meaning while we were in the air. He said, "Yea."

I was second position and the last man out of the plane. I followed Bill closely out of the door, but we opened far apart. I noticed I had a candy chute without tails—like my last jump. I was over the snags but drifting for the spot. Bill was between me and the spot; that was good because he was supposed to go to the top. He had tails so he'd make it easily.

Then Bill pulled his right guide line and held it. I yelled for him to release it and pull his left one, but he kept on coming. I couldn't figure what he was doing because a turn was unnecessary. I yelled and yelled and yelled. He wouldn't respond. He was turning toward me. I looked and saw snags and over mature trees that negated an option for me to turn, so I again yelled. It's easy to hear one another up there, so I got mad and let go some foul language to try and impress the point. Now he was completely turned and facing me. He seemed to be a couple of hundred feet away, but I don't know. Suddenly I think he realized the danger and started to steer away. Me too, but I didn't have tails and couldn't move quite as fast as he could. I saw him get bigger as he got closer and realized we were very close to being at the same level above ground. I saw his glasses reflect the sun and get big. I worried about hitting the lines of his chute, so I put my feet together and cocked them to the side— still pulling on the guide line. This all happened very fast. We came together with a combined impact speed of 10 to 15 mph. Because my feet were cocked to the side, my rear end hit his risers just above his head and I bounced off, jolting him rather severely. Our chutes rubbed, but we didn't tangle in each other's lines. For that I was thankful, but, boy, was I mad. All that room and he had to come back my way.

I quickly put it out of my mind, however, because I wasn't over the spot. I planed as hard as I could, my arms carrying all my weight on my front risers, but *reaching the spot looked hopeless. I thought I'd land in snags for certain. Then I hit an updraft close to the ground and it carried me to the bottom edge of the spot. It didn't make much difference where I hit within the spot because it all looked the same, so rather than work my chute all the way to the ground, I prepared to land. I lifted my feet in front of me slightly and shot into the trees. I could feel the tops "give" as I crashed through them, but I must have closed my eyes when branches slapped across my face mask because I don't remember seeing a thing. I landed on the ground flat on my back. It was really a soft landing. I know now why they refer to jumping into young second growth as a "featherbed landing."*

We hiked to the fire and met several of the ground crew working on the fire as well as the jumper crew that had jumped on Wednesday. We helped them with the line they were building on the main fire, but because burning snags were spitting sparks in advance of the main fire, it was decided that we could do more good by hunting for spot fires. As it turned out, there were about 30 of them, and it was important to put them out in a hurry because any one of them could quickly turn into a large fire.

I was impressed at night as the burning snags spit sparks showering down like Roman candles. It was quite beautiful.

Friday we really knocked the fire down. In the evening a plane dropped hay, oats, food, water, and another liquid refreshment cherished by most of the crew. The hot chow was great—better than C-rations by a long shot.

We had gotten up in the morning while it was still dark and fought until after dark. It really beats you, and the dirt caked on you adds to your discomfort. When a plane dropped a radio Saturday morning Fred found out that half of the jumpers were wanted back in Missoula, so the other crew returned except Fred switched places with Doug Wilkerson who then assumed leadership of the jumpers.

Those of us who remained continued the mop-up work. Whenever we saw smoke we mixed it with dirt. If we found fire in a log, we'd chop it out. We widened the fire line and had the fire secured, but not to the stage where it could be declared "out." The main fire was estimated at seven acres and we measured 15 chains [almost 1,000 feet] of fire line around the spot fires.

[That night I noted in my diary, "I'm so dirty I feel like a pig. My legs are just caked with dirt. I'm finally to the point that I can drink coffee and enjoy it, at least while on a fire. Wish I could take a shower tonight."]

We left at 6:30 a.m. the next day (today). It was a four-mile cross-country hike, and we took it at a leisurely pace and enjoyed observing some beaver dams along the way. When we reached an old dirt road our ride had not arrived, so we went swimming in a stream close by. What a good feeling to get clean even though we didn't have clean clothes to put on.

We got to Missoula at 2:00 p.m. today.

Love, R.

*   *   *

Monday, September 1, 1952

Dear Ma,

Monday the 25th I left Missoula for project. They split us up in groups according to how late we wanted to work. Since I was very low on the jump list, and wanted to work late, I was sent to Idaho—the Priest Lake Ranger District, of all places.

I had hoped to jump on a fire with Ted, but we didn't even see each other during the fire season, much less fight fire together. Now that the fire season was over we found ourselves in the same crew going on project to Priest Lake. Did I tell you that Ted and I plan to room together in the new men's dorm when school resumes?

Anyway, we got on the train at noon and spent the rest of the day in a long drawn-out ride. We had not eaten lunch and the train didn't sport a diner or club car. We were starved. Ted and I spoke to the brakeman and he said the train stopped for six minutes at some hick town a few miles down the track. When the time came all eleven of us sprinted the hundred yards to the general store and bought the first things we saw. Some old lady about 65, or is it 66?, [this was a joke to my mother who was 66] couldn't add 28 and 4, so we were nervous as all "get out." And when one guy pulled out a ten and she had to go look for change we about stole the stuff, we were that pressed for time. As it turned out, we got back to the train just as it pulled out, but at the rate the darn thing moved I think we could have chased it a mile and caught it.

We stopped at some place for a long time picking up milk. For something to do we got out what fire equipment we had (head light, hard hat, logger boots, smokejumper T-shirt) and put them on a little kid. What a fun time it turned out to be, and the kid loved it.

We ate dinner at Sandpoint, Idaho, and went by truck to Priest Lake Ranger Station. The ranger said four men would go to a remote site and work on bridge construction. The job would involve Saturday work with time-and-a-half for overtime work. As you know, we are only paid straight time for overtime on fires, so this was a very coveted opportunity. The other seven would stay at the ranger station and pile brush with no Saturday work. Of course everybody wanted the bridge work, not only to get out of piling brush, but to get the time-and-a-half pay. We drew straws and Ted and I both lost, but Gene Tuininga decided he wanted to stay at the station so I eagerly swapped with him. I kind of wanted to work with Ted, but, Ma, if I can make enough money, I may try to get home before school starts.

[Two years had passed since I left home to study forestry in Missoula and I felt a strong need to return, even if only briefly. The time-and-a-half overtime pay seemed to be the only prospect for making the trip a financial reality.]

We're six miles up from the station on a beat-up road. Nobody is here but us bridge builders. We stay in four-man tents. They have wooden floors, cots, stove and sleeping bags. Intermingled with the tents are giant Western red cedar, Thuja plicata (see, I learned something in school), about five feet d.b.h. (diameter breast high). It gives the place a nice atmosphere. We're camped right on a stream, which no doubt helps keep the place cool.

In the future it is planned to build a road through here as a short-cut to the Alaskan Highway. That explains this concrete bridge being built way out here in the sticks, but it sure looks strange to see the high structure with no road approach and nothing but a heavy stand of timber on the far end.

The cook here is terrific—every meal is tops. Plenty of pastries, etc. We don't have lunch here because lunch is dinner and dinner is supper. The noon meal is as big as the evening one. It's more than I need to eat, but it's a good pastime.

We've been shoveling sand, gravel and cement in the mixer to make concrete, helping carpenters with forms, helping put tie wires on re-enforcing steel . . . helping anybody . . . helping everybody—I feel like a life saver. Sleeping is wonderful here. It gets quite cold at night and the sound of the stream just puts me right into "la la land." I wish I could sleep this well at school.

Saturday evening (after we made 19 bucks for one day's work) we went in to the ranger station. We joined the other jumpers and went about 20 miles north to a dance in Nordman. I had a lot of fun. Some girls were up from Washington and we really whooped it up. In the morning (we stayed at the ranger station over night) we went to the lake close by and rented a boat for $2.50 for the whole day. The weather was fine, which sort of surprised me because of how cold I felt where I was staying at the bridge site. I guess the mountain streams and taller trees along with a little higher elevation makes the difference. In the evening we went to another dance. We didn't wake up until eleven the next day (today) so *we decided not to go to the lake. We laid in the sun all afternoon and then came back here.*

You know when you're out here you feel like there's very few big cities and very few people in what cities there are. Few outsiders are seen and even when you go to town in Nordman it's just one big log cabin containing a post office, grocery store, bar, night club, and dance hall—all in one. People come in from ranches, farms, logging camps, etc. to see the big city.

It's hard to get used to (maybe especially for me, being raised on the east coast) but I like it, for a change anyway. A bear regularly raids the garbage can at the ranger station each night. One night while I was there we heard him dump the can. Ted picked up his flash camera and we went out. We saw him by moonlight but by the time we got close enough for a picture, he high-tailed it into the brush. Bear season opened today. I hope he doesn't get shot.

You asked me what kind of noise a porcupine makes. I've never heard one make any oral noise, but when he moves in the brush he can be plenty noisy, especially on a quiet night when you're alone. [I must have been referring to my first fire jump with Bill Demmons when we were hiking in the dark.]

I've enclosed a tag that we seal our gear with when we've retrieved it after a jump. We have two—one for the jump gear and one for chutes. Once the tag is clipped into place it can't be undone except by breaking it. It provides a means for the guys at the loft to tell if the stuff has been tampered with or not.

The fire season is about over even if we haven't had our big rain. Lots of fellows quit this weekend and a lot more will go in a week. Who knows, we may jump again, but I doubt it. I enjoy writing these long letters, and not just to please my mother (although it's a big part of it), but also to bring to mind the things I've done. It also satisfies my writing hunger, and passes the evenings. Besides, I like to get letters.

Love, R.

*　　*　　*

Friday, September 5, 1952

Dear Ma,

Day before yesterday we went on a fire. The day before some big wheels started a fire to burn off the slash created by logging. The cut area was about 90 acres and after they set it afire, it got away. The nuts should have known it would because we still haven't had our fall rain. Ted said the fire that night was horrific. He and the other jumpers at the ranger station, plus the other workers at the station, fought all night long. At 3:00 a.m. we were also called. We got up and took off in short order. Boy, was it cold in the open truck. We laid down and put a blanket and canvas over us, so it wasn't as bad as it could have been. The fire was under control by the time we got there so we more or less watched it. During the day we worked improving fire line, knocking down hot spots and checking for spot fires (over the line). Since we smokejumpers (I forgot to mention that we didn't jump on this one except from the rear end of a truck) were a lot younger than the rest of the crew, we were sent tramping over the mountains looking for spots. It was fun working with Ted, even if we didn't jump to this fire, and we found quite a few spot fires a half mile from the fire and over the ridge. They were the size of some two-man fires that we routinely jump on.

Because the spot fires can be difficult to find once they are left, they must be put out, not just controlled. We spent the day working on them and looking for more.

The appearance of a dead fire impressed me. The view of that dull, grey, ashy hillside makes a guy feel half dead himself. When you walk through the ashes it's like walking in flour. And where the fuel was heavy, the remaining ash can be several inches deep, resulting in big clouds of ash dust with every step. I got my boots soled just before my first jump, but they didn't hold up very well because every time I fight a fire I burn my soles. This time I really did them up brown. Gad, there just wasn't much left, and they were really smoking. My feet were a little warm, too. Warm?—they were downright hot.

We left that evening and got seven hours overtime, paid at time-and-a-half. Strange isn't it, the government rationalizes that fighting wild fire is an emergency and will therefore not compensate with increased overtime pay, but fighting a slash burning fire is overtime. Oh well, I knew the score when I signed on. Tomorrow is Saturday and I'll be back on the bridge—another time-and-a-half day. Yes, I always like to see Saturdays roll around.

Love, R.

P.S. Ain't it a dishonorable way to fight a fire? Travel by truck!

*   *   *

The dispatcher from Priest Lake Ranger Station came to our camp and asked me if I wanted to cruise timber (gather field data to determine the volume of timber in a potential timber sale) with Ted until school started. I was really tempted because it sounded like valuable experience for a forestry student, but I told him no because I was planning to go home soon. After reconsidering, I tried to get on the crew, but John Hautzinger had already signed on in my place.

I continued to work at a variety of jobs including rigging steel, making forms, and mixing concrete. The nights were getting colder and I was grateful an older guy in our tent was an early riser and liked to start the morning fire. He would load the stove with cedar kindling to get a roaring fire quickly started, and the loud crackling was an effective wake up call. It felt good to emerge from the sleeping bag to a warm tent.

Bill Hoskinson and John Williams came to work with Jerry McGrazo, Harold Heyes and me as gofers on the bridge crew. We sometimes worked together, but usually we were distributed to assist the journeyman bridge builders. Daylight was waning after we finished supper, so we mostly read, wrote letters, or played cribbage. Occasionally when we had free time during daylight hours, we would horse around at the sand pile that had been dumped over a 15 foot bank. A concrete mixer was at the base of this huge sand pile, but slightly off to the side. We would race along the firm ground above the pile and jump out as far as we could. Even though it was a long drop, the angle of our descent approximated the angle of the sloping sand pile, so when we hit it was soft. We would slide for some distance before coming to a stop. At first the objective was to see how far we could jump, but when that got old we started doing flips. No one got hurt and it was great fun until we moved so much sand on our landings that we decided it was time to quit before someone did.

After several days, John Williams left and Herb Oertli came from Missoula. Even though Herb was a foreman, the fire season looked so bleak he decided to go on project to extend his work season, and I'm sure the Saturday work was an attraction. Entries into my daily diary (we all accounted for our time and activity in a small notebook) stopped after September 11, indicating that shortly thereafter I left for Missoula to arrange for a train ticket to Maryland.

*   *   *

I never considered flying back East for my visit. I knew plane fare was more expensive than the train, and even though I didn't have much time, I had less money. Two days traveling each way still left a week or 10 days and that was a reasonable visit, at least for a person in my situation. My brother Earl in

Lanham, Maryland, held an all day picnic in his spacious backyard. Most of my family was there.

I was a bit chagrined when it came to seeing my high school classmates. Some had gone into the service, others had already left for college, and some were just so wrapped up in whatever they were doing that they were indifferent. I didn't expect a brass band would herald my return, but I never expected that my friends would get along so well without me.

I began to realize my circle of friends was in Montana, not Maryland. I went to see Jeanne, a girl I dated in high school and to whom I had written since going West. She was attending the University of Maryland and lived in a sorority house. Our meeting was delayed because her sorority had called a meeting to decide which pledges to admit as new sisters. She told me about the "black ball" system they used in reaching a decision. The Greeks at M.S.U. were much the same, leading me to conclude that I was a GDI (goddamn independent). It was late in the evening before we had the chance to converse for a few minutes.

I knew I needed to be back among the friends I had made the past two years, and found myself anxious to be on my way. I was very grateful, however, to have been able to see things as they really were and not how I imagined them. It gave me a much better opportunity to enjoy my remaining two years at school in Montana.

My mother was particularly glad to see me. She and I, along with a few other family members, spent a great day at Atlantic City on the beach. I was surprised the weather was nice enough to permit swimming in late September— my thinking had obviously recalibrated since going to the Northwest. We had a particularly good visit, walking and talking along the beach. She had a way of making me feel good about myself and spoke approvingly of "my adventure to the Rocky Mountains." This was close to the end of my trip and I knew she was sending me on my way—with her blessing.

*　　*　　*

Monday, October 6, 1952

Dear Ma,

I guess I owe you an apology for not writing sooner, but really it couldn't be helped. When I got to school I had an awful mess with my clothes and trying to matriculate. I got my schedule straightened out except for ROTC [Reserve Officers Training Corps], but as you may remember I couldn't pass the physical for Air

ROTC because of my eyes and therefore had to switch to Army. The change caused conflicts in my schedule that were not easily resolved. Some of my classmates had the same problem and worked it out somehow, but I decided to take my chances with the draft and drop ROTC all together; besides I was fed up with military science.

Just as I was getting straightened out, the loft called. They had no jumpers at all and fire requests were coming in like crazy. They asked if we (Ted and I) would go to a fire on the Bitterroot National Forest near Lost Trail Pass on the Idaho/Montana border. It would have been nice if Ted and I could have caught a "two-manner," but we felt ourselves fortunate just to be jumping on the same fire, so seven of us jumped at 1:30 Tuesday afternoon on the Shields Creek Fire.

[Since most of the summer crew were students from all over the United States, it's not surprising that five of the crew were from Montana State University, and perhaps it wasn't even surprising that we were all from the Forestry School, but remarkably we were all juniors. Included were Bob Walkup, Danny O'Rourke, Dick Faurot, plus Ted and I. Len Krout was the foreman, and Dee Dutton was evidently not going to school but seemed committed to pursuing the jumpers as a career. He displayed an ability for hard work exceeded by no one.

For the sake of record keeping, smokejumper fires within the region are successively numbered throughout the year, so when Bill and I made our first jump on Count Peak in the Flathead National Forest it was recorded as Number 29.

My last fire in Sheep Creek on the Beaverhead was Number 55. Since the Shields Creek fire (the one we were now going to fight) was Number 79, it was obvious that several jumps had been made while I was on my trip back home. Also recorded for each fire is the accumulated number of jumps made to date. For example, on the Shields Creek Fire the fire number was 79 and the accumulated number of jumps was 367.]

Bill Woods, our spotter, told us the fire was 80 acres (the largest I had jumped on all summer). When Bill dropped a drift chute over a potential jump spot near the fire it descended in an irregular pattern, so we circled and he dropped another. It's hard to get a good view unless you are by the door, and even then, if the plane is banking in a turn it's difficult to orient to what level is. The spot, close to the fire, was a grassy opening surrounded by a dense stand of lodgepole pine snags— obviously the result of an old burn. Bill warned us of a cross wind—up high it was gently blowing one way—but down lower it was blowing strong in the opposite direction. He said if we felt we weren't going to make it to the spot, we should turn in another direction to get well away from the snags patch.

Len and Bob jumped first and managed to stay out of the snag patch. Ted and I were next and left the Ford close together in good fashion. I was glad when I checked my canopy and found I had tails—those who didn't had a lot tougher time managing the wind. I tried to anticipate the change in wind direction, but really didn't have anything to gauge by, so I had to wait until I felt it. I was well over half way down before I felt the gush of wind coming from the opposite direction. It was much stronger than I imagined it would be. I quickly pulled a guideline, reversing my direction and planed into the wind. From the air I thought the spot was more on a slope than I now found it to be. It was, in fact, level, and Ted and I both hit it. One of the guys without tails opted not to try for the spot and headed for a safer place some distance away. He had a tougher hike back to the fire than the rest of us, but it was nonetheless a smart maneuver.

Dick was the last to jump. He was much too slow starting his turn when he passed through the wind layer. We yelled, trying to tell him to head down the hill toward green timber, but he continued to try and make it back to the lower edge of the clearing. It was obvious he wasn't going to make it, but he kept coming. His canopy enveloped a snag and collapsed, breaking the snag at ground line. Dick was falling on his back with the snag coming down on him. Below was a jackstraw of dead lodgepole that prevented any chance of his landing on sod. What happened next I wouldn't have believed if I hadn't witnessed it. The snag he was falling with didn't tip very far before it hit another lodgepole pine snag. Miraculously this close by snag was forked and his falling snag hit exactly in the center of the fork. The resulting collision caused much creaking and swaying, but the forked snag held—he dangled by his shroud lines just barely above the hazardous maze of downed trees.

The fire was in grass (meadow) as well as timber. We started slapping it out with the backs of shovels, but Ted had a better way. He had fought lots of grass fires where he grew up in eastern Montana, so he knew enough to get a sack, put some dirt in it, and slap with a much more effective tool than a shovel. Grass burns as fast as paper, if not faster, but luckily it was burning downhill, so we had it at a disadvantage. Ted's sack worked well and we were tearing around the grassy portion of the fire in a hurry.

All of the fire's edge was not in grass, however, so we had considerable line to dig. A plane dropped a power saw that we were able to put to good use. Even with a seasoned crosscut saw team there is no comparison between what can be accomplished in an hour with one versus the other. We had the hot spots knocked down and the fire wasn't running any more, but a lot of work remained. In the evening a ground crew arrived on horseback.

[When we quit for the night Ted and I walked to a spot where we could see down the Bitterroot Valley to Darby, 20+ miles away. All we saw were the lights from the little town, but still it was rather spectacular in the dark.

Ted said, "I wonder if there're any coyotes around here."

"Likely," I said, "but I wouldn't know how to prove it."

"Well, I do," he answered. And he proceeded to howl. I joined him, but with less authenticity. In a few moments a whole passel of coyotes joined in a howling chorus. In time another chorus a little more distant joined in. Shortly, it seemed every coyote within a hundred miles was whooping it up with Ted and me. When we went back to our camp, some of the guys were already in bed and expressed no appreciation for our coyote calling skills. *C'est la vie.*]

The next day a larger ground crew showed up to finish the mop-up, and since we wanted to get back for our Friday classes, we left. We hiked out ten miles and then were driven the 90 miles back to Missoula.

We expected to head right back to the campus, but before we even had a chance to think about it we were loaded in a Ford Trimotor and left for another fire. It was about 500 acres and was going like hell, but it was too windy to jump and eight jumpers couldn't have done much more than watch it burn, so we returned to base.

On Friday at 1:30 p.m. we took off in a Ford Trimotor for a fire in the Bob Marshall Primitive Area.

[Again there were seven of us, but only Walkup, Dutton, Ted and I from the crew on the last fire. Paul Carpino, Lund, and Rawley filled out the crew. This fire was Number 83, so this was the fourth fire since our last jump.]

Len Krout, the spotter, had a tough time finding a suitable jump spot. We settled on a location a half mile from the fire, but it was so terrible we all later commented that we were fortunate to have landed safely. In addition to that difficulty, two guys on the same stick had inversions, meaning their chutes opened inside out. I never understood how that happens, but it does sometimes. It doesn't cause the chute to descend any faster, but it does make it difficult to steer because the slots (and tails, if you have them) are in the front portion of the canopy instead of the rear. I understand it can be tough to tell which line to pull in order to close a slot (thereby guiding the chute). Further complicating the problem, the propulsion pushed you backward instead of forward. Ted was one of the guys who had this experience on this jump, but he still managed to hit the spot. The other guy almost hit a cliff. He was one happy jumper when he hit the ground safely.

The fire was only three or four acres and wasn't too aggressive, but it was tough to build a fire line because of the numerous rocks in the soil. When trying to

151

scalp the surface our Pulaskis would clank ineffectively without moving any vegetation or soil. Fortunately a nearby stream provided an opportunity for efficient use of the hand water pumps. Ted and I, however, operated a crosscut saw much of the time.

Most of these fall fires had been started by hunters. This wouldn't happen if it would rain a bit; nevertheless, it's pretty basic to always put out your campfire.

A plane dropped some juice, bread and canned meat—a delightful supplement to our C-rations. We all praised the great bird in the sky. On Sunday two men on horseback got there to watch the few smokes left, so we took off. We had to carry our gear, weighing 90 pounds, a mile-and-a-half to the trail so the packer could pick them up. The effort about beat me. We met the packer when we reached the trail and took off, 90 pounds lighter, for Black Bear Guard Station. There are no roads, just an airstrip. What a nice log cabin. Not only was it large, it was well built and plumbed with running water. The stove was not only used for heating and cooking, but rigged with a system to provide hot water. It was great to be able to wash with hot water. After spending the night a plane came in this morning and flew us back to Missoula.

I have to mention how fortunate I am to have once again flown over the full length of the Bob Marshall Primitive Area. It's such beautiful country and it's breath-taking to be able to see for many miles without any roads. I'd love to spend a summer working on the ground just to get more of a feel for how it must have been in yesteryear.

I got here for my 11 o'clock class.

A fellow got chewed up by a grizzly bear in the Flathead National Forest (a hunter, not a jumper) and eight smokejumpers parachuted in to clear a spot with a chain saw for a helicopter to land. The guy will live. I think they will be doing a lot more rescue work with the helicopter in the future.

I'm going to work 14 hours per week for the Forest Service at the federal building (for Woolfolk) and each evening in the dorm as a resident assistant (RA). Of course I'll continue my job with the food service, only I'll be checking [student's names] instead of washing dishes.

I'm way behind in school work and can't afford to jump again even if it means money. I got 80 hours on the last two jumps combined.

Love, R.

P.S. Wish it would rain. What a funny fire season—hot in the spring and fall and nothing much going on during the summer.

Concrete bridge without an approach road.

CHAPTER 7

Junior Year

I welcomed the opportunity to jump on two fires after school started, but had to scramble to catch up in my studies. Two of my courses were forestry subjects: silviculture (relating to tree culture) and mensuration (mathematics associated with determination of forest volume, growth and yield). The remaining two courses were outside the forestry school—basic geology and technical writing.

Several changes occurred since last year. Corbin Hall was converted to a womens' dorm and we were obliged to move to newly constructed Craig Hall. Ted and I continued washing dishes at Corbin and had several classes together, but since I was majoring in "timber" and he in "range" (both options in the forestry curriculum) our journey to a degree had begun to follow different paths.

I also purchased a car. Mr. Woolfolk offered me his '37 Ford for $100. Ted and I decided to own it together, each paying $50. It was easier for me to get to work at the federal building, and it was great to be able to go downtown to a movie or to church without having to brave the elements.

Sometimes kids from Wesley would pack into the back seat until there was scarcely room to breathe. The brakes were mechanical, so we never drove fast and usually geared down when coming to a stop. The engine was a little hard on oil and we used to kid about pulling into a gas station and filling up with oil and checking the gas. We carried a five-gallon can of used oil.

Enrollment dropped to a little over 2000—the lowest since the war years. There were rumors it dropped under 2000 during winter quarter, but from then on, the student population steadily grew. Construction on new buildings for music, liberal arts, a men's dormitory, and a new field house, brought a sense that the campus was expanding.

Ted had several friends who had joined a fraternity and thought it might be fun to join one, so we pledged. From the start we didn't like it much. The required study hall might have been alright for freshmen, but for juniors it was ridiculous. We had long ago established study habits and didn't respond well to paternalism. The demerit system and consequential paddling of pledges was just pure harassment, and not easily endured by an upper class student. But the last straw was a fall formal dance where many of the fraternity members got so drunk they couldn't see their dates home. Ted and I ended up giving rides to several girls whose dates were incapacitated. Thus ended our taste of fraternity life.

I had taken a beginning mensuration course in spring quarter the year before and earned an "A," but didn't care for it. I did well because I was intimidated and worked hard.

The professor, Fay Clark, was at one time a forest supervisor (working for the Forest Service) who appeared to have come out of the Black Forest in Germany. He wore a monocle attached to a string around his neck and would periodically widen his eyes so the glass would fall from the eye socket. Then, when he referred to his notes, he would place the monocle back into place, stare at papers, and then look at the class while raising the eyebrow of the unmonocled eye. We sometimes suspected his actions were for dramatic effect, but if they were, he played the part so well we could never be certain.

We all knew, however, that his mensuration courses were the bottle neck causing many forestry majors to change to a different field. Prof. Clark said he reserved the right to ask questions on any of our previous courses when he gave his final exam. He also said finals were open-book and we could take as long as we wanted, up to eight hours. Also permitted were cribs, cheat sheets, old tests, and anything else we thought would help us pass. We didn't accept this as generosity on his part, but as an indicator his test would be as difficult as he could make it.

The best students didn't seem to be intimidated by his approach, but most of us sweated bullets just trying to survive. I worked hard but didn't learn much even though I averaged a "B" in his three courses.

All of the calculations in mensuration were done with the use of a slide rule technically named a "log, log, duplex." I don't know what the nomenclature meant, except that it was based on logarithms and was crammed with fine calibrations on both sides. It was complex. We all carried one in a holster attached to our belt, a practice unique to forestry school students, and we usually referred to it as a slip stick because of its sliding parts.

Most of my other junior courses were a continuation of study in the sciences: wood technology, range management, forest entomology (study of insects) and forest pathology (study of diseases). We did, however, have to take a course in the principles of economics. It felt expanding to study a subject so unrelated to science even though it was not a course that drew my interest.

The biggest change during my junior year was meeting Corky. She was a freshman majoring in music, played the cello, and was working towards a teaching degree. We met playing volleyball at a Wesley Foundation gathering. She easily took the top spot in the long list of good things that happened during college.

We enjoyed the school dances and the special artists brought to campus such as Duke Ellington and Les Brown and his Band of Renown. Corky was a serious student, and we were both busy, but we enjoyed one another's company when time permitted.

Sometimes we just walked around campus and nearby neighborhoods. Once, on a Saturday afternoon, we went shooting with my .22 caliber rifle. We walked around Mt Sentinel, following the railroad tracks into Hellgate Canyon, away from any buildings or traffic. After about a quarter-of-a-mile, we came to a draw coming down from the mountain. I set some cardboard targets and we shot a box of shells for practice. We couldn't have been more than a half-mile from the campus, but the environment felt remote—another reminder of the MSU's unique setting.

I learned later she had been the head drum majorette for the Butte High School Marching Band and was the one I had seen two years before when I went to the football game in Butte.

I continued to work in range research for the Forest Service as my class schedule permitted, but it was different from the year before. Attached to the offices where I worked was a green house several floors above the ground. Mert wanted me to conduct germination tests on various seeds, but the green house was without shade and the sun was sometimes too intense. I was told to devise a means to provide shade, and designed an apparatus with two-by-fours and heavy wire to support a bamboo curtain that could be rolled out beneath the sloping glass roof and dropped down the sides. It was quite effective.

Although assigned a variety of work during the year, I spent a substantial amount of my time testing seed viability, which allowed me to spend significant time away from a desk. I liked that, and the work was educational.

There were two other scientists working in range research beside Mert (and E.J.), and I got to know them well. One of the fellows, Roald, was an extrovert who loved to play devil's advocate during coffee break discussions. He was well-liked and always considerate of others even though he had an inquisitive mind and liked to create controversy. I admired his wit and competitive nature.

Something was wrong in the office, but I couldn't determine what until Roald took me aside. He said I would be hearing negative things about him and wanted me to hear his side of the issue before I heard it elsewhere.

The McCarthy hearings were in full swing in the Congress. Roald had belonged to an organization in college that was later labeled Communistic. It was assumed he was a Communist, and was forced to quit his job with the Forest Service. It seemed preposterous to me, but it didn't become any clearer no matter how many questions I asked. It was brutally unfair—surely a way could be found to exonerate him. It couldn't, and he had to leave.

I had followed the hearings from a distance. A part of me felt that they wouldn't be in progress unless a real threat existed. But now that it hit close to home, I formed a lasting impression that McCarthy was on a witch hunt, and was gratified a year later when he was toppled from his place of power, even though it didn't help Roald.

*   *   *

Christmas turned out to be extra special in 1953 because Jim came to Montana for a visit. He was my brother Earl's son with whom I had lived the last five years of my pre-college days. He was more like a brother than a nephew and his parents decided to give him a train ride to visit me as a Christmas present. I was working over the holidays, but took a few days off to spend with him. One evening we drove in the old '37 Ford on a secondary forest road in fresh snow. I tied a rope on the back bumper and Jim hung on and "skied" in the moonlight with nothing but boots on his feet. We must have been easy to please because we thought it great fun.

We spent Christmas with the Woolfolks and then drove to Butte to visit some of my friends there. Because the price was right, we stayed in a room over a bar on Montana Street that can only be described as a flophouse. For both of us that was the most memorable part of the visit. We couldn't sleep for the loud noise from the bar, but the worst of it was the sound of a firearm discharging. It scared the hell out of Jim.

We visited with Tom and his family. Tom's mom was an excellent candy maker and their house was well stocked for the holidays. We also stopped by to visit with Corky and her family although we didn't stay long in Butte because Jim's visit wasn't very long.

Jim's memory of the things we did is not much better than mine. He said we went to see a friend of mine, a black foreign student. It impressed Jim that he was still in bed in the afternoon, allegedly claiming he wouldn't have to eat as much if he slept. He was a long way from home and was trying to save money.

We also visited the new field house on campus and Jim was struck by the fact that the basketball floor was on blocks and you could look underneath and see dirt. I have no recollection of that.

Jim had never seen a sawmill operate. We visited one, and we did lots of other fun things. It was the only Christmas I spent with family in my four years at college. The absence of holiday blues was a welcome change.

*　　*　　*

I earned more as a smokejumper than I did the previous summer, but my funds were still low. Traveling home at the end of summer was an expense, but I thought I had made allowances for those costs. No doubt I missed some working days while Jim was visiting and I had contributed $50 as my share of the cost of the car with Ted. Perhaps my class schedule had prevented me from working as much. At any rate, I couldn't cover my spring quarter expenses and applied for a $200 loan. It was a little more than I needed, but the extra money would allow a less frugal existence. The Ford Foundation came through with a loan that accrued no interest while I was still in school, and only three percent per year after graduation.

*　　*　　*

The Wesley Foundation and the forestry club continued to play a significant part in my school life. Both provided diversion from the daily grind. I didn't function well with all work and no play.

I did reasonably well scholastically and was never satisfied when my GPA fell below 3.0. Perhaps I should have raised my sights a bit higher, but working at a higher level often required more tenacity, commitment, and focus than I was prepared to give. My friends in pre-med studied hard every night to maintain high grades, but I could study that way only for those courses that attracted me most. For the others I sometimes allowed participation in intramural sports to take a higher priority for a portion of my evening study time. That's not to say I could have aced all my courses if I wanted to. Some courses came hard for me no matter my effort. Economics, for instance, was a humbling experiences because I worked so hard, but could muster only average grades.

In May, just a little over a month before the end of the school year, I received the surprise of my college career with the notification that I had been selected to become a member of Phi Sigma Society, a biological honorary. I didn't even know what it was. Surely someone had made a mistake. A hand-written note to me read:

Frank,

Phi Sigma will meet in room 207, Natural Science, at 7:30 p.m. Thursday eve. Your attendance is required. All day Thursday you will have the following items in your possession and will bring them with you Thursday night. A jar containing at least one yard of colored cloth, a needle, a spool of thread, and samples of silt, loam, clay and sand. You will also obtain a white "lab" coat to be worn all day and to the meeting.

Dick Solberg, President, ΦΣ

I obtained all the items and carried them to my classes wearing a white lab coat. I felt a bit self-conscious, undeserving, and pleased all at the same time. It happened a blood drive was in progress that day. (At least two times a year the Red Cross would draw blood to help furnish the supply needed for the service men in Korea.) My friends and I donated routinely, so I went to the gym in my white lab coat.

When I started to get in line a nurse gently tugged at my arm and asked me to come with her. We went behind some curtains and she said they were having difficulty reviving one of the donors and asked me what should be done.

"Prop up the feet and apply a cold compress to the forehead," I said, a bit confused why I had been singled out for this inquiry.

"Is there anything else, doctor?"

"Doctor? I'm just a forestry student trying to give blood," I answered in total confusion. Then I realized the white lab coat had mistakenly identified me as a doctor. It didn't take long to escort me back to the other side of the curtains. I hoped the situation wasn't serious because I couldn't help but chuckle at the scene.

An article in the Kaimin carried the following account:

Biology Group Initiation Includes 13

Wear white lab coats and carry a jar full of small miscellaneous items—that was the order of the day for the 13 students initiated into Phi Sigma, biological honorary, last night.

The honorary's informal initiation was at 7:30 and formal initiation will be Thursday, May 7, said Dick Solberg, president.

Those initiated . . . [were seven juniors, two seniors, and four graduate students. They came from several fields of study: Premed, 3; medical technology, 3; bacteriology, 2; wildlife technology, 2; forestry, 2; and zoology, 1. The other forestry student was working on his masters degree.]

To be considered for membership in Phi Sigma, students must have a 3.0 grade average in biological science subjects, and a 2.5 over-all average.

It wasn't difficult for me to verify that I met the grade point requirements, but it still seemed unrealistic for me to be selected over some of my peers who earned higher averages. Certainly the requirement of "good moral and ethical character" was not a deterrent for consideration of my classmates. I concluded my edge was working in range research for a summer and part time during each of my school years, since by definition the organization was formed to promote academic achievement AND *research* in the biological sciences. Whatever the reason, I was honored to be selected as a member.

Following one of our meetings, Dr. Diettert, a botany professor from whom I had taken several courses, spoke with me. He was a highly respected teacher, an exceptionally kind man, and easy to talk with. Questioning me about my summer work in the smokejumpers, he said one of his sons had been a smokejumper but had died in the Mann Gulch Fire in 1949 along with 12 others. It was obviously a great loss to him, but he said he supported his son's decision to jump and refused to try and lay blame on the Forest Service for the tragedy as several parents were doing.

I thought he might caution me against continuing to fight fire, but he only asked if I found it enjoyable work. I think he knew the answer, and sensed he had a need to talk with someone who worked in the same outfit as his deceased son. It was a moving experience.

The Mann Gulch tragedy was discussed many times during our smokejumping training, but because of the accusations brought by some of the parents, details were not volunteered. It wasn't until reading Norman Maclean's book, *Young Men and Fire,* in 1992 that I realized the depth of bitterness felt by some parents. I had met one of the killed jumper's father, Henry Thol, Sr., several times when I worked on the Flathead National Forest in the late 1960s and early 1970s. He had been retired for many years and my impression was that he was a gentle, easy going man. I couldn't recognize him as the same person described in Maclean's book. The tragedy must have had a profound affect on the personality of all those close to it. As Maclean points out, some never were able to adjust.

*   *   *

Even though I had a "B" average two of the three quarters, I still ended up with a 2.9 GPA for the year. My goal of earning a 3-point would have to wait another year.

CHAPTER 8

Clarence Creek

Excerps from a letter:

February 22, 1953

Dear Ma,
　It snows, it gets warm, it rains, it does everything. Just like home. The experts say the coming summer will be the worst fire season for the past 20 or 30 years.
　I got a letter from the Forest Service asking me back to the jumpers this summer.

Love, R.

In the spring of 1953, refresher training for the Smokejumper Project began on June 15, the Monday after the spring quarter ended at the university. Even though my grade point average goal had eluded me, it had been a good year at school; nevertheless, for several months I had been anxiously anticipating another summer in the mountains and was glad it was about to begin. Although Ted was going back to work for the Forest Service, it was with the Beaverhead National Forest and not the smokejumpers. Since he was majoring in forestry with a range management option, he believed he needed some grassland work experience. I understood his reasoning, but was disappointed we would not be working together.

As in previous years, the training for "old men" was not as physically demanding as it was for those just entering the program. On the first day, for example, we brushed up on how to calculate the acreage of an extinguished fire: not exactly the kind of activity that taxed muscle power or got the heart pumping. Emphasis was placed on gaining a better understanding of the mechanical equipment. We set up and operated marine pumps so we would be prepared to use them if we found ourselves lucky enough to have a water source close to a fire. While chain saws were still not routinely provided, they were seen as valuable tools on large fires, so we trained using them, focusing on safety.

Harold Wicklund, or "Wick," as he was called, was a mechanical engineer whose sole job was to invent equipment for Forest Service use. On our second day he gave us instructions on how to operate a trenching machine he had invented. It resembled a rototiller except in place of the tiller blades, a disk with four short pieces of chain turned at high speed. On the ends of the chain were small hammers designed to tear into the ground and throw soil, roots, and rocks in a huge cloud of dust, primarily to the side, but there was no telling where the plume would drift. In its wake, a path through the soil would serve effectively as a fireline. It seemed to work well, but we all realized it would be useless on steep terrain or in heavily wooded areas. Consequently most of us never saw one in operation on a wild fire, and it never was accepted as part of the arsenal in the fight against fire. Wick, however, diligently tried to promote its use.

We also refreshed our skills making let-downs and jumping from the towers. It was "old hat," but we enjoyed being back with the outfit and eagerly exchanged "silk stories" about the events of last summer that were not mutually experienced. The term "silk stories" came from the times when parachutes were made of silk. While the stories are basically true, it is also generally understood that they may be embellished to add color or mystique.

While taking first aid training on Wednesday we joked that it was probably in preparation for the jumps we were to make the next two days. We weren't apprehensive about jumping, it was just fun to banter about it, particularly at meal time in the presence of rookies.

The jumps went smoothly, from the Travelair on Thursday, and from the Ford on Friday. Upon completion we were ready and qualified to jump on fires. We knew, however, we would likely be on project for several weeks before there was substantial fire activity. Soon after the completion of the second jump, Fred Brauer stood before us and spoke in his notorious "Good Deal Brauer" manner: "Do I ever have a fantastic list of projects for you guys. Each and every one is a golden opportunity."

He was proud of the work smokejumpers accomplished on projects and sincere in believing the program a winner for everyone affected—especially the jumpers and the ranger districts. No matter the job or location, he spoke of it like it was absolutely the greatest opportunity on the face of the earth. He went through the list of requests various ranger districts had submitted and made assignments. I was to go with Dave Owen and Skip Stoll to Ant Flat Ranger Station to mark bug infested spruce trees for harvest by logging crews.

On Monday, June 22 the three of us started out in Dave's car, a black 1939 Ford Tudor. I knew them both from school; they had started in the smokejumpers a year before I did. Dave was a bit older than Skip and I. He had delayed going to college until after he served a hitch in the service, so he was a year behind us in school. Skip started school when I did but was pursuing a five-year course in pharmacy. We had become acquainted in our freshman year when we lived in Jumbo Hall.

Our route took us through St. Ignatius, a small town 40 miles north of Missoula, Skip's hometown. The majestic Mission Range was the backdrop for this quaint town and we enjoyed Skip's many stories about it and the surrounding area. Dave commented about how much snow there was on the high, rocky slopes of the Missions. Skip said the townsfolk often bet on whether all the snow would be melted by Labor Day. Even at high altitudes it was hard to imagine temperatures cool enough for snow to last through July and August, but he assured us it was common.

It wasn't long before we reached Flathead Lake, the largest fresh water lake west of the Great Lakes. I was familiar with it because of my participation in the annual spring break retreat sponsored by the Wesley Foundation, but the massive area of water with dense timber lining its shoreline always impressed me each time I saw it.

By noon we had passed through Kalispell and reached Whitefish where we decided to eat. I had never been there and found it an intriguing little town. It was an attractive recreation community near Whitefish Lake that boasted a golf course and a nearby ski hill, Big Mountain. We were determined to come back and explore it when we had time.

At 2:30 p.m. we reached Ant Flat Ranger Station, headquarters for the Fortine Ranger District of the Kootenai National Forest. We were welcomed by Assistant Ranger Bob Gillespie, a forester who had graduated from Montana State University in 1950. He immediately put us to work mopping the barrack's floor. He also told us we would be leaving the next morning for Clarence Creek where we would live in tents with limited facilities. He advised us to take only essentials and to leave the rest at Ant Flat. Although we didn't have much luggage, we did as he suggested and parceled out the minimum needed to live in a tent camp and stored the rest at the ranger station.

*   *   *

The early 1950s were a time of accelerated logging in the Northern Region (R-1) because of the spruce bark beetle epidemic. Anywhere Engelmann spruce grew, beetles were increasing their activity. The educated guess was if the trees were not already infested, they soon would be, and forest managers desperately looked for ways to stop the spread.

It was easy to locate infested trees. As the bark beetles chewed their way along the cambium layer (just inside the bark), the tree would try to "pitch" them out, that is, the tree would exude pitch through the bore hole made by the insect and often "wash" the insect out.

This combination of pitch and sawdust would form a wad of "frass" at the site of the beetle's entry into the tree, and one could often find a pitched-out beetle in the mixture. The frass looked like a glob of light tan chewing gum stuck to the tree, and in areas where the infestation was heaviest a single tree could show evidence of numerous "hits."

The commonly used defensive technique was called the trap tree method. Sites were selected about a 1/5-acre in size where all the spruce trees were cut and left on the ground. The bark beetles were attracted to these trees because they did not exude pitch. Experience proved that the beetles would concentrate in these felled trees and not in standing timber. When it was determined that the beetles had invaded the trap trees, an insecticide was used to kill them.

In spite of these efforts the epidemic spread. It was decided to log the most heavily infested areas across R-l as rapidly as possible. As a part of that effort, some smokejumpers were sent to Clarence Creek to help mark the timber to be cut and to fell trap trees.

*   *   *

The Clarence Creek Camp was located close to the junction of the Clarence Creek and Grave Creek Roads. We felt like we had arrived at the end of the world. It was remote, cold, damp, and the rawness of the hastily erected camp was ugly and depressing. The opening for the campsite had been hacked out of the heavily forested landscape.

The huge trees and the stark contrast of the opening with the dense stand of surrounding trees, immediately impressed us. Frames had been erected to support a dozen or so wall tents, and planks had been laid on the ground to avoid sinking in mud. A shack had been built to house a mess hall, and carpenters were working on a shower house, but it would be weeks before it was operational.

Ralph Johnson, the camp boss, assigned us to cots and we headed for the woods. Russ Cloninger, the district ranger, visited our camp several times pleading that we work safely. The district had such a large crew and the work was so hazardous that accidents were mounting up drastically.

Sawyers were dropping trees so fast the marking paint was hardly dry before a chain saw was making stumps. They were often so close the sound of their saws was deafening and we couldn't help but look up when someone yelled, "TIMBER!" The danger was not exaggerated and one marking crew was almost hit. We made a concerted effort to get ahead before the odds caught up with us and resulted in serious injury or death.

The criteria for marking was not complicated. Since we simply marked all the big spruce trees, why bother to mark them? The hierarchy obviously didn't want to be put in a position where they could be accused of allowing the sawyer to decide which tree to cut, even though the results would have been the same.

We had two kinds of marking guns. One was a quart can equipped with a trigger-pump that operated on the same principle as a kid's squirt gun. It was effective but because paint could only be sprayed a short distance the operator had to be close to the tree.

The second gun incorporated a gallon pressurized tank. It could send a stream of paint 20 feet, but because it was so much heavier it had to be carried on a Clack[7] frame.

---

[7] Clack was the name of a man who invented a light-weight frame to carry fire packs. Made of hardwood slats 2" wide and ¼" thick, it was 22" high and 10" wide, except for the bottom cross piece which was 16" wide to provide a more accessible place to tie off the shoulder straps. In addition to the bottom cross piece, there were three others, all 10 inches wide and located in the upper half of the frame. The pieces were joined together with two copper rivets at each overlap. The two-inch webbing used for shoulder straps was also riveted to the frame. It was sturdy, light (one pound, 13 ounces), and inexpensive. It worked fine for light loads such as fire packs, but because of its lack of padding and poor adjustment capability was uncomfortable with loads of more than 35 pounds.

We pumped vigorously for several seconds before mounting the packs on our backs because it was difficult to do when the frame was on our shoulders. A hose extended from the tank to a triggered nozzle.

Both types tended to plug if paint started to dry in the nozzle. Sometimes the problem was so severe we had to return to camp to perform a thorough cleaning or time consuming overhaul.

On Wednesday it rained hard, but we continued to mark. We couldn't stay dry and it was sheer misery, scrambling over slippery logs. Porcupines were abundant and we sharpened our spraying skills by giving them all a yellow stripe down their backs. A person visiting from another part of the country may have suspected the squirrels in the Clarence Creek area were related to the porcupines because so many had similar yellow markings. However, since the latter were much faster on their feet, the stripe was seldom cleanly delineated.

The work situation was rather chaotic at first. We never knew from day-to-day where we would be sent next. On Thursday, Dave and Skip were sent farther up Clarence Creek while I was sent to pile brush for an hour with John and Ray, two non-jumper seasonal employees. After cleaning up the brush, the three of us went back to marking, but John busted his paint gun and went back to camp. Mine also plugged up after lunch, so I too went back to camp and helped the carpenters building the shower house. To my surprise Tom Clawson, Bruce Ferguson, and Dave Graham came into camp. They had finished their job felling trap trees high in the mountains and were now assigned to the camp with us. I had taken my rookie training with Bruce and Dave the year before.

*   *   *

We frequently encountered wildlife in camp. A cow moose and her calf occasionally sauntered in looking for salt. We gave them a wide berth since a cow can be very protective if you get between her and her calf. In addition, bears had found the garbage pit on the edge of camp. It was covered with stout logs with only a small opening to dump garbage through, but the bears would worm their way in. The cooks made such an issue of their presence that we were drawn to watch as they yelled obscenities and pounded on the pit covering to chase them away. Skip had suggested (out of earshot of the cooks) we put some biscuits from the mess hall in the pit. He was convinced no self-respecting bear would ever return after taking a single bite.

The cooks, however, had their own scheme for dealing with Mr. Bear. Since it was close to July 4, the firecracker vendors were doing a brisk business in Whitefish and Eureka and the cooks had bought an ample supply. When they were sure a bear was in the pit, a string of firecrackers was dropped in the hole. We had never seen a bear move so fast. He came up out of the pit like he had been shot from a cannon. One of the cooks yelled, "I swear he came out of there with his asshole up around his neck!"

The cooks whooped and hollered for several minutes, satisfied their scheme was effective. All bear activity ceased, at least while we were there.

*   *   *

On Friday I marked timber with Dave and Skip in the higher country. It snowed and we were soaked. It seemed to us we had been there a month, not just a week. That evening we went down to Ant Flat to take a hot shower and to wash clothes. Except for a brief sojourn to Eureka we hung around the ranger station, reading and playing cards. On Sunday we drove back to the Clarence Creek Camp. Across the road from the camp on a bench above the road was a corral where mules were kept. They were used to pack equipment into remote areas where trap trees were felled. I went up to the corral to offer some feed from my hand to a mule, just to pass the time of day. It wasn't long before all the stock began to whinny and nervously stammer around.

I looked down toward the road and saw the cow moose and calf headed our way. Just the smell of them frightened the mules. I waved my arms and yelled, but the big old cow wasn't the least bit threatened—she kept coming. I reached in my pocket and retrieved several cherry bombs I had purchased in Eureka. They were round, about ¾-inch in diameter, and had no fuse. If they were thrown at a hard surface they would explode with a loud "BANG" on contact. I lobbed one in the direction of the old lady and sure enough she stopped. I had imagined she would take off like the bears did, but she took her sweet time reversing direction and ambling back up the road with her calf.

*   *   *

The second week began with the same regimen as the first. However, by the second day a wisdom tooth began to bother me. By the third day it was extremely painful, so I decided to find a dentist in Whitefish. I caught a ride on a logging truck and headed for Ant Flat that evening. I spent a sleepless night there and started hitchhiking the 40 miles to Whitefish the first thing in the morning.

I went directly to a dentist's office, but since I didn't have an appointment he told me I'd have to wait until after lunch. I walked around town in agony, and found myself standing on the bridge over Whitefish River staring at the water passing below wondering how much more pain it would take before I would consider taking a high dive into shallow water. I quickly moved off the bridge.

The Novocain was welcomed when I finally got in the dentist chair, and the relief from pain promptly brought sleep. It was marvelous. After the extraction I was on top of the world, and headed back for Ant Flat. As the effects of the Novocain wore off, my jaw began to hurt again. The pain was unexpected, but I consoled myself with the thought that it would continue to get better, not worse. After reaching Ant Flat, it was easy to catch a ride with a logging truck to Clarence Creek.

While I was gone there had been a terrible wind storm. Fortunately it occurred while men were in the woods and not in their tents. Several large spruce trees had fallen, and one scored a direct hit across several tents, smashing them and the cots flat to the ground. We knew it was just luck to have missed a tragedy.

I spent Friday in camp helping the carpenters. My jaw ached all day, but let up in the evening, so I went with Dave and Skip to Eureka, about 15 miles NW of Ant Flat (in the opposite direction of Whitefish). They drank beer, but not feeling up to it, I went to a movie. Later in the evening, we made plans for the weekend. Since the next day would be July 4, we felt we should do something special.

*   *   *

We left in Dave's car the next day for Glacier Park. My jaw was still swollen, but I felt much better. After we poked around the park for a while, we went to see the construction taking place at the Hungry Horse dam site. It was impressive, but a short stop was all we needed, so we visited Kalispell. Even though the day was pleasant, we agreed we'd rather be fighting fire on a high-mountain two-manner.

On our way back to Ant Flat we stopped in Whitefish and watched a golf tournament. My attitude was that "the only thing more boring than playing golf is watching somebody else play." Since I had never played the game, Dave and Skip were determined to get me on the links.

*   *   *

Rain and snow were a thing of the past and the days became hotter. The week started with more marking but since we were reasonably ahead of the sawyers it was decided we were needed more on trail and telephone line maintenance. Dave and I used a chain saw to open up some trails obstructed by blown down trees. The job didn't take all day, so we had time to blaze a trail for a telephone line to be strung.

We spent the next day on tree-climbing spurs, rehanging telephone line torn from its insulators by trees that had fallen since the last field season. The line was number nine galvanized wire supported by trees along a trail. The wire usually didn't break because it was draped between insulators, allowing it to stretch. We would cut the fallen tree, freeing the line, and then climb to the insulators on several trees to redistribute the slack by slipping the wire one way or the other. Occasional we would find the line broken, or the insulator pulled from the tree. We carried a supply of splices, a Nico-press (a plier-like tool used to crimp a splice between broken wire), and insulators to replace the broken ones. We liked to climb and found the work a welcome change from the constant diet of tree marking.

In the evening, Bob Gillespie came to our camp to recruit a softball team. He asked if we'd be interested in a practice to prepare for a game against Eureka on the weekend. We had kept our skills sharp in our numerous games at Camp Menard during training, so we joined up with employees from Ant Flat and drove to Eureka to practice.

We were a little disappointed that our play didn't go as smoothly as anticipated, but we felt confident we could make a good account of ourselves and looked forward to the competition the following Sunday.

The shower house was still not operational, but the warm days made it imperative that we wash more thoroughly than we could in a wash basin. We decided to bathe in Clarence Creek. While the days had gotten hotter, the creek water had not. We unanimously decided not to make it a daily event.

Saturday we played golf. Learning the proper technique came harder than expected—I had a terrible time getting any lift with a driver. The temptation to use only a putter was negated by Dave's and Skip's insistence that I learn properly. We played 27 holes, and while I did fairly well putting, driving was an all day struggle.

The next day, as we drove to the softball diamond for our big game in Eureka, Dave mentioned he sometimes had a tough time judging fly balls and might be subject to an error or two. Skip said Bob wanted him to play catcher even though he had never played that position. He speculated that some situations might arise when he wouldn't know how to respond appropriately. I also confessed that if the pitches were fast, hitting the ball could be a problem for me. Even with this candid recognition of our faults, we felt the other players would compensate for our minor shortcomings, making us a highly competitive team.

When we arrived we found we were not playing Eureka, but Libby. When uniforms were provided we really began to wonder what we had gotten into. We were amazed at the hustle and athleticism of the Libby team, and our confidence was somewhat challenged. We played hard, but despite two men getting on base we lost the game 28 to 0. The young pitcher was so fast that I wasn't the only one having a tough time at the plate.

Again we talked about wanting to be high in the mountains on a two-manner.

*　　*　　*

Our fourth week at Clarence Creek had barely begun when we were called to Ant Flat at 2:30 a.m. on Monday to fight fire. Tom Clawson and Bruce Ferguson had already been dispatched; Dave Graham missed it because he had been in a car wreck. By the time we reached Ant Flat the men already on the line had stopped the fire's run, so we were held at the ranger station. We assisted in loading supplies needed at the fire and other related chores.

At 1:00 p.m. a call came from the Smokejumper Project to return to Missoula. Because we had to go back to Clarence Creek to get our gear, we were delayed, but that wasn't the worst of it. The day was so hot, the radiator boiled over twice. This was followed by the carburetor vaporizing, a condition that locks up the flow of gasoline.

It made for a long day, but we were thankful to leave Clarence Creek and enter another phase of our summer's work. We tried to accept the delays philosophically. Still, as we drove back to Missoula, each of us privately felt the excitement that comes from knowing we would soon be winging our way to some remote spot to fight a fire. I think Dave and Skip shared my wish.

CHAPTER 9

A Record Fire Season

In hindsight the 1953 fire season was a banner year, at least from the perspective of a smokejumper stationed in Missoula. First, this was Hale Field's final season as the base for smokejumper aircraft. The next year we would move to a location adjacent to the paved commercial airfield now called Johnson-Bell International Airport. This new complex would also replace the spring training facility at the CCC camp (Camp Menard) near Ninemile Ranger Station and the summer billet accommodations at Fort Missoula.

The old facilities fit with the comfort of a worn shoe and had become a part of who we were. Those of us who made the transition knew the new facility was more efficient, but also felt something was lost. We had become accustomed to the seclusion of the wooded, rural area of Ninemile; to the bucolic surrounding of the turn-of-the-century buildings at Fort Missoula; and to the rustic buildings and primitive runway at Hale Field. Rarely did visitors or Forest Service brass observe our training or our departures as we lifted off the runway at Hale Field, but our closed fraternity was breached in 1954 when we moved into a fishbowl.

As I look back from the vantage of 50 years, this change marked the beginning of the loss of a certain innocence. We were coming into an age of sophistication and increased regulation which was as inevitable as lightning starting a fire.

But another feature was more memorable—fire occurrence in 1953 was greater than any year since smokejumper operations began in 1940. As the fire activity escalated, it became routine to come off one fire and find yourself at the top of the jump list for the next one. After putting a fire out, we normally stacked our gear on the nearest trail for a Forest Service packer to retrieve with his mules. But we were ordered to carry out our jump suits and parachutes because they were in short supply due to the increased fire activity. When the walk out was long, it was an arduous task because the packs weighed up to 100 pounds. It was made tougher because we carried all this weight on a flimsy Clack frame—a killer even with a sane load. Stories floated around about jumpers returning to base and hiding so they could get a few hours sleep before being sent out again. It had nothing to do with shirking duty, they were just dog tired.

*   *   *

Without further explanation it may be a little difficult to understand how the escalating action during the fire season affected us. While each of us had a different experience, we all shared a basic commonality: long hours, little sleep, and many fires. I documented the details of my fires in letters to my mother. A review of them clearly reveals the affect of the fire season on me, and to a large extent, on my comrades as well.

Tuesday, July 14, 1953

Dear Ma,

It's 6:15 in the morning and I'm dragging. We were called into Missoula yesterday, but didn't get here until 9:00 p.m. I'm first on the old man jump list. Eight men left this morning, but they were new men except for the foreman.

I didn't sleep much last night for all the racket caused by men arriving from project or the commotion made by the crew that left for a daybreak flight to their fire.

It was 105 degrees in Missoula yesterday. That's a record.

I could tell you about the moose we had in camp, or the tree that fell on our tent, but I'm too tired and want to try to get some sleep before breakfast—now that it's quiet.

I'll write again soon.

Love, R.

Sunday, July 19, 1953

Dear Ma,

I never did get this letter mailed. A call came at 6:40 a.m. for a two-man fire on the Flathead National Forest. A smokejumper's dream: a high-mountain two-manner. Remember that my first fire last year was a two-manner on the Flathead? Only this time I was going as the old man, not the new one.

I had never met my jump partner, Gus Ulrich, and we didn't have time for much of a conversation as we prepared to leave. We were taken to Hale Field without breakfast, donned our jump gear and climbed aboard the Travelair. We were airborne in just one hour from the time we got the call.

We had flown for an hour when we arrived at our fire. The smoke was obvious; thankfully the flames were not.

[The spotter was Jim Wait. It was common for spotters to be periodically observed by another qualified spotter as a part of the certification process. Hugh Fowler, no relation, was along for that purpose.]

Jim picked a jump spot close to the fire and dropped five drift chutes on five different passes. He was not comfortable with the chosen spot because the wind was so erratic. Neither was I. Gus had never jumped on a fire and was without any actual fire fighting experience—like me on my first jump last year. He was worried Jim didn't know what he was doing, but Gus didn't realize that the reality of smokejumping brought some situations not replicated in training. He wasn't prepared for the repetitious circling over the fire searching for a safe place to jump. It could be psychologically unnerving as well as physically nauseating.

After conferring with Hugh, Jim dropped a drift chute over an open hillside a mile from the fire. It blew over the ridge. He dropped another from a different position and found its descent to the spot was satisfactory, so I jumped on the next pass.

[The jump spot was a steep slope with few visible hazards such as big rocks, logs or trees. I exited the Travelair over a creek with ample distance between me and the ground to allow deployment of my emergency chute should the need arise, but there was no difficulty. My main chute opened properly and I rapidly drifted towards the open slope, a much shorter distance than straight down.]

I tried to approach my landing on the contour, but the stiff wind quickly slammed me into the slope with no possibility of a roll. I hit with a much greater force than any of my previous jumps, but was okay. When I got up and removed my helmet I saw that I had landed just six feet from a Forest Service trail and had barely missed the telephone line following it to Green Mountain Lookout. Gus jumped on the next pass and landed without difficulty.

The fire was a mile away so we picked up our fire packs containing a shovel, Pulaski, grub, flashlight, first aid kit, and canteen. We left our sleeping bags, five gallons of water and a crosscut saw because we wanted to get to the fire as quickly as we could. It was a hot day, 90 degrees, and we tried to use our water sparingly. When we got to the fire it was 100 feet long and 75 feet wide. We immediately hit the hot spots, spreading heavy burning fuels and slapping them with shovels of dirt. The brush was thick and the line building was slow. I figured it was easily a four man fire, but still thought we could get on top of it if we hustled right along. We got a line cleared and dug across the bottom of the fire and hit the hot spots again. We were making good progress and it looked like we were on top of it. By that time it was 11:30.

I had only eaten a milkshake the night before and neither of us had eaten breakfast, so we were hungry. We decided to stop for a can of beans. A patrol plane flew over to check on the fire. All was well. He rocked his wings to say "Howdy" and left. Just as I started to put my can opener to the lid of a can of beans, a hot spot sprang back to life. No lunch!

We worked our guts out trying to cool her down, but the wind picked up. This turn of events shifted the advantage decisively to Mother Nature. We just couldn't stop it. We ran out of water and my throat was so dry I couldn't spit. Then she crowned—meaning the fire ran into the crowns of the trees. Gus was terrified. In truth, I was rattled myself, but tried to keep confident for us both. I told Gus the safe place to go if the fire started to trap us, and that added to his uneasiness. He wanted to stop and get water and eat, but I insisted we continue. In spite of our continued efforts the fire doubled in size in half an hour. Evidently the cloud of smoke drew the attention of a lookout. His report to the ranger district resulted in the patrol plane coming back. He sized it up and left. We knew we couldn't stop the fire alone and felt better knowing help would soon be on the way, though I must admit I felt badly that my first fire in charge turned out to be one I couldn't handle.

I decided to concentrate our efforts on holding the line we had already built and let the rest go. We had left our gear alongside the fire, so I sent Gus up to get our food and flashlights before they got burned. [The run of the fire was up-slope, not laterally.] *I tried to keep the fire from backing down across our line. He came back shortly with all he could carry, but some had to be left behind. I lost a hat and gloves, but more importantly we lost a lot of our food and the files to sharpen our tools.*

[Like many new recruits, Gus's first exposure to the smokejumpers had been the movie, "Red Skies of Montana." The movie roughly followed the events of the Mann Gulch tragedy of 1949 in which 12 smokejumpers and a fire guard were burned to death. Many of the scenes included Hollywood exaggerations. One of them was the frequent exploding of trees as they were sucked up in flame. I'm not talking about "exploding" as in suddenly bursting into flame; I'm talking about "exploding" as in a loud BOOM, like TNT being detonated. It just didn't happen that way.]

The gear left beside the fire was eventually enveloped by the fire as it spread. The cans of food heated up and started exploding. Gus said, "My God, the trees are blowing up." I would have laughed if our situation weren't so dire.

I didn't want to leave Gus alone on the fire and since he was willing to go back to the jump spot for water, that seemed like the best thing to do. But he found a creek 200 yards from the fire, so he didn't have to make the long trek back. We both drank five quarts of water that afternoon. I tried not to drink so much, but couldn't lay off the stuff. We didn't have salt[8] tablets and I felt bloated.

The fire got our files so we couldn't sharpen our badly dulled tools. My Pulaski felt more like a club than a cutting tool. It was pathetic.

In the evening a DC-3 came. We were jubilant, at least for a few moments. After the spotter dropped a few drift chutes, the plane turned and headed back to Missoula—it was too windy to jump. I felt like a guy in the middle of the ocean treading water with a ship going by and not seeing me. By then the fire had gotten so big we couldn't even estimate it size, and it was burning ferociously. We stopped and ate for 15 minutes and then scouted the fire. It had reached the top of the ridge and the convection currents had deposited burning embers in numerous spots on the reverse slope. It looked like a job for 50 men.

In the evening, we hiked back to the jump spot for our sleeping bags and the five-gallon can of water and returned to the fireline we had built on the bottom of the fire. We continued to extend it until midnight when we lay down for some sleep. At 1:30 a.m. we were back at it. The fire was out along our fireline, but because it was so difficult to build more with dull tools, we decided to work at cooling down the hottest spots and left our line. The cool night air had slowed the aggressiveness of the fire considerably, so we spread concentrations of fuel, chopped brush and limbed trees so the fire would be less likely to climb into the crowns. We kept at it through the night expecting the DC-3 would arrive shortly after daybreak, but they didn't. I found out later the take-off was delayed to repair the safety strap across the door and to fix the intercom, so it was 9:00 a.m. before the plane showed up on the Big Bill Fire.

[I thought it would take more than 16 men on this fire but was nonetheless glad to see them arrive. Skip was one of the re-enforcements and he also experienced a difficult landing. He slammed into a snag so hard the force drove his face mask against his chin. Although the mask was padded in the chin area, the collision knocked him unconscious and split

---

8   Our individual first aid kits, which were a part of our fire packs, contained salt tablets; however, ours were consumed by the fire when it blew up.

his chin open. He quickly revived, and though uncomfortable, was still able to work.]

Paul Dennison was the foreman and immediately took charge of the fire. He was a tall, quiet fellow and was well-liked. He directed most of the men to stay on the upper end of the fire, but sent four down to help Gus and me. We all welcomed six men on horseback who arrived from Spotted Bear Ranger Station to work with us. They brought our fire fighting force to 24 men.

We built fireline all day, and when we stopped to eat at 6:00 p.m. we were only about 400 yards short of having completely circled the fire, but it was through heavy brush and would be slow going. After eating, Paul sent Gus and me to patrol the existing fire line while the rest of the crew tackled the final 400 yards. Their work was made somewhat easier because they had brought a chain saw, but it was still 2:00 a.m. before the line was completed and the fire declared controlled.

We got up at 6:40 a.m., Thursday, and retrieved our parachutes, stowing them in Beamis seamless sacks for pickup by a mule string. It didn't take long and we hustled back to start mopping up the fire before the day got hot. At 2:30 p.m. we stopped to eat, but the spot fires on the other side of the ridge started boiling up, so we missed another meal. Skip and I were the only old men on the fire besides Paul and two crew leaders. We found ourselves helping the new men with a lot of on-the-job training. Not that they hadn't learned the fundamentals in their rooky training, but there's a lot of difference between training and actually working on a grueling, gut-busting, galloping fire. It certainly wouldn't have been my choice for a baptism into fighting fire.

At 5:30 p.m. a plane flew over and dropped hot chow. What a morale builder! C-rations would certainly keep you going, but a hot meal was like manna from heaven. After chow we continued mopping up and extinguished all fire within ten feet of the fire line. We quit at 2:00 a.m.

The next morning we continued with the mop-up and attempted to completely extinguish all the spot fires. Nine men left to return to base. Skip left because he wanted to be able to take better care of his injury. Gus and I could go because we had been there longer than the rest, but I volunteered to stay because the next day was Saturday and I wanted the overtime. So did three others.

[Charlie Shaw, the Spotted Bear District Ranger, came to inspect the fire on his white horse. He questioned me about how the fire had gotten away. I told him of our efforts, but made the mistake of mentioning that we had stopped to open a can of beans when the fire blew up. No matter what I said, he had it in his mind that we were more interested in eating than attacking the fire.]

There was no smoke when we left at 2:00 p.m. Saturday. Of course the district men would have to patrol it for several weeks to be certain sleepers were not missed. The trail wound around the countryside in such a manner that we had a clear view of Big Bill Mountain and the blackened fire area. It was interesting to note how the fire backed down the slope around the point where Gus and I had built fire line. It seems apparent that we did prevent some additional area from burning. It turned out that the main fire was 50 acres in size, but in addition there were 80 spot fires.

The nine-mile hike to the Spotted Bear Ranger Station included stretches of beautiful vistas down to the Spotted Bear River. The area was not in the Bob Marshall Primitive Area but it was contiguous with it and just as primitive and just as remote. We arrived at Spotted Bear at 5:30 p.m., in time for dinner, and then took off in a Ford for Missoula. We were home at 8:30 p.m. and I found that I was ninth on the old man jump list, so I'm not sure when I'll be able to write again.

Love, R.

I learned the Big Bill Mountain Fire was the eleventh for the Smokejumper Project in 1953. I also heard from Fred Brauer that Charlie Shaw questioned my initial attack efforts, but Fred was already satisfied it wasn't an issue and told me not to worry about it.

Charlie retired in Kalispell and 15 years later I worked there for the Flathead National Forest. We were members of the same church and became close friends. When I questioned him about our meeting on Big Bill Fire he had no recollection of it. I also thought it interesting when I met Gus at the 1995 Smokejumper Reunion (for the first time since our jump together 42 years earlier) that the thing he most vividly remembered about the fire was my unwillingness to let him eat when the fire blew up. I thought it rather ironic that while Charlie was disturbed because he thought I had taken valuable time away from fire fighting to eat, Gus was disturbed because we *didn't* stop to eat. After the passage of 15 years, Charlie totally forgot about the food issue, but Gus would never forget it, proving an empty stomach has a longer memory than an irritated ranger.

*   *   *

The recent fires created a flurry of activity at the loft, so those of us waiting to go on another fire had plenty to do. I was so far down on the jump list that my number didn't get to the top until Thursday. A fire in Swartz Creek on the

Lolo National Forest was close to Missoula, but the jumpers on the first attack force couldn't hold it, and it began to spread. Because the weather was hot and the burning conditions so hazardous, re-enforcements were sent.

Before the day was out 48 of us jumped, including Fred Brauer. Those on the ground who could see the aerial activity must have been impressed because in a relatively short time span 28 jumpers arrived on four separate trips by the Ford, four arrived on two trips by the Travelair, and 16 arrived on a trip by the DC-3. I have no idea what the record is for the most jumpers on a single fire, but surely the Swartz Creek Fire ranked high on the list.

As it turned out, however, fire fighters had the upper hand by the time the eight of us in the last Ford jumped. When we landed our job was to retrieve the gear that arrived on a massive cargo drop. It was the only fire I can remember having to wrestle 10-gallon milk cans of water. Since the fire was in a logging area, there were access roads, and we began loading some of the surplus gear on trucks. Hot chow was dropped, so we helped take care of that and then many of us returned to Missoula.

Swartz Creek had obvious potential for a large fire, and hitting it hard was seen as a good investment, particularly since so many jumpers were available and the fire was so close to our base. I must say it was a good feeling to be part of at least one over-manned fire. Lord knows we knew about the others.

Thursday, August 6, 1953

Dear Ma,

One year ago today I made my first fire jump. This year I've got four already. I mentioned my second in an earlier letter; that's all it warranted, a mention. My third one, however, was a dandy.

A call came in for 16 men on the Flathead Forest near Kalispell, Montana. The DC-3 (our biggest plane) was already out so we split the load into two Fords and took off in tandem. I was sitting across from the door because I was to jump in the first stick (usually the old men jumped first). It was much more enjoyable situated where I was because the view from sitting on the floor at mid-ship was poor. From my perspective the door opening seemed to be a picture frame and beautiful pictures continued to appear. Snow capped mountains, rocky cliffs, sparkling lakes—a continuous array of beautiful scenes held me in awe. I fully realized one of the biggest benefits of my job was being able to fly at low altitudes over undeveloped mountain country.

[The call for the Mill Creek Fire had come at 3:35 p.m., but because the dispatcher on the Flathead Forest reported high winds our departure was delayed until 6:45 p.m. The other seven jumpers, comprising the crew I was part of, were Paul Dennison, Paul Carpino (he trained with me in 1952), Pete Peterson, Dan Merrell, Jim Clinker, Jim Forbes, and Charles Taylor. The latter five jumpers were all new men.]

We easily found the fire—a big one. If you see a light smoke, you know there's a fire. If you see heavy black smoke, you can bet there's flame and plenty of hot spots. But if you actually see flame you know you've got a whopper on your hands. We saw flame.

The spotter dropped a drift chute and it went three miles over the ridge. He dropped another which decided to roam around a bit before it reached the ground. The wind was bad. [It was 8:20 p.m. by the time the spotter made his decision for us to jump.] *The foreman was Paul Dennison, the same guy who was the leader on the Big Mountain Fire. He took his position in the door and I was standing behind him feeling like a dog being held back when he wants to chase a cat, I was that pumped up. The spotter said to hold into the wind and head for the brushy spot a quarter of a mile from the fire. The motors were cut, Paul got the slap on the shoulder and left, and I followed—yelling as I went after my cat.*

Paul couldn't hold into the wind and shot the ridge, crossing over the fire and landing in the next canyon. Somehow I managed to hold against the wind until I had just time enough to turn around and come in forward against the hill. I landed in good shape and headed for the fire to see if Paul was okay. He was, so we stood by the fire waiting for the cargo—knowing they would drop it closer to the fire than we jumped. It took three more passes for the other six jumpers to make their exits, so several minutes went by before the cargo was dropped. By this time we were starting to lose light, and wouldn't you know, every cargo chute hung up in a tree. I was "elected" to use the climbers and get 'em down before dark. Since I didn't have a rope to let the stuff down, all I could do was cut the cargo free of their chutes and let the contents fall 60 feet to the ground—THUD! In spite of the long drop, the cargo was fine, and by that time most of the other men from our plane were there as well. The other plane turned and headed back for Missoula for fear someone would get hurt jumping in the heavy wind. I didn't think it was that bad, but my judgment may have been clouded by the fact that I had made it safely to the ground.

A ground pounder arrived while we were getting our gear together. He said a few men were working below on the main fire and another 50 were coming. We were to stay up top and fight the two large spot fires and prevent them from shooting over the ridge. He left to return to the main fire and we started building line on one of the large spot fires. We could see a small fire starting above us. Paul sent me to work on it. I didn't mind working alone and felt good that he felt I could handle it. After I got the spot controlled, Paul sent me to the top of the ridge where the second large spot fire was located. I hot spotted—meaning I cooled down the places where the fire was most active—by throwing dirt and separating fuel concentrations.

An ember had landed over the ridge and started to burn, but it was easily taken care of because it had just started. I was up there to try and keep the fire from growing until we could get a line around it all. The boys finished the first large spot and I joined them attacking the second. At 2:30 a.m. we stopped to eat a bite—seated in the brush next to the fire line so we could take advantage of the light from the fire. We all were wearing helmet lights, but we tried to use them sparingly in order to conserve our batteries. Then we heard it. "SQUEAK!" Like the buzz of a rattlesnake, even the first time, you know it means danger. We all flicked on our flashlights and looked towards the sound. A snag had burned at the base and was falling. We all scrambled and it landed six feet from where we sat. All falling trees don't squeak; thank God that one did.

[The night air was noticeably cool once we stopped working, so after I ate a can of pork and beans I mixed a cup of instant cocoa. It needed stirring so I broke off a sprig from a huckleberry bush close at hand and used it as a swizzle stick. Sitting there in the flickering fire light was a bit eerie in itself, but me sitting there rotating that heavily leaved huckleberry branch in my hot drink prompted Paul to say, "Damn, Fowler, with that black soot on your face and that stick in your hand you look like some kind of voodoo witch doctor brewing up a magic potion!" Somebody picked up a heavy stick and started beating on a log to make a drum sound and all of us wailed in an unharmonious chant. It felt good to laugh.]

I forgot to mention that my personal gear, including my coat, got mixed up when we loaded onto the aircraft in Missoula and mine ended up in the other Ford. Believe me, the mountains at night are no place for shirt sleeves.

It wasn't until then that I looked down the mountain and saw the twinkling lights of Kalispell. Off to the left the moon was shining on Flathead Lake and it was "beautonic." That's a word I coined; it's prettier than beautiful. We could see the valley clear up to Whitefish, but our scenic gander was short lived because Paul said, "Back to work."

It's a funny thing when the fire is hot and running—nobody says a word. The only sound from the guy next to you is the noise made by his Pulaski as it scrapes and cuts away to mineral soil. By four o'clock we had the hot spots down and a line around the most threatening part of the fire. Paul decided it wouldn't do much until morning, so . . . . Morning? Heck, the sun was coming up then. Anyhow, we sacked out and it didn't take long to get to sleep. At 5:00 a.m. I awoke with the sound of a Ford flying overhead, and stuck my head out from under the sleeping bag just in time to see two men hit the silk. That was a real show. We just lay there and watched them float down. They included not only the eight who turned back the evening before, but also a second Ford with eight more, so now there would be 24 jumpers.

By 10:00 a.m. there were 60 or more ground pounders, so it wasn't long before the fire was under control—that is, all of the fires had fire lines around them. We slacked off a little, but continued to work mopping up the two large spot fires.

That night the last 16 to jump patrolled the spots. [The ground pounders were mostly older fellows. They worked hard, but they needed rest in order to function the next day, so they were not required to go on the line that night.]

Our crew patrolled the main fire which was a little easier than the spots because it was closer to being dead out.

The fire was so quiet we decided six could watch while two sacked out in the brush. My coat finally caught up with me, but it was still plenty cold, especially when not moving. When it came my turn to grab a few winks I was afraid I couldn't sleep without a sleeping bag—or something to wrap up in. There was nothing, so I improvised. I remembered a place beside the fireline that had been a source for dirt. It had been tough to find a place where digging was not impeded by rocks and roots, but this location was fairly easy to dig in, so when dirt was needed to cool down a hot spot, this location was often the source. The result was a pit resembling a grave. I also remembered a lot of bear grass had been scalped off at ground line and was in a pile near the "grave." Bear grass is a not a grass at all, but a grass-like plant with course leaves that grow from a tuber. I lined the grave with several inches of the stuff and then lay in it. One of the other jumpers spread the remainder on top of me—about a foot deep. I was as warm as a bug in a rug and slept like a rock for two hours. It really wasn't near long enough, but it sure helped.

The next day we retrieved our chutes and packed up most of our gear. We were not anxious to leave because we were into the weekend and wanted the extra time, so we didn't mind the dull task of mopping up the fire. But when night came it was again decided the smokejumpers would do the patrolling. It didn't seem fair, but as I thought about it, I wanted the extra hours on my paycheck. So did most of the others, so when it was announced that ten of us would work and the rest would sleep, we drew straws—I was one of those who would patrol. Had I known how long the night was going to be I wouldn't have done it.

We started patrolling at 7:00 p.m. on the main fire (the spots were declared out). We worked separated and alone. It isn't bad alone if there's something to do, but just standing or walking a little is awful. I put out a few smokes near the line and watched for awhile. Hot coals don't always put up smoke and I found that if I watched for gnats hovering close to the ashes that it meant there was heat below. I would dig in the ashes and expose the hidden embers so they would die in the cold night air.

As it began to get dark I got in a position where I could see Flathead Lake and Kalispell. I watched the sun sink low and finally out of sight. I watched the lights come on in town and saw headlights of cars making their way through patches of timber in the valley. The golden fields of hay were now black. I was cold.

During the night a guy came with sack lunches. It was good and it satisfied my hunger, but it didn't help my sleepy eyes or my chilly body. I sang and exercised and walked to keep awake. What a fight. Have you ever had to really fight sleep? I could have done it easily with a buddy to talk with, or if there was work to be done. At 3:30 a.m. I was so cold that when I found a piece of canvas I sat down in the fireline and put it over me. I fell asleep. At 3:45 the guy in charge of the patrol got me back on my feet again. I don't know how, but I stayed awake.

It began to get light at 4:00 a.m. I watched the sun come up and the lights go out in the valley, and heard the cooks moving around down in the camp. The fire in my sector was cold and dead—and so was yours truly. At 6:00 a.m. replacements came to relieve us and we went to camp and ate. We hiked out in the morning and rode in a mule truck to Missoula. They say it smelled rather badly in the truck, but I never knew. I slept all the way.

In the evening I enjoyed seeing some of my college friends at a Wesley Foundation picnic, but I didn't stay long. By 8:30 p.m. I hit the sack.

That was fire number three for me this year. I'm just coming off of number four now. The last few pages are being written returning to Missoula on the bus, so excuse the writing.

I sincerely hope I'll never have to go three nights again on just three hours sleep.

I'm back in Missoula now and it's almost 10:00 p.m. There's a big bust and there aren't enough jumpers to man them. I'll go out again in the morning.

Love, R.

*   *   *

The day after I got back from the Mill Creek Fire it was Tuesday, August 4. Those of us not on fire worked in the parachute loft preparing for more fire activity. In the morning I helped unpack jump gear coming in from fires. The apex of each personnel parachute (as opposed to a cargo chute) was attached to a rope so it could be hoisted up for its entire length in the tower. The floor was littered with needles, twigs, and sometimes pine cones because the chutes were often harboring debris.

A rigger would inspect each chute before repacking it for use on another fire. The standards for packing the personnel chutes were never compromised, but when the repacking got behind some short cuts in packing cargo chutes were taken. It was not uncommon in 1953 to watch a cargo chute open with a cloud of dust and debris drifting away from it, they were packed that hastily.

Even though the rash of fires had drained our standby supply of fire packs, we had a large supply of the components: flashlights, C-rations, files, Pulaskis, shovels, first aid kits, and canteens. However, they needed to be wrapped in a manty (a piece of canvas about five feet by seven feet) and tied to a Clack frame. In the afternoon that's what I did, until 4:23 p.m. A fire call from the Kootenai National Forest was received and Ralph Hurt and I were top on our respective lists (Ralph was a new man). While we suited up the Travelair taxied close to the loft and the loading crew stowed the cargo. Ralph and I were lifting off the runway at Hale Field, with Norm Allen as our spotter, in just 17 minutes from the time the call was received.

Tuesday, August 11, 1953

Dear Ma,

I had a new experience the other day. I came off a fire on Monday [August 3] *and went on another jump on Tuesday* [August 4]. *It was raining on the take-off and we were headed for the Kootenai on a two-manner. We flew under the clouds to miss the turbulent air, but there were still spots of clouds below. They looked a lot like smoke. We flew for two hours in turbulent and rainy weather before finding the fire four miles from its reported location. Oddly enough the wind calmed to almost nothing when we jumped. This was the first time I jumped in the rain. It was nice. The heavy air slowed my descent. The parachute acted as a giant umbrella, and at times completely blocked out rain, but since I was hanging so far below the chute, sometimes a fine spray would reach my face.*

We jumped into a little opening in the timber. I skinned an elbow on a rock, but all turned out okay. If the jump jackets weren't heavily padded, it could have been a different story.

This two-manner didn't get away. Lightning had hit a snag 30 inches in diameter and it was burning all the way up to the top, although not violently due to the coolness and rain. [I thought this fire was a good example of the value of smokejumpers because the lightning strike and flare-up were spotted during a storm, and before the fuels had time to dry out, we were on it. Rapid attack prevented many fire-starts from ever getting larger than a spot. No doubt some would have died on their own because of wet or sparse fuel, but others like the Big Bill Fire may have been controlled as a spot if we could have gotten there sooner.]

Ralph and I felled the snag with our crosscut saw and put a line around the fire. It stopped raining and soon the sky was clear as a bell. At 3:00 a.m. I decided to sack out, but I don't sleep well when I'm responsible for a fire. When Ralph would roll over in his paper sleeping bag it would make a noise that sounded like a rapidly burning fire. I'd jump up, but nothing ever happened. I think my Big Bill experience had me spooked.

The second day we mopped up and by mid-morning there was no sign of smoke. The fire was small enough that we could feel each stick and twig to determine it had no fire—it would be discarded outside the burn area. [It seemed to me Ralph didn't take the work as seriously as he should. At first I passed it off thinking this fire wasn't the threat that many are, and didn't have the characteristics that excites a guy into an all out effort, but nevertheless, it was always our practice to attack each fire like it might get away—at least until we got a line around it. That wasn't Ralph's approach, and I couldn't help think how I'd hate being on a "gobbler" with him in a dire situation.] *While we were still "feeling out" the fire two ground pounders arrived, but there was nothing for them to do. At 5:00 p.m. we walked out with the ground pounders to a truck and drove ten miles to Fairview, a guard station on the Fisher River Ranger District—arriving at 8:45 p.m. We spent the night there.*

The next morning a truck picked us up and took us to Libby, the headquarters for the Kootenai National Forest. We were issued travel vouchers and meal tickets and left at noon via bus. It was a long trip due to a two-and-a-half hour layover in Kalispell. We got back to Missoula on Thursday evening at 8:30 p.m.

Those of us who weren't on fires were at the loft Friday morning [August 7]. *The available equipment was pretty slim. The fires were so numerous that jump gear and parachutes were in short supply. It was almost 11 o'clock when the Nez*

Perce National Forest sent in a request for more jumpers than were available. A storm over the Moose Creek Ranger District in the Selway/Bitterroot Primitive Area left numerous small fires in its wake. Fourteen of us loaded into the DC-3, completely depleting the small force of available smokejumpers. Before we loaded I was somewhat confused when handed a map case. I couldn't imagine me being in charge of a 14-man crew. Well, I wasn't. There were four fires and this plane load of jumpers was to provide two men each to three of them and eight men to the fourth.

As we flew into the heart of the two million-acre primitive area, it intrigued me to think about these fires scattered over it. They had just started and were inaccessible by roads, but in just a couple of hours we would have jumpers on all of them.

[My partner was a new man, Bob Meier. I didn't know him at all. We sat and watched as the spotter, Al Cramer, and the assistant spotter, George Ostrom, sent jumpers to the first fire on Isaac Creek. It seemed to take forever to drop the drift chutes, drop the jumpers, drop the cargo, and finally make a pass to ascertain they had landed safely. Around and around we flew. It was hot and uncomfortable and everyone was feeling a bit woozy. We went through the same ritual for the Isaac Lake Fire, a mile from where the first fellows jumped. Our fire was only seven miles to the southwest, so little time was lost getting there. I wanted out so badly I didn't much care what the jumping conditions were, "Just let me out!" I felt sorry for the guys who had to wait it out for the last fire. I later found out one poor guy was so air sick he couldn't jump.]

This fire [the Rhoda Creek Cabin Fire] *was a lot larger than my last one, but I felt a lot less like fighting it. When I landed I didn't see a log hiding in the brush and slammed into it. What a charley horse!*

It was 1:45 p.m. when we reached the fire. Pretty fast time considering two fires were manned before we jumped. Of course the travel time was much faster in the DC-3 than it would have been in either the Ford or Travelair. About 11:00 p.m. a man walked to our fire and asked if we'd carry our gear to the trail in the morning so he could load it on a mule and pack it out. [This seems a little bizarre to me now, and I can only vaguely remember this unlikely meeting. Obviously there was a general concern in the region about the lack of available parachutes and jump gear at the loft in Missoula and the districts were being pressured to assist in returning smokejumper equipment posthaste. It seems extraordinary, however, that a man would walk to a fire alone in the dark to satisfy this request. On the other hand, this was an extraordinary fire year and many of us were working far beyond what would be considered business as usual.]

We worked all night to get the fire in shape so we could leave it for a few hours. By 2:00 a.m. we had a line around the fire and I noted in my diary that it was controlled, but we aggressively began mop-up to take advantage of the cool night air and lack of wind. By daylight we felt we could leave it long enough to haul our jump gear to the trail. We came directly back and the fire was still inside the line—I was relieved. The risk was not high, but nonetheless I hated leaving it unattended.

We worked all day digging out fire that had followed roots deep in the ground. As the day warmed, the smoke increased, but because we had removed all unburned fuel, it could not generate enough energy to burst into flame. Like all mop up, it was dirty, tedious work, and since we were working mid-slope in a heavily timbered forest, there was no view of the surrounding area. [Disqualifying it as an ideal high-mountain two-manner.] *Of far greater concern, our food supply was rapidly disappearing.*

[Each fire pack contained two boxes of C-rations, one box providing sufficient food for one day. A box contained five cans of food, a small tin of crackers, a small tin of pound cake, and an accessory packet containing plastic eating ware, small army can opener, salt, pepper, toilet paper, chewing gum, cigarettes, coffee, cocoa, and matches. One of the five cans of food was fruit, most commonly fruit cocktail, but it was sometimes pears or peaches. The other four cans of food were randomly selected from the following six types: pork and beans, lima beans and ham, spaghetti and meat balls, sausage patties and gravy, stew, and hash. Pork and beans was a universal favorite, but the spaghetti, stew, and hash were also generally considered good. Lima beans were not a favorite, and sausage patties were by far and away considered the absolute worst. This was all pre-cooked food, so it could be eaten cold, but it was much more palatable if warm.

Jumping with two days rations did not mean you only had two days in which to put out a fire, although it was probably thought two days was sufficient for most small fires. It was the responsibility of the requesting unit, in this case the Nez Perce National Forest, to determine if an additional food drop was needed. This was done by the aerial observer—the man who flew with the pilot of the patrol plane on routine fire detection flights. He could size up the situation and make a decision of our needs or we could use our orange crepe paper strips to signal for more food.]

The patrol plane must have thought we would return before we used up our food. We couldn't signal out because the crown cover of trees was too dense. Anyway, we tried to conserve our food knowing it would be the next day before we would leave.

I declared the fire out at 10:00 p.m. Sunday evening, but we had to stay until early afternoon the next day to see if any "smokes" showed up. It's standard policy, after the last smoke is seen, to remain on the fire through the heat of the following day. If nothing shows up, it's usually safe to leave.

At noon we each had half a can of beans. Our grub was just plain gone. We had turned over the soil on every inch of the fire so it looked like a garden plot waiting to be planted. All burnable material had been thoroughly inspected with the eyes and hands to determine it was cold, and it was cast outside the fire line. After a final hand inspection of the entire area we decided there was no need to wait any longer, so we left at 2:30 p.m.

All we had to carry was our personal gear, shovels, Pulaskis, and the crosscut saw, so our packs were light. It didn't take long to reach the trail along Rhoda Creek. It was only a short distance to the North Fork of Moose Creek, and because it was all downhill, the going was fast and easy, but we were really hungry. After traveling about eight miles we came to the Moose Creek Ranch, an isolated piece of privately owned land in the midst of the primitive area. Perhaps it was a patented mining claim, but it was used as a dude ranch. Access was confined to air travel or trail.

As we approached, we could see tents, but no people. All we could think of was food and were delighted to catch the aroma of freshly baked bread. It didn't take us long to find the kitchen. They have a swell cook. She immediately gave us some of her bread and milk right from the cow—and homemade butter, too. Then she fixed us a dandy meal. What a way to come off a fire!

Four more miles got us to Moose Creek Ranger Station, an isolated facility with the only access by trail or airplane. A DC-3 had landed and was waiting to see if more jumpers would trickle in before he lost daylight.

[When we arrived at the airstrip it was hot. Although my pack was not excessively heavy, it was not comfortable, my back was soaking wet, and the straps were digging into my shoulders. I had the crosscut saw bowed into a teardrop shape and lashed around my pack. Without thinking I leaned back and let myself fall to the ground, landing on my pack. It seemed simple enough, but I forgot the saw. The teeth were covered with a sheath but the back side was exposed. When I fell back my left elbow came against the back side of the saw blade and hit with such force that it gave me a nasty gash. Not only that, it was exactly on my "funny bone," and the pain from hitting the nerve was much greater than from the gash. Dumb.]

It was interesting to talk with the guys who had just come off their fires and to compare notes—none of them had jumped from the same ship as we did on August 7.

Someone said this was the first time a DC-3 had landed at Moose Creek, and I admit it concerned me a little. The airstrip is on a gentle slope, and it felt weird not to be taking off on level ground. The mountains are close to the field and some maneuvering was necessary right after take-off. Steep banks in an airplane, particularly at low altitudes, really get my attention. We were back in Missoula at 8:15 p.m.

I'm second on the jump list now and will probably make my sixth fire jump tomorrow.

I need some sleep.

Love, R.

*   *   *

My last day off was Sunday, July 26 and it was now Monday, August 10. I had jumped on three fires in that time span and there had been no time to wash my clothes. Now it was a priority. Several of us hurried to a Laundromat in town, all the while wondering if a fire call would come in. As it turned out, my position on the jump list wasn't reached until Wednesday, so there was ample time to get my clothes back in order and some letters written. I had been working in the loft putting up fire packs and helping to hang up parachutes when Fred Brauer came to me and said,

"Frank, this has been a big fire year, and I'm thinking about a new approach for manning our two-man fires."

"Really. I haven't heard a thing about it," I answered with great interest.

"Yeah, well, it's something I have been mulling over for the past couple of weeks and I think it's time to try it. What I have decided is to pair up old men and new men to form permanent teams. It looks like we're going to have a lot more fires and maybe it would be more efficient to work with the same jumper on a continuing basis."

I was surprised. It was a radical departure from what we had all accepted as a good working system. I should have smelled a rat because the new men significantly out-numbered the old, leaving a large body of new men who would never be considered for a two-man fire.[9] Fred paused while I struggled with my thoughts, then he continued, "I'm matching you up with Ralph Hurt, if that's okay with you."

---

[9]   The composition of the work force on the jumper project in 1953 was 25 overhead (two administrative assistants, seven foremen, and 16 squad leaders), 46 old men and 65 new men.

189

"No, it isn't," I shot back.

"I know you went on a fire with him on the Kootenai not too long ago. Didn't it work out all right?"

"We got the fire okay, but he's not the kind of guy I'd like to go to every fire with," I answered rather lamely.

"I've already made the pairings and if you don't have a better reason for not wanting to work with him, I'm not going to change it," he said with an element of finality.

I then unloaded several gripes I had concerning Ralph's work ethic and lack of initiative.

Fred then leveled with me, saying, "What you have said is in agreement with what I have been hearing from other fellows who have been on fires with Ralph[10]. It helps me to know how you felt about working with him on your fire."

"Then there's nothing to this business about pairing up old and new men?" I asked.

"No, there isn't. I figured this was the best way to get a candid response from you. Thanks."

At first I wasn't sure how I felt about Fred's approach on this issue, but after more thought, I respected it.

*   *   *

Sunday, August 16, 1953

Dear Ma,

What a glorious feeling to be full again. I'm saying this in connection with my condition coming off my last fire—the Bear Creek Fire. This is really a story for the books.

Wednesday [August 12] *I was working in the fire loft, still kind of tired from the last fire and was hoping I wouldn't go out until Thursday. No luck. I had eaten a tremendous meal for lunch and felt it wouldn't take much to make it rebound. Then a call came for a four-manner. Squad leader Bill Demmons, two first-year men, Jerry Soaps and Hunt Hatch, and I lifted off Hale Field in the Ford for the St. Joe National Forest. I never had a rougher ride. Up and down. Up and sideways. I almost asked for a burp cup, but I*

---

10   "Ralph" is the only intentional psuedonym in *High-mountain Two-manner*. The event, however, has been related as it happened.

managed to keep everything down, though I felt mighty woozy the entire trip.

When we arrived at the place where the fire was supposed to be, there was no sign of one anywhere. Our spotter, Norm Allen, could see smoke in the distance and decided our fire had been mis-located. Instead of being on the St. Joe, it was actually on the Clearwater National Forest. It didn't look very big; in fact, I figured it to be a two-manner. Later Bill said the same thing.

The fire was in heavy timber with a few scattered snags. Bill and Norm decided it was not a good place to jump. Had it been a two-manner with me in charge, I would have asked to jump there. As it was, it was their call and I respected it. There were a few spots a half-mile from the fire but it was too windy to try them, so we jumped on a big open hillside two miles away. Bill and I jumped first, me right behind him. My chute opened below his, but he rapidly dropped past me. In no time at all he was 100 feet below me. Gee, it looked like he was descending much too rapidly. I looked at his canopy to see if he had a line-over, but he didn't. I don't know what made him drop so fast. He wasn't headed for the spot and he had an oscillation. Later he said he couldn't turn his chute at all. The way he was swinging and dropping it appeared he might get hurt on the landing, so I said to heck with the spot and followed him in. He landed fine, however, and I did too. Shortly thereafter, Jerry and Hunt landed fine as well.

The cargo was dropped in one of the openings a half-mile from the fire. Now for the hunt. Distances appear shorter from the air than they do on the ground, consequently we erred and started looking for the cargo too soon. For four hours we combed the hillside, looking in every open spot. At times we were widely separated, but we had taken the precaution of agreeing on a central meeting place, so we felt comfortable we wouldn't get lost from one another.

Now listen to this, Ma, it's a scream! I was looking in the brush and saw some fresh bear sign. I've seen plenty of that, so I wasn't thrilled, but then I saw a cute little cub. Then I saw an ugly mother!

I heard a voice within me saying, "Be calm, keep your head, don't run."

To heck with that. I hightailed it to the closest climbable tree and went up faster than I could even imagine. Ole mama bear was right behind me, but she was too big to climb the tree—thank God. Or maybe because the cub ran off, the sow simply followed. At any rate I no longer felt threatened, but when I finally came down the tree I ran for several minutes in the opposite direction taken by the bears. In all the chaos I became somewhat disoriented. Since the ground was fairly level, it was easy to become confused.

I decided to make my way to steeper ground in the hopes of regaining my orientation. When I did, I could see for miles across a wild landscape. Far below me and off in the distance I recognized the view I had seen from the Ford—the Little North Fork of the Clearwater River. There were no roads or visible signs of any development as far as I could see. I yelled and yelled, but no one answered. I sat down and just thought for a few moments, and was pleased that I was so calm about it. I had long ago eaten the two candy bars I had in my personal gear bag, so I was without food. My canteen was on my fire pack, but I knew I could find plenty of water, so that wasn't a primary concern. What I really needed was a compass and a map; only Bill had those.

I found myself planning my survival—isn't that stupid? I knew it would take a long time, but by continuing to go downhill I would eventually get back to civilization. I yelled again and way off in the distance I heard a faint reply. Eventually Hunt came into view and when we met up he was thoroughly disappointed—he thought I had found the cargo. We made our way back to the rendezvous point and joined up with Bill and Jerry. Finally we (or they—I'm not smart enough) decided the cargo was farther down the ridge.

At last! The cargo was found. What a relief to have food and water in our possession. Now to find the fire. We had quite a load on our backs and ten gallons of water in two five-gallon cans. We switched off carrying them in our arms as we beat the brush down a steep hillside trying to see smoke. We were used to cross-country travel with fire packs, but the addition of a forty pound can of water was a challenge.

Our luck changed when Jerry climbed a tree and yelled, "Smoke, 200 yards down the hill to our left!"

We left one of the five-gallon cans of water, because a stream was nearby, and hastily tramped our way the final distance. So much for a rapid arrival to a fire with smokejumpers. The fire didn't look bad. It was all on the ground and the wood was punky and wet. By this time it was dark so Bill decided to just knock down the hot spots and hit the sack. So that's what we did.

Early the next morning we lined the fire and mopped it up. It was so wet that it went out easily. By noon she was dead—I never saw the likes of it. We lay around until three or four to see if any smokes came up and then left it for out. Since the fire had been mislocated, we were not certain where we were, so we needed to orientate ourselves on the map in order to determine the best way out. Not knowing how long the walk would take we ate pretty light so our two-day food supply wouldn't run out.

We packed our tools, grub, personal gear and sleeping bags uphill in search of the cargo drop spot. Gee, I hate cross-country travel with a pack. You can't imagine how slow and depressing it is—and the little pack frames about kill a man.

Missoula was so short on equipment that they had exhausted the supply of paper sleeping bags, and dropped kapok bags in their place. They are cloth, expensive, heavy, and not dispensable. Consequently we had to pack them to a trail as well. When we found the cargo spot again we picked up the cargo chutes, added them to our packs, and continued cross-country uphill in search of a trail where we would leave a lot of our gear for a packer's retrieval. More uphill, more sweat, more gripes. When a trail finally found my clopping feet—and when a Forest Service blaze appeared on a tree beside it—I just fell over backwards [you'd think I would have learned not to do that after my experience at Moose Creek] *and heaved a sigh of relief. Little did any of us know that a lot worse was yet to come. Oh brother, if I had known the misery coming before us, I don't think I ever would have made it.* [In hindsight, a youthful exaggeration. I was referring to the required physical effort, but I learned most of us are capable of much more than we think and seldom are pushed to test the limits of our physical capability. Years later I worked with a fellow who had survived the Bataan Death March. He was usually an office worker, but in the winter he would often help mark timber on snow shoes. He was not nearly as physically fit as those of us who spent more time in the field, but when the going got tough, he griped the least because he knew what *tough* was. That observation led me to believe most of us reach some kind of mental limitation long before we cross a limiting physical threshold.]

With our packs off we felt like birds and just flew up to the jump spot where our personnel chutes were. When we got there a patrol plane came over. We thought he had seen us, but he hadn't. He dropped a message (it had a streamer on it and we could see it clearly while it fell). It landed a half-mile down in the brush, and since we knew it was futile to even think of looking for it, we didn't. We sacked our jump suits and parachutes and strapped them on the dinky pack frames and set them on the trail. We could see a lookout tower a couple of miles up the hill and decided to go up since we were on the trail leading to it. We not only wanted to confirm our location, we thought there might be some food we could commandeer.

I was pretty griped because I was the only one who packed a canteen. Bill lost his (I had no gripe there), but Jerry and Hunt said a quart of water was too much to pack. As long as I have a canteen, I carry it even if I'm on the river. Anyhow, it got hot and they almost came begging for water. The lookout tower wasn't manned. Many aren't these days because the jumpers have been used so much [reducing the need for firemen] *and patrol planes do so much searching* [negating the need for lookouts]. *A few, however, continue to be used.*

We found a few fresh oranges and some canned fruit—which tasted mighty good. Canned fruit is a real treat on a fire. In the center of the room (high above the ground) the Osborne fire finder was in good order. The finder has a map orientated so the location of the lookout tower is in the exact center. An alidade is mounted over it in such a manner that it rotates on an iron ring around the map allowing the lookout/fireman to read an azimuth to a distant object—or to a fire. Now we knew exactly where we were and could see the easiest way out was to follow a trail to Canyon Ranger Station, six air miles away, perhaps 12 miles by trail. However, we were routed to come out at Buzzard Roost, five air miles away, but most of it was cross-country. Not only that, Canyon Ranger Station was all downhill; but in order to get to Buzzard Roost we would have to cross a major river drainage with a lot of uphill hiking.

Bill said we were expected to come out at Buzzard Roost, and it was emphasized in our training to follow the route back that was designated in our fire orders. On the other hand, the fire had been mislocated and it only seemed logical that we were therefore free to use our own judgment. We wondered if that wasn't what the message from the plane conveyed. Ultimately Bill decided we would head for that ominously named lookout, Buzzard Roost. Perhaps if we had vigorously objected, he could have been persuaded to take the Canyon Ranger District route, but we all accepted his right to lead the group as he thought best. His decision was obviously a mistake, but our silence was, too.

It was getting late so we dropped back down to our chutes and jump gear and packed it the two miles down to the rest of the stuff. By then it was dark and we were all tired, so we slept. The next morning, Friday, we put the tools, cargo chutes, crosscut saw and climbing spurs together and hung orange crape paper from surrounding branches along the trail so the packer could easily find them. Due to the record breaking number of recent fires, we were told to pack out our jump gear and chutes—both the back pack [main chute] and the emergency, so we put them on our Clack frames. That, plus our jump suits, personal gear, food, and manty weighed between 50 and 60 pounds [or maybe more]. The main reason for carrying the manty was to protect our backs. We would fold it several times and insert it between our backs and the pack to keep the Clack frame from rubbing. It's quite effective.

More cross-country with packs. The only good thing was it wasn't uphill . . . yet. It was steep and the pack kept catching on branches and throwing us over. It got so we didn't even notice the scratches and bruises. Jerry took a nasty fall once, but evidently didn't get hurt very badly.

It always seems to take forever while you're in the worst of a thing, but it actually wasn't too long before we hit Bear Creek, the stream leading to the Little

North Fork of the Clearwater River. Just before we got there, however, I walked into a mess of yellow jackets. Wham! Wham! Wham! I got socked three times before I knew what was happening. I really tore down that hill. Hunt had some stuff called sodium adrenalin that was quite effective in keeping the swelling down. I had one on the face and two on the arm.

[I have noticed in hot, dry years the yellow jacket population noticeably increases. They are very difficult to avoid because they build their nests in the ground with no visible structure warning of their presence. Once you arouse a nest, you feel like you are walking through a mine field, not knowing whether your next step will bring a sting.]

We knew there'd be some kind of trail by the stream even if it wasn't one built by the Forest Service. At least we thought we knew. Well, we were wrong. What a miserable hike down that stream to the river. We plopped through the water when the brush was impenetrable on the banks . . . over logs and across the stream . . . back and forth . . . again and again. Jerry slipped and fell and got his pack partially wet. His chute sopped up some water and added a few more pounds to his load. I got stung again—on the knee and on the hand. Gee, I hate walking on brush and grass when you don't know whether there're rocks, or water, or what beneath. It's a wonder we didn't sprain an ankle at least. More sloshing in water and over logs. Several times I'd reach for a branch to catch my balance only to grab a thorny bush. My language was only fit for the devil to hear. I really sounded off when I badly skinned my knuckles. Yea, there I was working my hands to the bone. Ha!

Sweat just rolled off of us and our backs felt glued to the manty. I was thankful I had salt tablets, but they didn't help stem our hunger. Gad, was I hungry. We helped each other over large boulders and logs and stopped frequently to rest. The straps dug into our shoulders 'til they were raw, and wet feet added to the discomfort.

At last we arrived at the Little North Fork of the Clearwater River. We waded across to the other side. Since the rivers at high elevations aren't very deep this time of year, they only come up to your pockets in the deepest parts except for an occasional hole or two, and fortunately you can easily see the bottom. As well as clear, the water is also clean and cold. Once on the other side, we decided to rest and eat. Our C-rations contained something new in them—dehydrated soup. Among us all we had eight packs of the stuff, four chicken and four pea. Jerry, Hunt and myself had fishing line and hooks, so we caught a mess of fish— about twenty. Nobody gets down there to fish, so they were plentiful and easy to hook. We roasted them on a stick and crushed salt tablets for seasoning. Bill had taken the band out of his aluminum hard hat and had soup boiling in it. Pea soup and roasted fish: boy, that tasted mighty good to me. We ate ravenously, and because of our fortunate catch, were able to save a few cans of food we otherwise would have had to consume.

Our clothes had been water-soaked from the thighs down from walking in the river and from the waist up from perspiration, but by the time we ate, everything had dried out. Rested, dry, and fed, we took off up the river. Still no trail. Bill figured it was two-and-a-half miles to the base of Buzzard Roost Mountain. There was supposed to be a trail following the next big stream coming in from the left leading to Buzzard Roost Lookout. Did I say dry socks? The first thing we did was wade back across the river, and it wasn't long before we waded back again. The current tugged at our legs and tried to push us down stream. It was breathtaking to feel the cold water creep up my legs when we reached deep water. It really amazed me that not one of us slipped and got his pack wet. I didn't take all this like a man at all. I seriously thought I'd quit when I got back. I just couldn't see carrying that heavy pack up any river for anyone, particularly not knowing whether we'd be out today, tomorrow, the next day, or when. My legs were wet and heavy and my feet sore from being wet so long, but I felt much better when Jerry, who had been up ahead, said the side-stream and trail were just ahead.

I rejoiced as I waded the river for the last time. When I reached shore again I flopped on my back and just lay there, thankful the water trek was over. After a bit we went swimming and dried our clothes. For dinner we had another mess of fish and chicken soup. I was trying to think of something to put in the soup to flavor it up when I remembered a couple of extra cans of C-rations I had stowed in my personal gear bag before we jumped.

"How about a can of beef stew?" I shouted. Into the soup it went.

"And would you believe a can of chicken and noodles?" I added. "Great," said Bill, and he dunked it into the mixture as well.

[We had walked all day, and a long day at that, but we really didn't cover a long distance—seven or eight miles at best. The terrain and the weight on our backs, however, had made those miles tough, and our meager food supply and uncertainty of our route back to base challenged us physically and mentally. We had dropped 4000 feet of elevation traveling from Goat Ridge Lookout to the Little North Fork of the Clearwater River. We now had to climb 2400 feet to reach Buzzard Roost, but we felt confident that the three or four mile hike to get there would be on a good trail. Most of all, we knew district personnel were expecting us and would have transportation at the lookout since there was road to it. Most of our assumptions proved to be wrong.]

We slept in our chutes that night and I was thankful I had my manty to spread over the ground. During the night Jerry got up yelling. He had heard a porcupine on Hunt's bed and tried to catch him. He didn't, but if he had we would have eaten it.

More soup and more fish for breakfast. Also hot cocoa. I figured we'd have a good trail up the mountain, and so did every one else, but we lost it and tried following game trails. We'd lose them or they'd peter out and we'd beat the brush. We tried to get started early enough to miss the heat, but no good. The mountain had been burned-over in past years and was just a mass of brush, and we had a southern exposure to boot. I never sweat so much in my life. It just rolled off. It seemed like we just inched up the hill. Do you remember reading "Water Babies" to me when I was a kid? There was a scene where somebody was walking up a hill on rocks and he kept thinking he was approaching the top, only to find he had farther to go. It was exhausting just to hear you read it. The feeling of dejection was overwhelming. That's the way I felt beating through the brush up Buzzard Roost. If I was alone, I would have stopped. I am sure. If we could have seen the lookout tower or something else to hike towards, it would have been easier. The journey seemed endless.

Jerry had his canteen secured to his back pack and couldn't reach it, so he asked for a drink of mine. I gave it to him and he started guzzling the stuff. I had to almost yank it away from him and told him that was a good way to get sick. [Before we left the river I had taken two salt tablets and drank heartily. I was convinced it fortified me against the raging thirst that often follows heavy exertion. In later years the use of salt tablets was not as vigorously promoted, but I remain convinced they provided something that kept my system in balance.]

Up, up, up . . . rest; up, up. It was discouraging to think we were climbing for a ridge that lead to the lookout, and not the lookout itself. I really didn't think I had the stuff to make it. It was by far the hardest part of the trip. Jerry got hold of his canteen and gulped more water—it fagged him, but good. When I really thought I was burned out, we heard someone yell. "Hot dogs, they're looking for us," I said to myself in a prayer of Thanksgiving.

We all yelled and made it clear that we were on our way to the lookout and would meet him there. We couldn't see him, nor did we hear a reply, but now the lookout was in sight. It was only 100 yards up the hill! We had side-hilled much more than we realized. Our spirits rose and strength seemed to pour into my legs—the end was in sight.

Jerry threw up, and he actually had to crawl part of the way, but nothing was going to keep him from making it to the top—carrying his own pack without assistance[11]. *We were disappointed the lookout was locked and not manned, but were encouraged that we were standing on a road, even if it was primitive. We could see a truck parked by the road a mile away. We ate our last can of grub and left our packs in a pile on the bank. Everyone left their canteens except me—I never part with it until I get back to Missoula. I suggested we take our personal gear, but there was no second, in fact, they were tearing down the road, so I did too.*

Bill decided the lookout we had reached was not Buzzard Roost after all, and that the one three miles over was it. [But he was wrong. The more distant lookout was Stubtoe at 5700 feet of elevation—800 feet higher than Buzzard Roost. The road, however, would descend to 4200 feet, meaning we would have a 1500 foot climb to reach it.]

When we descended to the parked pickup it seemed obvious it belonged to a fisherman who had departed. It was then we realized the voice we heard earlier was that of a fisherman yelling to his buddy. How crazy can you get? Hiking up and down that mountain to fish!

So, up to the other lookout we went. Without packs we seemed to sail along, but that feeling wore off in a bit. We picked a few huckleberries and serviceberries, but still kept up a good pace. Down and then up, up, up. Oh how I hate that word. It didn't take long for the four of us to drain my canteen.

Then we reached the place where the trail to the lookout departed from the road. It was less than half-a-mile away, so we didn't hesitate going there. To our disappointment Stubtoe wasn't manned either, and while we were able to get into the lookout, the telephone wouldn't work, and there was no food or water. Bill finally discovered a box of C-rations after a hard hunt, but that was all. The fruit in the rations helped to kill our thirst for water. Well, there was no way around it, we had a 25 mile hike down (and up) the road to Roundtop Ranger Station. We took off right away

[The road was built by the CCC Boys in the late 1930s. Like many roads built in those early years it was accomplished with a minimum of dirt moving, therefore the road meandered up and down, left and right, following the contour

---

[11]   It seems likely that Jerry suffered from hyponatremia, or water intoxication—a condition that occurs when the body's sodium level is below normal and a large amount of water is imbibed. Exercise-induced hyponatremia usually doesn't occur unless there are prolonged periods of exertion. We all qualified on that score. Jerry's nausea and vomiting are classic symptoms of the disorder. The wonder is that he continued to walk so many miles after being so sick.

of the ground. Stumps and trees were left in the fill-slope to add support. The width was so narrow that turn-outs were a necessary part of the design, to allow vehicles to pass. This kind of road usually penetrated deep into the national forests and dead-ended, providing vehicular access to remote areas. Since we had started at the end of the road, we knew the only vehicle that could come from behind us was the fishermen's truck we had passed, but we also knew they had hiked down to the river and were not likely to be coming out any time soon.]

We hoped we would meet a fisherman driving towards us and he would give us a ride to Roundtop, but it never happened. Before long we passed a small stream and were able to drink our fill. [Even though we weren't without food over the past two days, we never had enough to completely satisfy our hunger. We had expended so much energy that our bodies demanded more calories, but we had substantially less than usual.]

We had one can of food apiece left [from Stubtoe Lookout], *but none of us dared eat it for fear we'd be hungrier later on. Up and down, up and down. We steadily stepped along . . . five . . . ten . . . fifteen miles. Oh, I was hungry. I could think of nothing but food. I longed for a big stack of pancakes with lots of syrup. Then a rather bizarre thing happened. We were on a stretch of road that traversed a steep, heavily wooded slope. A grouse was perched high in a tree on the downhill side, but because of the steepness of the terrain he was situated at very nearly the same elevation as we. Without breaking stride Bill scooped up a rock, awkwardly brought back his arm, and sailed it at the bird. As fate would have it, he hit it square in the head and it fell to the ground way below the road.*

[I find it interesting that I wrote to my mother that *"we roasted the grouse over a fire we made on the road and ate it,"* but my notes reveal, "Walked 17 miles by road. Alternate ranger picked us up just before we roasted a grouse." I don't believe I normally exaggerated my experiences to my mother, but obviously this was too good a story not to fudge a little. It's also interesting to rediscover that it was Bill who threw the rock at the grouse. In my telling of the story through the years it was I who killed the bird—and I came to believe it! The truth can be elusive.]

My legs felt like they'd fall off and the soles on my boots were badly worn, but they held out until the ranger from the Roundtop Ranger Station came up the road in a truck. We were happy boys! That meeting saved us twelve miles of walking.

I was asleep when dinner was served that evening. There's no question where the body's priority is when you are both tired and hungry. Nevertheless, I got up and enjoyed the dinner at the ranger station and the breakfast in the morning.

We're just about to catch a train to Missoula. We're in Idaho. [The Roundtop Ranger District was remotely situated in a heavily forested landscape with no development closer than Avery, 18 miles away. Someone from the ranger district had driven up to Buzzard Roost and retrieved our gear, so it went with us when we were taken to Avery, a town so isolated that only narrow, dirt roads linked it to St. Regis, Montana in one direction and St. Maries, Idaho in the other. The main east/west line of the Milwaukee Railroad, however, came through Avery, and stopped there to switch from diesel to electric engines before beginning the climb over the divide between Idaho and Montana. We boarded the Hiawatha at Avery and the train began its climb up the North Fork of the St. Joe River, passing through numerous tunnels in steep, heavily timbered country. Instead of climbing over the highest part of the Bitterroot Mountains, the train entered a two mile tunnel in Idaho that ended in Montana. We all marveled at the beauty of the ride and the engineering feat in the construction of the route. It's difficult to understand why such an outstanding facility was allowed to perish, but it was. All of the track has since been removed and in some places a road occupies the right-of-way.]

I'm glad that's an experience I can look back on and not forward to.

Love, R.

P.S. We got back to Missoula at 5 p.m. Everybody goes out tomorrow. In the last two weeks more money was spent on extra time for fighting fires than the whole of last season. All records of previous years have been broken—more jumps, more fires, more everything.

An August 16 letter to my mother was written while traveling back to Missoula. The post script, "Everybody goes out tomorrow," was added after returning to Missoula. Fifty-nine of us were on the jump list—all just back from fires. That's a lot of jumpers for me to say with such certainty that every one would jump the next day. On the other hand, you could feel the call to action floating in the air. The fire season had been steadily getting worse and weather forecasts indicated it had not yet reached its peak.

There had been considerable evening lightning on the Bitterroot, Clearwater, and Nez Perce National Forests, and although spotty, the Flathead was hit hard. Early morning flights were already planned for 12 men to three fires on the Bitterroot and Clearwater.

When we checked-in the evening of August 16, the loft was so drained of fire equipment that those of us on the bottom of the jump list were asked to work after supper to prepare fire packs and other gear needed for the upcoming fires. Many of us worked until 10:00 p.m.

August 17 proved to be a red letter day. Shortly after daybreak a Ford lifted off Hale Field with eight jumpers for the Bitterroot. Not far behind another Ford with four jumpers went to the Bitterroot to drop two men on two fires.

Many of us continued to build fire packs, rig five-gallon cans of water for drop, assist the riggers with the parachutes, and anything else that needed to be done in preparation for the rash of jumper requests we knew would come.

Dave Owen and Skip Stoll were there. I had seen Skip on the Big Bill Fire, but I hadn't seen Dave since we were marking spruce together on Clarence Creek. Bob Graham, the guy who had been in a car accident when the rest of us left Ant Flat, was also there. It was nice rubbing elbows with old friends and comparing notes on our recent fires.

It was shortly after 11:00 a.m. when a Doug loaded with nine jumpers left for the Nez Perce National Forest. Shortly before, two Travelairs headed for two small fires, and one of the Fords was making its second trip of the morning, this time with four jumpers to the Nez Perce.

One of the Travelairs returned from the Bitterroot with the jumpers still aboard—if the fire hadn't gone out, it was not putting up enough smoke to be seen. The Ford also came back with its four men because the small contingent of jumpers stationed at Grangeville, Idaho, had already manned it.

With so much activity, the Missoula base was out of aircraft, so when a call came in for the Flathead, the jumpers had to wait. I was particularly interested in this one, named the Tango Cabin Fire, because it was located just west of Big Salmon Lake, a place I was familiar with from my several flights over the Bob Marshall Primitive Area. I envied the five guys assigned to jump there, but they left without me shortly before noon when a Ford became available.

At noon we were down to 31 jumpers. By 2:00 p.m. 24 more jumpers were flown to six more fires, but three of them were dry runs, so eight men returned and their names went back at the top of the jump list.

Next, Dave Owen, Bob Graham and four others took off in a Ford with crews for two fires on the Flathead: one on Red Plume Mountain 15 miles north of Big Bill Mountain, and the other on Helen Creek, five miles east of

Black Bear Guard Station. I was always a bit envious of those lucky enough to be sent to the Flathead and was hoping mine would be in the same direction.

At 5:00 p.m. George Ostrum and Hunt Hatch left in the Travelair for a two-manner on the Flathead, reducing the jump list to seven.

At 4:30 p.m. a call had come in for 16 jumpers for a fire on the Nez Perce National Forest. We didn't have enough jumpers, and no aircraft were available. Nevertheless, Martin "Oni" Onishuk, Al Casieri, Bob McGraw, Jerry Soapes, Bill Frame, Gus Ulrich and I prepared ourselves for a flight. Oni, Al and I were old men, the rest were new; however, everyone was well seasoned by then. At 6:00 p.m. a Ford was available and we left immediately, knowing darkness could have been a problem had we been delayed any longer. The fire, named Battle Creek Ridge, was located in the Selway/Bitterroot Primitive Area. It's very name seemed to portend a difficult time ahead.

Thursday, August 20, 1953

Dear Ma,

What a fouled up mess! We went out the next day after we got back from the Bear Creek Fire. I'm sitting by a creek waiting for the other six to get dressed so we can hike to a road. We jumped Monday just before dark, a good mile from the fire. Five of us hit the clearing (our jump spot), but when I came in a down-draft caught me and I really sailed. After my feet hit, they slid right out from under me and I landed in a perfect three-point position. Only one point hurt. Naw, nothing hurt, but it scared me.

We arrived at the fire at 7:30 p.m. and it was burning with gusto. Sixteen jumpers had been ordered, but only seven were available—that's us. Four ground pounders came in about 2:00 a.m., but they were worthless. [That now strikes me as an unkind way to characterize them, although I don't doubt they were able to do much. It was miles to the nearest road and their hike had to have been tough.] *We worked straight through the night and by 10:00 a.m. the next morning we had a line around it. The fire was a Class C (between 10 and 100 acres) and on steep ground. A helicopter was supposed to ferry men, one at a time, to assist in firefighting but the operation somehow got fouled up and none arrived. We were plenty tired, not only from working all night, but most of us were not fully recovered from our last fires. Even so, we had no choice but to stick it out and try to hold the line we had built. Unfortunately there was too much territory to cover, and the heat and wind in the afternoon were too high—it blew up.*

Just after we lost all the line some ground pounders arrived. Had they been an hour sooner we may have saved the line, but who knows. Four of us were on the bottom when the fire escaped. Shovels and Pulaskis were flailing as we tried again to establish a line of defense. Two of our group decided it was useless and went to the top of the fire to rejoin the others. Jerry Soaps and I remained. Granted, two or four men couldn't control the fire, but you had to start somewhere. The way we looked at it, every little bit helps. From the time it blew up until 6:00 p.m. we had about . . .

Tuesday, August 25, 1953

I started this letter to you while coming off my last fire, but never finished it. It seems the whole West is ablaze. Things are one big mess—chaos and confusion. In and out. That's us, the in-and-out-boys. The end isn't in sight and the future weeks are predicted to be worse. Suddenly the money I'm making doesn't seem to count much. Since July 14 I've put in 264 extra hours of work. I don't mind the hard work so much, but no sleep is exhausting. On the last fire we had no sleep the first night, two hours the second and none the third. I almost fell asleep walking out.

I don't feel like telling about my last fire now—it's getting to the point where I don't want to talk about any of them.

I'm not sick, or really run down—I'm just a little depressed and tired. Please don't worry. I've probably made things sound worse than they are.

I hope and pray we get early rains this year. We really need it.

Love, R.

P.S. They're letting us sleep 'til noon. We go out after lunch.
P.P.S. ZZZZZZZZZ

It makes me cringe to read those words. It's embarrassing to think I actually whined to my mother like that. It prompted me to delve into my diary to figure out some statistics. For the 25-day period from July 30 through August 23 I spent 22 days on fire (or traveling back from fire). I jumped six times. There were three non-fire days, but they were on week-days, so I worked every day in the 25-day period for a total of 361 hours. That averages out to 14½ hours a day. Considering the amount of energy expended on many of those hours, perhaps I can plead temporary insanity.

Only now, viewing the situation back through time, can I understand my feelings in late August 1953. Typically we were attracted to the demands of

FRANK FOWLER

our job: the long hours of hard, dirty work; being ready on a moment's notice; risky low altitude mountain flying; parachuting into remote areas in hazardous situations; and fighting fires in dangerous conditions—all in an atmosphere of high physical demand with little rest.

These things made the job attracting. We exhorted Zap, the god of lightning, to challenge us with demanding fires. We breathed it; we needed it, and loved that part of our job. What I didn't realize was that these same factors, when intensified, defined the dark side of the job as well. As rest became routinely less available, we began to increasingly walk that fine edge between love and hate.

Those things that had brought joy to the job became the anchor of our despair. I wanted desperately to be invincible, but I wasn't, and my inability to comprehend the love/hate relationship resulted in further confusion.

Now it seems clear that those fires in 1953 were a challenge that pushed us to the limits of our endurance. Our reaction was normal. And when we had the opportunity to become rested, the adversity melted away and we were once again eager to go.

*　　*　　*

I had started a letter to my mother about the Battle Ridge Fire on August 20, but didn't finish it before being sent on another. After I returned I tried on August 25 to finish the account of Battle Ridge, but only complained about how tough the summer had become. When I was rested, I continued with the letter started August 20.

I need to say a thing or two about my seventh and eighth fires. I started the seventh, but never finished it. I guess I left off down at the bottom of the fire trying to hold some line, huh? Jerry Soaps and I started putting in new line at the bottom. Conditions varied, but a lot of the loose ground surface was fairly easy to build line on. The problem was that the ground was also steep and burning pine cones would roll down the hill and bounce over the line, taking fire with them. It was necessary in many places to dig a deep cup-trench in an attempt to catch the rolling debris. It also required constant patrolling to find slop-overs soon after they occurred—otherwise you would lose the line.

Anyway, we put in line and held it, and put in more line. About 6:00 p.m. we were hungry so we flipped a coin to see who was to go up to the top for food and news about what was happening. I lost, so I dragged up the line, and I mean dragged. It was a long way, and when I got there I was so mad I couldn't talk. Guys were laying all over the place—both ground pounders and jumpers. Since

204

the fire was being supervised by a ground pounder, I asked to see the man in charge. He was standing there and said, "Fowler, go back down and hold your line. We'll send relief down at 7:45 or so, but remember—hold that line!"

My anger subsided because I thought he had recognized that Jerry and I were accomplishing something important. I went back down with some food for Jerry and me. We ate a bite and then put in more line in order to keep the fire from out-flanking what we had already built. At 8:00 we were starting to lose daylight and were concerned because no one had shown up. For almost 24 hours we'd been slinging that Pulaski and shovel, and for 36 hours we hadn't slept. Where was the ground crew?

At 8:30 we left and when we got to the top the leader acted as if he had never seen me before. As it turned out, the fire jumped our line and we lost it all. I was so angry I could have slugged him, but I was too tired and gutless. Jerry was mad at me because he wanted to go leave the fireline earlier, but I wouldn't go. I didn't attempt to hold him back, but he wouldn't leave me there alone. I really felt like I had been playing the part of a big martyr and prize chump. I apologized to Jerry, but that didn't make him feel any better about our many hours of burned up work.

[I never understood what others were doing while Jerry and I were working alone. When I asked, it became apparent that confusion and chaos reined. Oni was our squad leader, but because a ground pounder was in charge, Oni wasn't making fire decisions. While Jerry and I were working, the fire boss must have been attempting to organize for a concerted effort in the evening. Perhaps he was letting the ground pounders rest after their long walk to the fire, but I never could rationalize that as a reasonable approach. When I spoke to Oni about it at our 1995 reunion he remembered how mixed up it was, but couldn't recall any of the particulars.

Later, when writing about the fire, I decided to contact him again to see if he could help me fill in some voids. He was cooperative and rather philosophical. He started by saying that when he started jumping in 1951 he had had no previous fire fighting experience, other than a little mop-up work. But he did well his first year and by the end of his second year had jumped on 13 fires. The turn-over of jumpers was high in those years, so he was selected to become a squad leader in 1953. He gained more experience as the year progressed, but confessed, "We were not professional fire fighters. We were mostly college students who loved our summer job and worked hard at it, but we frankly lacked the breadth of experience the jumpers of today have."

I surmised Oni was saying that the Bear Creek Fire was bigger and tougher than anything he was used to. In fact, the whole 1953 season was beyond the organization's experience. Not that more knowledge could have kept the fire from blowing up, but it might have allowed us to more confidently figure out how to make the best use of our time after it blew.

Oni said he knew a cargo drop would come in the afternoon, so he put his efforts into figuring where the best location would be. All things being equal, the drop would occur at the bottom of the fire, but Oni wanted to avoid the parachutes hanging up in the big cedars in that location. He scouted the terrain and found an open area up slope to the side of the fire and marked it with orange crepe paper in the form of an "H"—the established symbol for a cargo drop spot.

I didn't ask Oni why he accepted the request of the fire boss for us (the smokejumpers) to patrol the fire at night because I felt I knew the answer. In those years we were trying to gain Forest Service grass roots support for the smokejumper organization, and often put out extra effort to help foster a good name for the outfit. Even though we were exhausted, we attempted to be invincible.]

Everyone worked on the fire that night, but we still managed to get two hours sleep before starting the next day. It's amazing how quickly a fire can "lay down" if its spread is prevented. Although we were tired, the second day was easier. We still had a long way to go, but our numbers were sufficient to catch slopovers as they occurred and the fire was never able to make another run.

That night the ground pounders were "too tired" to patrol the line, so Oni volunteered us. Nobody wanted to because we desperately needed sleep. We spread out 300 yards apart and watched, occasionally spreading a hot spot. I was glad when two of us were assigned to work together on hot spots in the center of the burned area because it was a lot easier to stay awake with activity and conversation. The night slipped rapidly by and at 3:00 a.m. the hot spots were cold. With the exertion over, so were we, and I didn't have a coat. The wind came up, but we were heartened by the fact that our fireline held. By morning the fire was declared controlled and since the ground pounders could now handle it alone, we began preparations to leave.

[We hiked back to the jump spot to retrieved our jump gear. It was quick for those of us who landed in the clearing, but even those who hit trees didn't have a difficult retrieval. We had left our tools and paper sleeping bags at the fire with the ground pounders. The cargo chutes had been deposited on a trail for pick up by a pack string, but we had to carry the rest out with us. Fortunately, the terrain wasn't steep and a trail was close by.

In short order we arrived on the East Fork of Moose Creek and turned north for the final 10 miles to Elk Summit. The trail along the East Fork was gentle and meandered among huge cedar trees. It was pleasant walking but we desperately needed sleep. Jerry was walking in front of me and he extended his arms to the side at a 45 degree angle and rotated them in tight, eight inch circles. He claimed it helped him "float" along. He looked like he was trying to fly and it amazed me he kept it up for so long.

At a point where the trail took a slight bend to the left, one fellow kept on walking straight ahead, then he fell over a log. He had fallen asleep while walking down the trail and was pinned with his face to the ground by his pack that had rested on his head and shoulders.

You may challenge the veracity of that event, but I didn't. I could easily have done the same thing, and didn't think anyone would fake falling over a log with a heavy pack on his back. I thought it interesting that even with the passage of 51 years, Oni still remembered that he was so tired during the walk to Elk Summit that he almost fell asleep on his feet. He seemed to confirm my story.

It was evening when we arrived at Elk Summit Guard Station located on the Powell Ranger District of the Clearwater National Forest. The fire guard called Powell on the grounded telephone line and while transportation was coming we ate at the guard station. We all signed a register at the guard's request, only I wouldn't have remembered it if I hadn't visited the station 10 years later when I was district ranger of the Powell Ranger District. I happened to peruse the register while I was there and was greatly surprised to find my name in it. I had been so tired and sleepy when I visited there in 1953 that it was little more than a faint memory.

The ride back to Missoula was 70 miles, most of it over dirt road, so it was 11:00 p.m. by the time we arrived.

The next day, August 21, we worked in the loft; fire activity was still in high gear. There had been a plane crash on August 17, the same day we jumped on the Battle Creek Ridge Fire. It was a Ford at Spotted Bear, the one Dave Owen and Bob Graham were in. They had flown over both the North Fork of Helen Creek Fire and the Red Plume Mountain Fire, but when Dick Conklin dropped several streamers to test the wind, they blew out of the country—it was too windy to jump on either fire.

Les Darling, the dispatcher at the Spotted Bear Ranger Station, requested that Dick instruct the pilot, Ken Roth, to set down at the airstrip at Spotted Bear to wait for the high winds to subside. Ken landed the Ford Trimotor and they waited an hour before trying again to man the two fires. But before they even reached a jumping altitude the engines started missing, and then quit all together. They crashed a mile from the airstrip on a moderately steep side slope less than one quarter mile from the road.

The pilot sustained a foot injury and a bad upper lip cut; Bob Graham suffered a broken leg; the spotter was shaken up rather severely; and Fritz Wolfrum had several broken ribs. Amazingly, Dave and three others were not injured.

I couldn't help thinking that with a very slight shift in my position on the jump list that day I could have been on that flight. It was a sobering feeling, but it was also reassuring that a crash didn't necessarily mean death.

We also found out that the guys who left for the Tango Fire on the same day had some tough luck. Their fire got away and burned up 700 acres, so perhaps Battle Creek Ridge wasn't so bad after all.

The next day, Saturday, August 22, Jerry Soaps and I drew a two-manner on the Deerlodge National Forest. The call came in at 9:45 a.m., but all the small planes were out. A Twin Beech returned from a cargo run and we were able to take-off at 11:30 a.m. It wasn't the quintessential high-mountain two-manner, but I looked forward to the solitude of a small fire and jumping from a Twin Beech, a new experience for me.

It was located nine air miles south of Anaconda on Crooked Johns Creek, about a mile from Sugar Loaf Mountain. Paul Dennison was the spotter and Oni was the assistant. Paul was located in the glass nose of the plane which is where the bombardier sat when the plane was used for military purposes. Not all Twin Beeches had glass noses—some were covered with a solid skin of aluminum.

With the glass nose Paul had an excellent view of the ground and could talk with the pilot and Oni on an intercom, an arrangement I knew nothing about. When we flew over the fire I was concerned because I thought Oni was the spotter and he wasn't looking out the door opening. I didn't realize he released the drift chute when Paul gave the order and therefore didn't need to look. The country was a mixture of lodgepole pine stands and open, grassy parks, not the typical heavily forested landscape of the more westerly national forests. It was immediately obvious the wind was very strong so it was only after several attempts that a drift chute landed fairly close to an opening near the fire.

We prepared to jump. Oni told me to hold into the wind or I'd be blown out of the country. He also said there were numerous open areas, so I could pick my own landing spot. I was concerned that we were on our final approach and he wasn't even looking at the fire or jump spot to give the pilot directions, so I asked him about it. Then he told me Paul was spotting from the nose of the plane—what a relief!

I remember dropping down to my left knee and sticking my right leg out the door to the step because it impressed me that there was no wind pushing at my leg. The Ford and the Travelair had high wings, (wings that attached to the top of the fuselage), thereby allowing the full force of the slip stream and prop wash to pass by the door opening. The Twin Beech, like the DC-3, had wings that attached at the base of the fuselage, and this must have made the difference. In the DC-3, however, we stood erect in the door opening and since there was no step, we didn't feel the wind blast until we jumped. In the Twin Beech, however, I didn't experience much wind blast even when I jumped. It strikes me that the flaps were lowered somewhat to reduce airspeed; perhaps they further deflected air from blasting by the door opening.

I jumped following Oni's suggestion—I turned into the wind and pulled my front risers down in an effort to hold against the strong wind. By looking down through my feet I could see I was still drifting heavily backwards, so fast that I continued the maneuver almost to the ground. Just before landing I reached with my right arm behind my head and grabbed the left riser, and with my left arm I reached across in front of my head and grabbed the right one. When I pulled from this position my body turned 180 degrees with my parachute remaining in the same position. This allowed me to avoid gaining speed (as I would have if the parachute were turned), but still allowed me to watch the ground for hazards just before I hit. Watching the ground on impact wasn't exactly the way we were trained, but I was much more comfortable looking at what was coming up while traveling so fast horizontally.

My letter to my mother continued . . .]

Saturday Jerry and I went on a two-manner. It was windy and we drifted one-third of a mile even though we held into the wind.

We jumped at 12:45 p.m. and were on the fire in 15 minutes. It was an easy fire, and made easier because Jerry is such a hard worker. This is my third time out with him. [I had gotten to know Jerry well and appreciated his eagerness to "go the extra mile." His energy seemed boundless. He was the one on the Bear Creek Fire who climbed the tree and located the smoke of our fire; and he forged ahead as we sloshed up the Little North Fork of the Clearwater River in search of the trail leading to Buzzard Roost. On the Battle Ridge Fire he stayed with me building fireline for many hours, only to lose it all; and he did that thing with his arms on the walk out that appeared like he was trying to fly, when it was all the rest of us could do just to walk.

What was his source of energy? He confided to me that he was only 17. My God, I thought the rest of us were young, but by contrast, we were well-seasoned. Most of us were college students; Jerry was clearly an exception.]

We got a line around the fire pronto and had all the snags cut when three guys arrived in a truck—right to the fire. I never would have thought it possible, but they did it. Boy, was that a rotten break. An easy fire on the week end and we had to be relieved. Seems like relief just comes at the wrong time. The fire was controlled at 2:15 p.m. and we left for Anaconda at 5:30.

Well, I didn't feel too bad because we were only 17 miles from Butte, so I went and saw a friend before catching the late bus to Missoula.

Things are quiet now and everybody is rested and ready to go again.

Love, R.

The "friend" I went to see was Corky, whom I had met at college the last school year. I would have preferred an opportunity to clean-up and change my clothes, and was a little embarrassed to show up in my fire clothes, but nevertheless, it was great seeing her, if only for a few hours. I suspected even then that we would be seeing a lot of each other in the coming years.

I caught the 1:00 a.m. bus to Missoula and was surprised to find that Al Cramer and five other jumpers had just come off their fire and were riding the same bus.

*   *   *

The dispatcher's log noted that the Crooked Johns Fire was number 153 for the year and 774 fire jumps had been made. Those of us who were late getting back were allowed to sleep a little extra in the morning. It was Monday, August 24, and many who had been on fires were returning. Productive work was scarce, but everyone at the base was working at the loft.

With rain in many parts of the region, the fire season came to an abrupt stop. Some speculated the weather might change and we'd be right back fighting fire again, but it didn't happen. Brauer sharpened his pencil and started lining up project work. We knew work assignments were coming and welcomed them since there were no fires. Not only was it costly to pay for meals three times a day, but it also made for long days when there was not enough to do. What a change a week can bring! I also noted that August 29 and 30 were my first days off for a solid month.

The Big Bill Fire at dusk the first day.
The foreground was our jump spot.

CHAPTER 10

Tango

O n the last day of the month, Monday, August 31, Good Deal Brauer had project assignments all lined up and Dick Faurot, a forestry student in my class at the university, Bill Hale, and I left together for Kalispell.

Tuesday, September 1, 1953

Dear Ma,

This is a real quickie. Although the weather has warmed up and the rain stopped, we are all going on project.

After we got to our project, it fell through and our orders were changed. In about five minutes, nine of us are starting on a 16 mile hike back in the boondocks to build a cabin. I may be there three days or three weeks—I don't know. So I may not be able to write. Must run.

Love, R.

Rumors were floating around about many different projects including a controlled fire patrol. It was obvious they didn't know what to do with us. The prospect of building a cabin was inviting; the mere thought of patrolling a cold burn was absolutely abhorrent. Since we were convinced it was the former, we felt good about the assignment.

Sunday, September 6, 1953

Dear Ma,

Even though I can't mail this letter to you until some time in the future, I'm going to write it anyhow. I'm afraid if I wait to write any longer, I won't remember what has taken place; besides, I have lots of time.

Last Monday a whole mess of fellows left Missoula for Kalispell, Montana. From there we were dispatched to various places on the Flathead National Forest. Five of us went to the Big Creek Ranger Station located up the North Fork of the Flathead River to mark timber. We looked forward to working there because Glacier Park was situated across the river and we thought possibly we'd have an opportunity to see some of it, but it never happened. When we arrived at Big Creek about dark, we learned about a change of plans. They wanted us on a 700 acre fire and we had to leave right away. The fire was controlled, and maybe out, but they needed a few men to watch it until they were sure it was dead out. Bill Hale and Bill Calder had both jumped on the fire when it was just a spot and had no wish to return, but had no choice.

It was 3:00 a.m. Tuesday morning when we drove into the base camp at Lower Holland Lake. Everyone was asleep and there were no lights, so we looked around until we found some sleeping bags. We just threw them on the ground and sacked out right there.

Early the next morning the cook yelled us out of bed, and we were surprised to find three other jumpers there. After getting lunches, we started our 17 mile hike to the fire. Nine miles of it was up and nine miles down [oops, another mile], but none of it was too bad because there were lots of switchbacks, making the climb tolerable. It was cool and mules were bringing up our gear, so we weren't laboring in the heat with a heavy load.

The country was terrific; the views fantastic. I'm fully convinced the prettiest pictures can't be taken with a camera or painted. There's always something missing. Maybe it's the smell of the forest or the feel of the breeze, I'm not sure. At any rate, there's no substitute for being there.

Upper Holland Lake was at 6,146 feet of elevation. We got there at noon after a climb of 2,100 feet, so we ate, rested and "smelled the roses," so to speak. Since we had worked up a good sweat, we decided to go swimming, at least some of us. Bill Hale cheered us on from the shore. Sure, it was cold—very cold, and it literally took my breath away when I dove in, but it felt good. We found a raft and really had a fun time, but couldn't stand it very long. From now on, whenever

I am exposed to cold water I will think of Upper Holland Lake because I have never swam in colder water.

By 5:00 p.m. we were at the Tango Fire. What a mess. Only five fellows were there and they hadn't seen any smoke for two days. We got two kapok sleeping bags apiece (one for a mattress) and went to bed early. There were ample pup tents around, so I pitched one just above the camp. Boy, did it rain that night. The next morning I could hardly get out of bed. I could write a book about getting up on a frosty morning when sleeping outside. Some guys leave their clothes on, but I have to strip down, or I can't sleep. Of course, that makes it more difficult trying to get dressed when leaving the warm bag. It takes a great deal of courage to start the day—Ha.

After breakfast, we started the long haul up to the top of the fire. It took almost three hours. Of course we were becoming acquainted with the fire and not trying for speed, but still, it was a long, hard climb. We dreaded the thought of spending another day at this place. The next day we only went part way up and looked around a bit. We worked alone. I took a book and read a good deal. It helped the time to pass more quickly. Now I don't mind the job.

So this has been going on for a week now. I'm glad I had the mules bring a change of clothes up from base camp. I've got some down in our camp to put on this evening—what a treat that will be.

I'm off the mountain and back down in camp now. I'm still working—Ha— boiling clothes in a tub of water. They will still be dirty, I suppose, but not filthy. And I'm hoping they will smell Oxydol fresh!

There's a bear that comes to the garbage pit now. It's a huge thing, the pit, that is. Maybe an eight foot cube dug in the ground. Last night Bill and I stayed up late (nine o'clock) and we almost walked on top of the devil. I don't know who ran the faster—the bear, Bill, or me.

A mule deer doe came into camp this morning and started eating something off the ground. I walked within 30 feet of her before she moved away.

The mountains are full of goats and elk and we see them frequently. I often think how spectacular all this wildlife would be to you folks at home; it's just a part of life here.

When the Tango Fire was at its peak, 200 firefighters were assigned here. When they left, a mountain of equipment and gear remained that has to be taken back by mules. I get a big kick out of seeing a mule string come in. Usually there are eight mules to a string and one packer on a horse. I like to hear his spurs "ting" as he walks and enjoy watching him in his chaps, beat-up hat, and whiskers. I'm no natural around stock, but like to help when I can. Usually that amounts to holding the halter rope while the packer loads a mule. It's one way of learning something about the art. I almost got kicked one day and I don't mind saying I was scared. They get ornery and pretty hard to hold at times.

At night we sit around the fire and talk, or somebody plays the harmonica. Sometimes I read, but the failing light makes it hard on the eyes. I rather enjoy sitting by the fire and hearing some of the old men talk. They relate some wonderful stories, and I doubt that they would be as lucid in a different setting.

Last Thursday Dick Faurot and Odis Powell left to help build a cabin four-and-a-half miles away. The next day Sheridan Peterson, Dan Merell, and Fred Hooker left for Holland Lake. We don't know where they were assigned, only that they were instructed to walk out.

When I pitched my tent I hadn't realized it was over a weasel's nest. I kept hearing things at night that I couldn't account for until one morning when I saw him—or her. Needless to say, I moved my tent to a new location.

I guess we'll be here 'til it rains. I don't mind. I've really gotten used to sleeping on the ground and not taking a bath. Saturdays and Sundays are just like any other day—just like the rest of the summer, come to think of it. I kind of look forward to returning to school again.

Well, I'm written out—more later.

Love, R.

David Greeson, a junior forester on the Coram Ranger District, was in charge of patrolling the Tango Fire. He had graduated in forestry when I was a freshman at Missoula. Although he made work assignments for us, I remember little of his presence except for two occasions.

The first was shortly after we arrived. Some of the guys were determined to snare a bear in the garbage pit. Why, I was never sure except that it was something to do. Rigging the trap took a lot of time and effort, but it was not well conceived. Cans were strung on a rope and arranged so they would rattle if a bear (or bears) should enter the pit. The trap involved a rope and a young, pole-size tree. The tree was on the edge of the pit and was pulled to a bending position by several ropes, but ultimately held by only one. The snare was simple. One end of a rope was secured to the top of the tree and the other was a loop arranged in the pit that would slip like a hangman's noose. The trigger mechanism was the most difficult part, but they devised something they thought would work. This was really dumb, for several reasons, but the biggest one was that a rifle was only in camp when a packer was there—and they were gone.

215

The guys tried to stay up after dark with flashlights in hand, hoping to witness the event, but all was quiet, so they sacked out. During the night came a great commotion. Cans rattled, a bear bellowed, and the breaking sound of wood was distinct. The camp became alive and flashlights were directed to the pit, but it was too late, the bear had escaped. The snare tree was tipped over into the pit, so it wasn't possible to see down into it, but the silence was taken to mean it was empty.

In the morning this was the subject of much discussion by everyone except David. He was completely unaware of any of the night's events because he had a severe hearing problem that required the use of a hearing aid. At night he turned it off and was able to sleep through anything.

The second incident occurred while we were patrolling the fire. For a couple of days when one of us would saunter past a particular area, we would smell smoke, but couldn't see it. Finally we decided we were looking too intently on the ground when we should have been looking high in a tree. Larch was the predominant tree species and they were large in diameter and height.

Where the fire had burned hottest they were dead, but most were still standing. One tree in the vicinity of the place where we smelled smoke was broken off about 30 feet up, but it was such a large tree that the diameter at the broken spot was a substantial 30 inches across. We went up slope to get a better view. It was still too high for us to see the top clearly, so we threw rocks, hoping that the disturbance would result in a puff of smoke. It wasn't easy, but we had lots of time. Finally we started lobbing the rocks underhand so they would come down on top of the tree. Occasionally one would hit the target, and we noticed those that did, stayed there. We expected they would bounce off the top and fall to the ground, but they didn't. It was then we realized the top was an open cylinder, like a drinking glass, and we continued to chuck rocks into the opening. At last a puff of smoke appeared—we had found our sleeper.

To fell the tree with a Pulaski required an extreme amount of work, so we went back to camp for a chain saw. David decided it was his job, so he eagerly packed the saw up the mountain. When he started to cut, those of us observing stepped behind trees above him, but were still very close. It took awhile to make the undercut, and when the wedge of wood slipped out he turned off the saw and said, "When the tree starts to fall let me know. I want to have time to step a few feet away so I'm not near the butt end when the tree hits the ground."

The battery pack for his hearing aid was attached to a lanyard around his neck and rested on his chest. The engine noise must have hurt his ear drums because when he started to saw, he turned down his hearing aid. The bar of the chain saw was shorter than the diameter of the tree, so it took several minutes to cut through it. It was almost imperceptible, but we noticed the top of the tree move, so we yelled. But because his hearing aid was turned down, he couldn't hear us, so we started throwing small rocks at him. Our pelting had no effect; he continued sawing until he noticed the kerf was beginning to widen, meaning the tree was starting to fall. He dropped the saw and scrambled out of the way. The tree fell with a tremendous crash and a huge plume of debris shot up into the air. David turned to us and yelled, "Why didn't you warn me when the tree started to fall?"

No matter what we said, he didn't believe we had tried to warn him. Later we privately agreed that if we ever found ourselves in a similar situation, we would throw much bigger rocks—in the interest of safety, of course.

Thursday, September 10, 1953

Dear Ma,

This is beautiful country. There's a lot of good clean air, lots of wild game, but . . . I'm tired of the joint. Every day we trudge up the mountain and look for smoke. Sometimes we find one, sometimes we don't. Mostly we don't. The Big Dogs say stay, so we stay. One thing that makes it hard for me is anticipating the summer coming to a close and classes starting. Sure, I like the summer and jumping, but I also like school, especially the newness of it in the fall. Did I tell you I'm going to be a resident assistant at my dorm this year? I appreciate being able to make a little extra money that way.

We just about ran out of grub here. Oh, we had four cases of cookies, three cases of beans and some canned fruit, but we had no meat, potatoes, jelly and vegetables, to name a few. Beans and cookies don't make for a very good diet. Well, when we all (David Greeson, Bill Hale, Bill Calder and I) got off the hill today we were greatly disappointed when we found the packer and mule train were not here. Bill (Hale) and I decided we were so cruddy we'd take a bath in Tango Creek, which, of course, runs right by our campsite. The last time I stood in the creek to bathe, my feet were numb for hours. So Bill and I got two wooden boxes and put them in the creek to stand on. We positioned ourselves six feet apart and started yelling insults. We each had wash pans and started slinging water at one another. Boy, did we howl! It felt like he was throwing ice cubes at me. When we both were good and wet we called a truce and soaped up. After we were well lathered, the battle resumed, and we kept it up until we were well rinsed. Finally we stopped and put on fresh clothes. Gee, does it feel good. Guess that means I wash clothes tomorrow.

When we came up from the creek the packer, Bruce Piles, had arrived. Hal-lay-lou-ya! Steaks, eggs, bacon, watermelon, milk, jam, bread . . . hal-lay-lou-ya! Our spirits really rose. But just after we finished a fine meal, Bruce really broke our morale. He said every jumper on the Flathead Forest, except us, had been called to Missoula for a fire bust. We felt rotten.

Well, now it's Friday. Last night Bruce decided to kill the bear in our garbage pit. It's against the law to shoot at night, but he decided no one would know the difference. The pit is about 25 yards from the kitchen and the same distance from where I sleep. Bruce and David waited in the kitchen for the sound of cans rattling in the pit—Bruce with the gun and David with a flashlight. I was asleep when a shot just about rose me through my tent. Another shot and I was wide awake. Bruce had hit the bear once and knocked it tin over tea cup, but it got up and crawled off. They couldn't find it in the dark, so they went to bed. I really felt great sleeping unarmed with a wounded bear nearby.

In the morning they followed the blood trail for a way, but soon lost it. They figured it was bound to die from loss of blood. If he isn't dead, someone will have hell to pay if they meet him.

The next day I decided to move down under the huge flap (or perhaps more accurately called a fly, a tent-like canvas with top and sides, but no ends) and sleep where everyone else was located. As our numbers dwindled, there had been a gravitation to this central living, and I was the last to join in. If we were going to meet a bear at night, I'd just as soon it be in the presence of others, and if possible, near someone with a gun.

The place is lousy with chipmunks. I know it's awful, but sometimes we lob pebbles at them.

After dark it's too cold to do anything but sit by the fire. I like it, but I'd rather be doing something.

I'll try to catch Bruce in the morning and have him take these two letters, but if you don't get them, don't worry, I'm fine. Ha.

Love, R.

P.S. Missoula, Missoula, please call these hungry jumpers. We're tired of this place.

After I moved under the fly with the other fellows it took a while for me to get used to my new sleeping environment. Five of us were bunking there—David, Bruce and we three jumpers. I don't recall any heavy snorers, but we were located just a few yards from Tango Creek and could hear the splashing and bubbling of the fast moving water, especially at night when human sounds were not competing. Laying in bed one could distinctly hear elk or bear plopping through the water, only to suddenly realize it was only the variegated sounds of moving water, intensified by an imagination run amok. At first the noise was loud and pervasive, but soon became familiar and melted into a friendly and intoxicating whisper of white sound.

After making the move a strange event occurred. During the night I was awakened by something heavy moving across my chest. It was too dark to see but I could tell an animal was slowly moving across my sleeping bag and onto the guy's next to me. I was afraid to say anything for fear my voice would provoke the animal to attack. When our visitor made his way to the end of the row of sleeping bags he turned and started back taking a route across the bags on the far side. Somebody yelled and somebody else turned on a flashlight and we caught a glimpse of a porcupine just as it left the tent.

Bruce charged across our bags in pursuit of the critter. We could hear him thrashing around outside. After several loud thumps in rapid succession, the porcupine was dead.

We all went back to sleep, but in the first grey light of dawn I was again awakened. This time it was not the movement of an animal but the sound of one. I couldn't figure out what it was at first because I had never heard such a sound before. It was a high pitched moan—a wail. But the sound was not continually on the same pitch. It would raise a few notes, as if to intensify, and then return to a more constant monotone. It conjured a feeling of sadness. I got out of my sleeping bag and strained to see in the pre-dawn light. Finally I was able to make out the form of another porcupine. It was huddled close to the one Bruce had killed and was obviously mourning over its mate.

It was profoundly sad. As I lay there, I speculated that many of us think of animals as being unfeeling, particularly with regards to emotions. This porcupine seemed to be in deep emotional pain. How pompous of humans to reserve the right of such feelings to themselves. I was glad that when morning blossomed the critter had left and escaped the fate of its mate.

*   *   *

Bill Hale and I often engaged in lengthy discussions. Of immediate interest to me was his accounting of the jump he had made on the Tango Fire, the one we were now patrolling. August 17 was a red letter day for several of us, but his experience was hair raising. The fire started when the Tango Cabin burned down, although how that happened, no one is certain. When the jumpers arrived it was putting up a heavy plume of smoke. Since the area was a productive growing site, the trees were extremely tall. Many were larch, a species always avoided by jumpers because its branches are small and brittle and will break under the weight of a snarled parachute. Bill was able to miss the larch and hung up solidly in a huge "some other kind of tree." Bill wasn't certain, but he thought it was a Ponderosa pine, but I didn't think Ponderosa grew there and concluded it was more likely Englemann spruce. In any case, he went through the steps to make a let-down with his 100-foot rope. When ready, he popped his single-point-release, slipped out of his harness, and smoothly slid down the rope. When he was about three-quarters of the way down, much to his horror, he could see the rope was not long enough to reach the ground. It wasn't just a matter of three or four feet, it was 30 or 40 feet, much too far to drop.

He easily stopped his descent, but solving the problem was another matter. He couldn't climb back up the rope. It was too long a pull, particularly with the weight of his jump gear. He figured he could follow a branch to the trunk of the tree, but there were no branches below 30 feet and the trunk was too large to slide down. He figured his only recourse was to climb back up through the branches to his parachute and untie his let-down rope. He did that, but it took a long time. In the process of retrieving the let-down rope his harness and emergency chute fell to the ground.

No matter, he had retrieved the rope and could now start to climb back down the tree. Meanwhile the fire burned beneath him, but fortunately did not crown. It doesn't take an imagination to figure what would have happened to him if it had. When he climbed down enough to be certain the rope would reach the ground, he tied it to a stout branch and descended the rope. This time he made it down and quickly ran over hot ground to safety.

Paul Dennison was the foreman, and he and the other jumpers were extremely glad to see he was okay. They feared he wasn't.

Bill showed me the stump of the tree in which he had landed. It had been felled in order to retrieve his parachute after the fire was controlled. We looked in the ashes next to the stump and found numerous buckles and snaps—all that was left of Bill's emergency chute and harness.

*   *   *

Sunday, September 13, 1953

Dear Ma,

Now that I've written the date I realize I wrote you a letter a few days ago; nothing much has happened since. Yesterday we had a wind storm that just about moved the mountain. I was looking for smokes in the middle of the burn when it started to blow. Snags were dropping faster than I could count them. I got out in a big hurry.

We were really living for a couple of days as far as grub was concerned. It was nothing real fancy and a person who's used to home cooked meals would probably look down on it, but to us it was nothing short of manna from heaven. It lasted two days, then flies blew the meat—bears got the rest.

I came up to the top of the burn today—what a pretty view. I can see the whole valley. Below is a little clearing full of charred stumps and trails where five tent flies are strung—home. I've been here for a long time watching the smoke curl up from the stove in camp. Way down the valley to the left I can see Big Salmon Lake and the stream going to it, the same one running by our campsite. Even though the lake is five or six miles away, it feels like I could throw a rock to it. On different places on the opposite mountain I can see long, narrow, bright green strips. They are brush fields which resulted after massive snow slides plowed up any tree in the avalanche path. On the right are big, high barren peaks covered with snow. It's getting dirty now because it hasn't snowed for a week.

A couple of fellows came by last night on horse back. They were going to Big Salmon Lake to do some fishing. Most of our group was pretty happy because the fishermen offered three shots of whiskey to each of us. I passed, but was delighted when they gave each of us a big chocolate bar.

Well, the three of us have decided to leave this coming Friday morning. We're going to strike out at dawn. You keep an eye peeled for these letters around Tuesday of next week.

I have to mosey on down the mountain now.

Love, R.

Sunday, September 20, 1953

Dear Ma,

Hooray, we're long gone from the Tango Fire, but say did we ever have a couple of hair raising experiences the last few days we were there. Bill H. and I were on the fire together and David and Bill C. were poking around the burn somewhere. The only guy in camp was Bruce, and he was fixing dinner for the crew. He was sitting under a tent fly involved in culinary chores when a grizzly cub approached, but Bruce didn't notice until it was almost up to him. He jumped and looked around and there was mama and another cub. The sow scooted the cubs away and came at Bruce. In those few seconds Bruce had grabbed his thirty-ought-six and blasted her one. She rolled over backwards and took-off at a run.

Grizzlies are notorious for their protection of their cubs. If you should wound a grizzly cub, the sow will likely fight until somebody loses.

Anyway, Bill and I heard the shot and came cautiously down to camp. I walked up behind Bruce who was kneeling and looking into the brush with his rifle in hand. I was going to growl, but decided I wouldn't look good with a bullet hole in my chest. Bruce was visibly shaking and I was quite concerned because he's always so cool about things. I guess anybody would have been rattled after what he had just been through.

The three of us started following the trail of blood into the brush and trees. One gun was hardly enough, but we all had eyes and ears, and we stayed close together and moved slowly. Of course, it's pretty hard to shoot a bear with an eye or an ear, but we could help Bruce find his target. For about a mile we tracked the blood trail. We all expected that bear to come pouncing on us at any moment. Then we heard a tremendous roar and growl. Bruce figured she was kicking-off out there somewhere. It was quiet for a few minutes and then I saw a bear's head off to our left about 25 yards away. Bill saw it, too, but not Bruce. Bruce had ejected a 150 grain shell and was trying to replace it with 180 grain round in order to have more shocking power. It should have been easily done, but he was shaking so badly he was having difficulty getting the round into the chamber. Finally he did it, saw the bear stick its head up from behind a log, took aim and fired. The head promptly dropped behind the log.

Later we found it to be only a cub, but it hardly seemed possible because his head had seemed so big. We all thought he was shooting at a full grown bear. The next day Bruce was right up close to the other cub. Had the sow been alive she would have been there, too. The whole affair was really very sad, but we were glad to be able to rationalize a wounded sow wasn't roaming about.

Friday, our last day there, Bill H. bumped into a pair of cubs as he was returning from his patrol of the far side of the burn. He evidently got a head start on the sow and started running along the fireline in the creek bottom towards our camp. He was one scared kid. He said he didn't have time to climb a tree. A man can't outrun a bear, but the fireline had several very sharp turns, and the bear must have lost interest when she couldn't see her target. Bill and Bruce went back after the incident and found her claw marks on the ground and could easily determine she had turned around. That made two close calls for Bill on the Tango Fire.

We had intended to leave on Friday morning, but were talked into putting in another shift. We agreed, but decided we wouldn't wait until Saturday to walk out—we would leave at 4:00 p.m. on Friday. Boy, I've never been so glad to leave a place. We knew we'd never make it to Holland Lake before dark, but we could get to Holland Pass by nightfall. We had 35 pound packs and really set a pace. Did you ever stop to think about walking, and how slow it is? All you can do is 30 to 40 inches in a stride. Eighteen miles is a long way when you just make 30 or 40 inches at a time.

Does the word "pass" conjure an exciting and romantic feeling for you? It does for me. It also smacks of adventure and intrigue. Anyway, just before we reached Holland Pass we came to a small lake. The wind was blowing up a storm, the clouds were black, the air was cold and the sun was just visible between two mountains. Standing in the water by the edge of the lake were two elk—a bull and a cow. It was impressive.

After going through Holland Pass, elevation 6,660 feet, we figured we had climbed about 2,000 feet since leaving camp. In short order we arrived at Upper Holland Lake. It was 7:30 p.m. It had taken us three-and-one-half hours to cover 12½ miles, and it had all been uphill. From there out it was all downhill, and it was a good thing because our legs were tired from walking so fast. After a bite to eat we made the final spurt to Holland Lake. We could hear a bear plowing his way through the brush somewhere along the way.

At 9:00 p.m. we arrived at Holland Lake and eagerly climbed into Bill's car.

Today is Sunday and I'm on standby to jump. I'm supposed to work in the halls [at college] *tomorrow, so I shouldn't go.*

Love, R.

CHAPTER 11

Fall Fires

As it turned out, I didn't jump again before school started. Most of the guys had gone back to college or other jobs and the smokejumper project all but closed down. It was good see my school friends and to begin classes. Since it was my last year, I had all the basic courses out of the way and was taking advanced forestry courses including forest utilization, valuation, and logging.

The forestry curriculum was so heavily laden with science and forestry courses that we really didn't get a very broad education. For the first time in my college experience I had room for an elective and decided to take something completely foreign to forestry—sociology. I don't know why I leaned in that direction unless it was because an aptitude tests I had taken in high school indicated sociology was a subject fitting my profile.

I quickly settled into a routine with my classes and part-time jobs. Anytime I had a block of two hours free, I could work for Mr. Woolfolk at the federal building mounting plant specimens. Some of the plants had been gathered the year I worked at Ft. Keogh and had been sent back to Washington, D.C. for positive identification by skilled taxonomists. There were hundreds of specimens, but they were of little value stored in cabinets between blotters and newspaper.

I would mount each specimen on 11" x 16" heavy white card stock with rubber cement, and then glue the identification label in an open corner. Finally, each one was inserted in a clear plastic jacket and filed systematically in the herbarium. It was an enjoyable project and the resulting collection was a tangible, useful product. My work in range research was always rewarding.

Ted and I continued to live in Craig Hall and eat at Corbin. I was a checker at the evening meal, recording those who ate and preventing unauthorized persons from crashing the line. I was also a resident assistant (RA) for my wing of Craig Hall. It usually didn't involve much, but during certain hours I was responsible for maintaining a quiet atmosphere.

Evidently I asked my mother to send me copies of two letters I had written to her about fires. It prompted the following letter:

Monday, October 5, 1953

Dear Roverboy,

I am sending you the two jumps you want, also a copy of the three letters you mailed at the same time about that 700 acre clean up job [Tango Cabin Fire]. *I feel hesitant about sending them after the way those first ones affected you, but since I am hoping that you want them to complete a most thrilling and wonderful summer story, I will let you have them.* [Unfortunately I can't recall why I requested the letters or why I was affected by some she had sent earlier.] *That is why I'm putting in those last three, for they complete the summer story. I bet you could make a grand magazine article from them. But if you do, you need the account of your first practice jump of last year and the rescue jump, also. I am even copying what you wrote when you got overtired and depressed and don't you dare let it bother you. Life is not all high-mountain two-manners, and if you were happy and on top of the world all the time it would be a NOT TRUE TO LIFE story. The sunshine afterwards shows up all the brighter because of those dark hours. O.K., Senior? O.K.?*

Love, Mother

It was uncommon for my mother to lecture or council me, but in this instance she would not let it pass. I thought it interesting that she not only thought about "high-mountain two-manners" but she had internalized the term and could easily use it as a metaphor to more clearly make her point. She was also suggesting to me that a high-mountain two-manner could simply be a state of mind.

*   *   *

My ninth fire of the season was described in detail in a letter to my mother on Sunday, October 11. I rewrote the account by combining the letter with information from newspaper articles, the dispatcher's records at the smokejumper loft, my diary, and my personal recollection.

In early October snows ushered in the hunting season. The woods were full of hunters and their camping fires, and many were left unattended. When the weather warmed and the snow melted, many of these fires started to creep. A check of the smokejumper records showed this phenomenon started on October 6 and ended October 15. During this 10-day span, 24 fires on the Lolo, Bitterroot, Clearwater and Nez Perce National Forests were manned by jumpers.

I had been back at the university for several days when a message came from the loft that jumpers were needed. I returned the call Wednesday morning, October 7, and was told several requests for smokejumpers had been refused because men weren't available. The Austin brothers, Jim and Dick, had also reported their availability, so the three of us were put on the jump list. In the meantime I continued to attend classes. At 4:00 p.m. the fire call came and since Hale Field was near the university, it didn't take long for me to get there. While I was suiting-up I asked Fred Brauer, "How big is the fire?"

He answered rather dryly, "Three acres."

Then I asked, "How many men are going?"

"One crew is going and you're it," he replied without the slightest hint of a smile.

Everyone knew the minimum size crew was two men, but even that seemed light for three acres. Fred was a great kidder and I decided to string along with his obvious banter. "Great, just send me with a big lunch," I replied rather cockily.

Since the Austins were also suiting-up, I thought the three of us were headed to the same fire. I should have suspected differently when Fred gave a map case to one of the Austin brothers as well as to me because customarily it was only issued to the leader. The three of us climbed into a Ford Trimotor with our spotter, Al Hammond, and at 4:45 p.m. lifted off the dirt runway and headed southwest in the direction of the Selway-Bitterroot Primitive Area. It wasn't a long flight, but we passed six fires on the way—all man-caused. In the last week 56 fires had been started in Idaho from hunters' abandoned campfires.

It was close to 5:00 p.m. when we flew over our fire. The evening air had settled; smoke was hanging low over Marion Meadows. The area was good elk hunting country and the meadow seemed a likely place for hunters to have camped.

Several things appeared in our favor—a big, open jump spot, light wind, lots of water, and level ground. Fighting fire on level ground was to be a first for me. Al said, "OK, Frank, this one's for you." Now it was clear that the three of us were not jumping together.

As the pilot made a pass over the fire, Al threw out a drift chute to check the wind's speed and direction. We knew from the smoke what it was like close to the ground, but we had to know if the wind aloft was different. It wasn't.

No question I was going to jump, but I regarded it ambivalently. Although I was pleased to have been judged capable of fighting a fire alone, I wasn't entirely convinced that going alone was such a great idea—after all, no fewer than two jumpers were ever sent on a fire. I didn't know at the time that Forest Service history was rife with examples of men who had been dispatched singly from ranger districts to small fires, so my going alone was unusual only in the sense that it was not usual smokejumper policy.[12]

As we banked for the final approach, Al yelled above the engine noise, "WE'VE GOT TO MAKE THIS QUICK. WHEN YOU LAND, IF YOU'RE OK, DON'T TAKE THE TIME TO SET A SIGNAL ON THE GROUND—JUST WAVE SO I CAN TAKE THESE TWO GUYS TO THEIR FIRE BEFORE IT GETS DARK."

It wasn't a situation permitting debate. As I approached the door I said, "OK, BUT I DON'T HAVE A PRAYER FOR GETTING THIS OUT IN TWO DAYS. I'LL GO IF YOU PROMISE TO DROP ME A WHOLE CASE OF C-RATIONS." I was concerned because several times during the summer I had experienced working with a short food supply. When he readily agreed I also requested a marine pump since the stream in the meadow appeared to have ample water and the fire was extensive enough to warrant one. He agreed to drop one the next day and to try to get more men.

The plane leveled out and Al made one last check of the harness snaps clipped to my parachute, checked my static line, and directed me to the open door. I gripped the sides of the opening and put my right foot onto the step outside the plane and knelt on my left knee. The air blast from the prop-wash made this maneuver awkward.

I watched ahead at the meadow and knew it was large enough so there would be no problem landing in it. Al's head protruded out the small window next to the door. He was also watching the meadow while using his left hand to give signals to the pilot so he could fly with precision to the jump spot. Al

---

[12]   In Norman Maclean's book, *Young Men and Fire,* he states that a smokejumper is never sent alone to a fire. Although generally true, there are exceptions. Martin Onishuk and Bob Nicol each jumped alone to a fire on the same day I did. Len Krout and Herb Oertli also jumped alone five days later. I have no information on solo jumps that may have been made in other years.

gave a signal, the pilot cut his engines, and I stiffened in anticipation of the signal to jump. The roar from the engines stopped, the plane started to glide, and Al slapped me on the shoulder.

The jump was routine—at least until I hit the ground. Instead of the usual "thud," I landed with a "splash." I was in water over my boots. I shed my harness and chute and got out an orange streamer (crepe paper about one foot by 12 feet) to signal Al. The pilot had circled and descended to almost tree top level. I waved the streamer as Al kicked out a cargo chute with my fire-pack and waved back to me.

The plane quickly disappeared over the tree tops and I was engulfed in a world of silence. I looked at my watch while retrieving the fire pack—5:15 p.m. It seemed almost impossible that just a little over an hour ago I was sitting in a lecture hall at the university. I hadn't looked at my map, so I had no idea where, or how far away, the nearest road was.

I started breaking up hot spots, exposing them to the cool, evening air, but didn't linger in one place because I needed to assess the entire fire situation before dark. The grass in the open meadow was essentially out, but numerous scattered lodgepole snags were smoking or flaming—a potential threat to spread. The fire had crept to the edge of the meadow and was beginning to work its way into the heavy timber on the fringe. Fortunately, the breeze was blowing the fire across the wet meadow and not into the waiting timber.

At the hottest area I tried to dig a fireline, but the duff was eight to 10 inches deep and so interlaced with roots that the time and effort required to reach mineral soil made this approach impractical. I had hoped to dig firelines around the hotter portions of the fire and secure them to those areas that had burned and gone cold, but all I could do for the present was to slow its spread. I worked from one side of the fire to the other trying to knock it down. To prevent the fire from crowning, I'd rapidly move from one chore to the next. I'd fell a snag with my Pulaski, limb a few trees, and cut some brush. The ground was damp, so if the fire was confined there, it crept slowly or smoldered.

I decided my time would be best spent working with the hand pump—a five-gallon canvas bag that rode on my back. A short hose extended from the bottom of the bag to a hand pump that was activated by a sliding motion, in trombone fashion, to produce a small stream of pressurized water.

Since the perimeter of the fire was "L" shaped, and I was at one end of the "L" and my gear was stashed at the other, it seemed logical to take a shortcut across the unburned area. As I walked, it seemed the ground was moving under my feet. At first I thought it was dizziness. It was like walking on a mattress—no matter where I stepped the ground was sloping toward me from every direction for a radius of 12 feet or so.

I then realized that under the thin sod layer was water—or soupy mud. I tried to backtrack but suddenly broke through the sod and instantly sank to my knees. I involuntarily yelled "Hey!" as I continued to sink slowly in the muck. I remember having a mental picture of rescuers finding my hard hat setting on top of the sod with no sign of me.

As I struggled to move my legs, a coyote howled in the distance—as if to put my feeble call for help in perspective. I dropped the shovel and leaned forward as I chopped downward with the digging end of the Pulaski. I was then able to pull myself to a prone position on top of the sod and carefully creep to firm ground, feeling both relieved and ridiculous. I had a lingering sense that nature was ready to punish me if I made a mistake.

As I walked the rest of the way to my gear, I mulled over this thought and concluded no mystical force was pitted against me, but I could indeed be hurt if not careful—an unwelcome fate at any time, but potentially disastrous if alone. I resolved to continually and deliberately weigh options and minimize risks.

I filled the five-gallon canvas bag and began to spray the hottest spots. After a few pumps, I used my shovel or Pulaski to spread the burning material and, where possible, mixed it with mineral soil—a difficult task in many places because of the deep duff layer. The night air became much cooler and I knew the more hot spots I opened up the greater chance they would cool and die before morning. While doing this I used the flashlight on my helmet sparingly to conserve the batteries.

I made numerous trips back to the stream to refill the bag, and because the nature of a canvas bag was to drip, my back and legs were soaked. At 10:00 p.m. I had just spread a hot spot, sprayed it with water, and dropped the pump handle so I could use both hands on the shovel. In the heavily shadowed firelight I tripped. As I fell, the pump handle caught on something and ripped free of the bag. Water gushed down the backs of my legs and into my boots. "DAMN!" The expletive ricocheted in my mind for a long time as I continued to work deep into the night.

Except for an occasional pop from a hot spot, or the distant intermittent howls from coyotes, it was remarkably quiet. Even a small sound seemed to magnify and captivate my attention. I found myself moving an arm or shaking a leg in an attempt to reproduce any strange sound, confirming I had made it. Tiredness had set in as my adrenalin flow subsided. My actions were somewhat bizarre, but I made no effort to control them. I wasn't frightened, just unaccustomed to working alone and needed to verify that nothing besides God and me was roaming about.

I hoped the snags would burn out in the night air, but they didn't. It seemed likely when the sun came up, and the day warmed, they would spit sparks that could drift into the heavy stands of unburned timber and brush. They had to come down. The bad news—I didn't have a saw; the good news—most of the trees had diameters of 10 inches or less. Some of them were almost burned in two at the base. A few chops with my Pulaski and a push was all it took for many to topple. I came upon a lodgepole a bit larger than the ones I had dropped—about 12 inches at breast height. The base was black from fire, but solid. It forked about 15 feet up and was spitting sparks and snorting smoke. When I tapped the Pulaski against the trunk, sparks and fine chunks of charcoal gently showered from the upper portions of the snag. "Whomp!" I jumped back instinctively. A large portion of the top slammed to the ground next to me without warning. It shook me so profoundly I couldn't have dropped another snag even if I'd been dumb enough to try. Obviously my "playing it smart" didn't earn a high grade.

It was common practice the first night on a fire to work until it was controlled, but under the circumstances I could do little until daylight, so I returned to the spot where my gear was stashed. The air was perfectly calm and the smoke stagnated over the meadow. If I stood erect, my head was in smoke, but if I bent over, it was clear. I had never experienced this strange stratification of smoke since fires on a slope just didn't act that way.

My clothes were still damp from the canvas bag and perspiration. I laid the paper sleeping bag on the piece of canvas that had covered my fire pack. Then I stuffed my parachute in the bag and mounded the cargo chute on top. I took off my wet clothes and gingerly slipped in between the folds of the cold nylon until my feet reached the bottom of the sleeping bag. I soon warmed up, but could not sleep. Each time I started to doze the cacophony of coyotes' howls drove any vestige of sleep away. I was satisfied, however, just to lie in comfort and think about the unique day and what tomorrow might bring . . .

*　*　*

I awoke with the first grey light of morning. I hated putting on my damp clothes, but did it hastily and built up my camp fire. I had figured how to get the remainder of the snags down safely and was anxious to do it before they became an active threat.

I took the 100-foot rope from the large pocket in the leg of my jump suit, and threw one end over a branch stub 12 feet up the snag. After tying a slip knot in the loop, I pulled on the rope forcing the knot to slide up to the stub. Then I jerked on the rope from a point as far away as it would reach. I did this until the snag whipped vigorously and one of the burning forks snapped and crashed to the ground in a spray of sparks. I chopped the rest of the tree down.

I repeated this procedure for the remaining snags. Not all of them had tops or branches that broke off, but I figured the test was adequate to deem them safe to chop down whether something broke off or not.

About 7:00 the Ford Trimotor came to drop a marine pump. I had put out the "H" signal with orange streamers to mark the cargo drop spot. When the cargo chute hit the wet meadow, I slogged to it and found a "message dropper" attached to the cargo package. I took it off and read, "Only one more man is available."

I sat on the pump box and waited for the plane to return and give me a parting wave. I was staring at Al's note, disappointed that he gave no time-frame for the arrival of help, when suddenly the Ford shot into the clearing just over the trees. I could see another load of cargo perched in the door, but it was too late to get out of the way, so I frantically waved my arms. The pilot or Al must have seen me because the cargo landed a hundred feet beyond the spot. I hastily moved out of the way and watched as three more passes were made. I should have realized it would take several passes to drop the pump, accessory box, gas, oil, and 1,200 feet of inch-and-a-half linen hose. When the plane finally left I retrieved the items essential to operate the pump and began setting it up by the stream.

The pump was described as a "Type Y, Pacific Marine Pump." Compared to pumps used today it was not user friendly. A printed list of steps had to be strictly followed or it wouldn't run.

While I had been briefly trained to operate this type of pump, I had never used one on a fire. I began reading the manual. It didn't take me long to realize two things. This model was different from any I had seen before, and flames had started to flare-up in several locations—a response to the warming sun. I was tempted to knock the hot spots down, but getting the pump to work was a higher priority. The manual read, "Put oil in the pilot gear," but I couldn't find it. "Put mixed gas and oil in gas tank." Hell, I couldn't even find that! On the model used in training its location was obvious, but not on this renegade.

It must have been a ludicrous sight—me sitting there reading the manual, licking my thumb to turn another page, and the fire racing through the crown of another tree. I finally moved a lever, revealing a chamber I thought surely had to be the gas tank. I poured in about half a gallon of fuel. It appeared sufficient to fill the tank, but didn't. No matter. I hooked up the intake and outtake hoses, adjusted several cocks and knobs and tried to start the engine. No good. It seemed to have a mind of its own, refusing to run no matter what. I even tried talking nice, but my cajoling made no difference—it refused to belch even a little blue smoke.

Noticing there wasn't gas in the carburetor, I poured some directly into it and tried again. At last it fired. "Ah ha!, it's not getting gas," I said jubilantly. I began to follow the gas line back from the carburetor when the Ford flew over again and dropped another jumper, Joe Blackburn.

Joe was a college classmate who, like me, was playing hooky. While he got his jump-suit off and retrieved his fire pack, I found that the gas line to the carburetor was open ended—that is, a separate gas tank needed to be attached. The gas tank was an integral part of the pumps I had previously seen, so I hadn't even considered this possibility. I found one in the accessory box and attached it as Joe joined in. He said that what I previously thought was the gas tank was the pilot gear, so he dumped some oil into it. We both saw an expanding oil slick on the ground and realized the oil Joe had poured into the "pilot gear" was coming out the exhaust port (just as the gas mixture I had earlier poured into the same chamber had done).

At last Joe found the correct location of the pilot gear, added oil and started the engine. He threw the lever to direct water through the linen hose. I had 800 feet laid out and ran to grab the nozzle at the far end as the water raced me to it. I lost. I had almost reached the nozzle when the hose stiffened and began to whip around like a gigantic snake. I dove for it and missed, and scrambled for cover behind a tree. I don't remember how my adversary was finally subdued, but do remember it was none too soon. The fire roared as it raced through the crown of another tree, but its ferocity was tamed when I directed a stream of water to it. As quickly as the crown fire died, so did the pump.

When I went back to see what was the matter, Joe was moving the pump. It had been obvious that the stream was not rapidly flowing, but it was three to four feet deep—at least we thought so. Now it was apparent that only the top few inches of the stream were free flowing. The pump had sucked the water from a small basin quicker than it could be replaced, and for this reason we had to move the pump several times. We took turns operating the nozzle and we had to actually stick it into the root laced duff and saturate the ground a foot under the surface. The pressurized water would frequently gush back from the ground like a geyser. We were continually wet, but we felt good about our progress.

We soon realized, however, we had wasted a lot of oil in our earlier efforts to get the pump started and we didn't have enough to mix with gasoline to finish the job. We wrote "OIL" with our orange streamers in the cargo drop area. Fortunately a plane came over and got our message—we knew he had because he rocked his wings in the familiar sign of understanding. Later in the day the plane returned, not only honoring our most recent request, but also my earlier one for a case of C-rations.

We were well fortified with oil for the pump and food for our bellies and ready to stay as long as it took to declare the fire out. As it turned out, the size of the fire was closer to four acres instead of three, and before we left we had crawled over all of it to be certain it was cold to the touch.

We left the fire at noon on Saturday. It was only about a five mile walk to Savage Pass where we hooked up the crank telephone and called Powell Ranger Station for a ride back to Missoula. I knew Wag Dodge was the dispatcher at Powell and was hoping he would be at the station because I had heard so much about him. He was the foreman on the Mann Gulch Fire where 12 smokejumpers and a smokechaser were killed on August 5, 1949. I had hoped to meet him earlier when we came off the Battle Ridge Fire, but it was so late I didn't even remember stopping at Powell.

This time, however, Joe and I did stop. Wag checked over our fire report and questioned us about the work time we had recorded. At first I thought he was going to make some reductions, but he didn't. I wouldn't say he padded our tabulation, but he added a half hour here and there based on what we had told him. He mentioned how unusual it was for a smokejumper to jump alone, but added that several others fires on the Powell District were also manned by a single jumper. He was a friendly, soft-spoken fellow and seemed to genuinely appreciate our help in getting the rash of fires out on his district.

On the trip to school we talked about how strange it was to end the fire season so late in the fall.

*   *   *

It turned out that I would feel stranger yet because the fire season was not over. Seven fires had been manned by smokejumpers since my last one, and requests for jumpers were still coming in.

My mother wrote on the top of my next letter:

Maybe sometime these smokjumping letters will stop. Frank seems to think this is the last. It was the twenty-fifth jump he made, counting last year's and the practice jumps. This makes two after school opened—the same as last year.

Jump #10 for 1953. Tuesday, October 20, 1953

Dear Ma,

When I went to work at the Forest Service on Wednesday [October 14] *I was told to call the loft. They wanted me right away, so I rushed back to the dorm to change my clothes.*

[My logger boots were worn out from a hard summer's use and were unusable for a long walk back from a fire. The stitching holding the tops to the sole was separated in several places. I still had my low quarters (shoes) that were part of my Air Force ROTC uniform, and since they were comfortable I decided to carry them in my personal gear bag in case I needed them to hike back from the fire. I wouldn't be allowed to jump without boots, and I hoped no one would notice that mine were not up to standard.]

When I arrived at the loft I learned that the fire was named Horse Creek and was on the Nez Perce National Forest in Idaho. Also, it was supposed to be going over the hill. Three ground pounders were on it and had a radio. They had called for help. Four of us left in the Ford with Paul Dennison in charge. He was in charge on my first and fifth jumps this year. Remember?

[Except for Paul, we were all forestry students. Fritz Wolfrum and Harlon Hayes were both starting their sophomore year. Harlon and I had trained together in 1952, and Fritz was the only new man, although at this stage of the season he was certainly not a novice.

The fire request was received at 12:35, but it took almost two-and-a-half hours to get the crew together, so we were getting a late start.]

We flew for a heck of a long time and we all began to feel that we'd never get there, but we did and the fire didn't look bad at all. The jump spot opportunity was another matter—the choices were all awful. I wanted to jump right by the fire, but didn't express myself because it is so tough to converse above the noise of the engines—it wasn't worth the effort. Besides, the spotter, Paul Wilson, and our foreman, Paul Dennison, knew a lot more about picking a spot than I did. They decided on one near the creek bottom a half-mile from the fire, and we all put on our helmets. I had been sitting on mine and crushed it a little—not much, but enough to make my head mighty uncomfortable when I squeezed into it. Fritz was in real agony. He had to relieve himself in the worst way, but couldn't do anything except tough it out.

We took a low pass over the jump spot and conditions weren't very encouraging. I asked Paul D. if we were jumping two on a stick. He took another look out the door and said, "I guess not." I was relieved because I sure didn't want the two of us pulling for the same little spot increasing the risk of a midair collision.

Paul was in the door ready to go on three separate passes over the jump spot, but didn't jump. The pilot was flying the wrong pattern. My head was about to split and poor Fritz was . . . well, grinding teeth. Finally Paul went and did well enough—he hung up in a tree a few feet off the ground.

I got ready and felt fully relaxed. I watched the ground and the fire up ahead out of the door. The prop wash was blowing in my face. It felt good. There was little wind so Paul let me out right over the jump spot. I was anxious to get my helmet off and when I got the signal to jump I leaped forward instead of simply jumping off the step—as if that would put me on the ground sooner. Later Fritz said he never saw a guy go so far out before he dropped. I don't know if my indiscretion contributed to the shock that racked me when the chute opened or not, but I had never before felt it so severely. My body seemed to be in two pieces, but of course it wasn't.

When I got close to the ground I became concerned with the terrain. There were trees over 100 feet tall, snags, down logs, and tall stumps—that were actually broken trees. I would have hung up except the trees were too tall to mess with [meaning I didn't want to have to retrieve my parachute from high in a tree]. I guided for a clearing on the side of the hill and pulled hard to get the distance I needed. I came down right between two broken-off trees and landed right next to one. Oh, I was glad to get up and find I was O.K.

Harlan jumped on the next pass and hung up in a tree about 40 feet off the ground. When Fritz jumped he ended up hitting the tallest tree there. It swayed ten feet when he hit it. It seemed to me it could have been avoided, but I felt sorry for him. If one of us needed to land on the ground, it was he. It took him a half-hour to make his let-down. He was obviously having some difficulty or it would only have taken a few minutes.

[We had jumped at 4:30 p.m. and it was an hour before we had retrieved our fire packs and reached the fire. The fire had several hot spots but was not running and the ground pounders had made a good start at getting a line around a portion of it. We pitched in and aggressively built fire line into the night. By 11:00 p.m. Paul declared it controlled. We stayed there mopping up the next day and part of the next, but then left the patrolling to the ground pounders. I must have been pressed to get back to my school work because I concluded the account of the fire to my mother with:]

The fire wasn't bad and I think I'll leave it at that.

[What I failed to mention to my mother was the difficulty I had by wearing my ROTC shoes for the hike out. The fire was about six air miles south of Selway Falls. Although the walk out may have been a little longer, it wasn't difficult, and we didn't have to pack out any of our equipment. My shoes felt comfortable and I was doing fine, but eventually the top of both big toes began to sting. I stopped and put Band-Aids on the sensitive areas, but my efforts did not entirely correct the problem. By the time we reached a road I knew it wasn't a very bright thing for me to have done, and my feet were a long time healing. My letter concluded:]

I find school difficult, but challenging and enjoyable. I've never been so dog gone busy. I leave the room at 7:45 a.m. and don't return until after 8:00 p.m., except for fifteen minutes at noon. All this time is taken by classes, my jobs, or meetings. My studies are suffering terribly from having been gone on fires.

Love, R.

The dispatcher's records at the smokejumper loft show two missions after the Horse Creek Fire, one a rescue and one a fire—both on October 15. The season finally ended.

CHAPTER 12

Senior Year

It may not have been advisable to continue jumping after classes began, but my thought processes were tainted by emotion. I could rationalize I needed the money, but I would have made it through school one way or another without the additional income. But the excitement of smokejumping was almost an addiction, one not easily ignored. Each jump was an adventure that seemed to sharpen my senses for greater enjoyment of other aspects of my life.

I also thought about the fact that when a fire started in some remote corner of the wilderness and smokejumpers were needed, only a handful of us could be called upon—especially late in the fall. I felt a certain pride in being one of them. It was special in a way that has not been repeated in my life.

Those after-school-fires put me behind in my class work, but several of my classmates had similarly jumped. The forestry school professors were helpful in providing us with the material we had missed and my sociology professor shared in that consideration. I enthusiastically began my studies.

The '37 Ford was sick. It would run but had little power, so Ted and I decided to get rid of it. Mr. Woolfolk said he had a '39 Ford I could have for $200. Although he never revealed how he just happened to have a car available when one was needed, it seems obvious he was simply looking after me. His kindnesses were unending, but despite his interest in my welfare, he was never over-bearing with his thoughts concerning my career decisions. There may have been others who were assisted by such a mentor/benefactor, but they were not obvious. I was indeed fortunate.

The '39 Ford's body was tight, it ran smoothly, and had hydraulic brakes—an important feature after our experience with the previous Ford. Again we bought it jointly. In the two years we owned a car together we never argued over its use, or who would drive if we were both in it. And we never had insurance. I expect this arrangement was unwise, but at the time it seemed workable and reasonable. Such is the nature of college-age guys who are good friends.

During my senior year I was president of the Wesley Foundation. The group always had a large membership and was well organized, so the workload was fortunately distributed among many. My job was one of coordination and follow-up. The cooperation and enthusiasm of the members made the job enjoyable.

I ended Fall quarter with a GPA a little above a 3-point. It was gratifying, especially the "A" in sociology.

* * *

It makes me a little sad when someone tells me they didn't enjoy college life. If asked how I regarded my four year's at the "U," it was easy to run off a litany of positive descriptors. But if asked to explain why I felt all those things, it would be difficult to verbalize a simple answer. It was a hundred little things—things like the school traditions: the participation in saying hello to anyone you met on "Hello Walk;" the gathering at SOS (singing on the steps) at the front of Main Hall after dark following every home football game—where we would sing school songs and our state songs; and the participation in Aber Day (named after a retired prof) where the entire campus would engage in a massive spring clean-up and share in a buffalo barbeque cooked over an open pit dug temporarily in the lawn, and students were prosecuted in kangaroo courts.

I liked the trees on campus: the elms that graced the oval; the lindens that lined the sidewalk in front of New Hall; and that single gingko that flourished on campus but was hard to find elsewhere. I liked the big chunk of rock that protruded through the lawn in the oval and the towering spruce and cottonwood trees spread across the lush campus.

I appreciated our occasional trips to "Brownie's In-and-Out" for after-study-hamburgers, and the many late night walks with Ted as we harmonized all the songs we knew. I liked being on a small campus where no one routinely gazed into a strange face. My friends were numerous and I appreciated the things we shared. And, of course, intricately laced through all this were my feelings for Corky. She brought an abiding sweetness.

* * *

When winter quarter started, my schedule allowed another elective. A philosophy or humanities course was my first choice, but neither fit well into my schedule, so I settled on psychology. My other three courses were in advanced forestry: forest management, economics of forestry, and forest engineering. I never liked economics courses, but was eager for the other two.

Six quarters of PE were needed to earn a degree, and one of them had to be in swimming. It was University policy for all graduates to be able to swim. For those who had difficulty fitting a swimming class into their schedule, the PE department allowed proof of swimming ability to be shown through a test. I was one of those, and easily passed.

My most devastating experience in college occurred in the forest engineering class. Jim Faurot, our instructor, explained that engineering was a very exact science, and answers to problems were either right or wrong. There would be no consideration given to understanding the process; only the final outcome determined success or failure. He further stated there would be no final and that four tests would be given during the quarter, each one having equal weight. The average of these tests would determine the final grade.

I liked the instructor and learning how to design roads, and felt I could do well in the class. However, in the first test I only carried my answers four places to the right of the decimal point; we were supposed to carry them five. As a result, my test score was zero. It mattered not that the problems were otherwise worked correctly.

That meant it would take a combination of "As" and "Bs" on the remainder of the tests just to make a "D" in the course. Even though Jim had clearly announced how grades would be determined, I could scarcely believe that so early in the course I was doomed to a substandard performance. If there was a lesson to be learned in the need to be accurate, this seemed extremely harsh. I had no recourse other than to bear the burden. The load was staggering.

*　　*　　*

Meanwhile the Foresters' Ball rapidly approached, and as seniors we provided the leadership for the event. Several articles appeared in the Kaimin that reflected the campus interest:

Alert Foresters Foil Intrigue

Over 100 hours have elapsed since the disappearance of 25-year-old Bertha, beloved mascot of the Forestry club—and still no word from the 'napper as to her whereabouts.

With the Foresters' ball only 36 hours away, the campus is growing anxious as to whether she will be returned in time for the big celebration.

John Lowell, chief push of the Foresters, told the Kaimin Thursday afternoon that they have leads as to who "moose-napped" her. However, they still have not been able to locate the head.

Bertha disappeared from the Forestry school some time Sunday night. At the same time the nose-piece of Babe, the blue ox, also was discovered missing.

The "moose-napper" contacted the Kaimin and has left clues daily. Monday he threatened to cut off Bertha's antlers. Tuesday's rumors were that her hair was going to be burned. Wednesday evening the nose-piece was impounded by Missoula city police on six misdemeanor counts.

Thursday morning before Judge William Logan the Foresters obtained custody of the nose. But with all this going on—still no word from Bertha.

Shortly before dawn Thursday, the Foresters captured Jim Ryan, high potentate of Kams and Dregs [an organization in the Law school], *and five Kams as they were in the process of painting schmoes and Kilroys on the Forestry building.*

Joan Brooks, one of the Kams captured in the surprise move of the Foresters, related the terrifying experiences of her few hours of captivity. The girls were painted with a rainbow of colors, pushed through cold showers, and then "driven" to the Student Union and displayed to the early-hour breakfast crowd.

The Kaimin reported a steady stream of articles about the ball and the pranks exchanged between the lawyers and foresters. Then an article appeared that put this ball in a class above those of the past:

Life Will Cover Forester's Ball

Life, national magazine, will cover the Forester's Ball Saturday on the Montana State University campus.

N. R. Farbman, Life staff photographer from San Francisco, and Charles Champlin, Denver Correspondent, will arrive on Wednesday. They will cover the Men's Gym decorating, beginning Wednesday night; beard judging contest Saturday afternoon; awarding of prizes for beards and costumes at the ball, and the ball.

Tickets were sold out Tuesday afternoon. Sales started Monday after the tracks of Paul Bunyan, and Babe, the blue ox, appeared on downtown streets and on the campus.

The Forester's Ball is the largest all-school dance on campus and the largest of its kind in the country. It is sponsored by the forestry students. Profits go to a loan fund which is available to forestry students who need financial assistance to continue their schooling. The ball originated in 1915.

Foresters will begin decorating the Men's Gymnasium Wednesday night with the 3,200 fir trees cut before Christmas. The trees were cut as part of a thinning operation on Grant Creek, northeast of Bonner. Cedar boughs cut on the Flathead Indian reservation near Dixon will cover the gym ceiling.

Another article reported on the convocation the foresters held to advertise the ball. High-kicking can-can girls opened the convocation followed by several skits and songs. I had written a poem entitled "Foresters—Peace-lovin' Men" which I recited. But the long awaited news came in the following article:

The Case of the Missing Moosehead Ends

The last demure freshman had been "pecked" goodnight on the North Hall steps. The last car lights flicked off in the driveway. The last street light dimmed, then died. It was dark.

The front door of the Student Union squeaked, then opened. One by one members of a week-long intrigue sidled through the shadowed opening then crept through the darkness to the Eloise Knowles room to wait.

Then one of the moose-nappers called Life men Nat Farbman and Chuck Champlin from their Hotel Florence Headquarters. A 'napper also summoned a Kaimin photographer, who—for obvious reasons—remains nameless.

At 2 a.m. the crew removed the head from her fourth floor tomb and lugged her to the Gold room parapet. A unique rope arrangement enabled the head to be hoisted to the Union roof. As the partners-in-crime made their way up through a series of trap-doors, the others prepared the moose-head for descent. Slowly they lowered it until it appeared as though Bertha was mounted on the Union brick wall overlooking the campus. Closing trap-doors and hiding ladders, the 'nappers made their way downstairs. It was 3 a.m. They went home.

Morning came. By 8:30 the Forester's had spied the beast gazing ludicrously over the campus, its countenance the epitome of feigned ignorance. Quickly they retrieved their lost idol. As they fondled her they whispered, "Whodunit Bertha?... Who done you this dirt?" But Bertha wouldn't talk.

Tuesday, February 9, 1954

Dear Ma,

I just can't seem to get on the ball—I wish I could get motivated and really rack the books, but for some reason I can't. [I hadn't told my mother about the depression I felt from that first test in forest engineering.]

Last Wednesday night we started the Forester's Ball rolling. We got the trees in, but boy were they wet! A crew had to stay up all night mopping the floor so it wouldn't warp (it might have anyhow). I'm not going to describe all the details because I'm in hopes Life Magazine will have a story and pictures on February 19 [which they did].

I don't know if I'm still tired out from working on the ball or if my eyes are being strained. Anyhow, I'm going to get a check-up if they keep bothering me.

Now that the ball is over the profs are laying the tests to us. We all are tired from the hard work involved with the ball, but it was worth it!

You still haven't told me how long you can stay here in the spring. Do you have any idea? [My mother and I had previously discussed plans for her to come to Missoula for my graduation in June.]

I realize my letters aren't much lately, but perhaps they'll get better.

Love, R.

In order to reach the dining room at Corbin Hall I had to walk past New Hall where Corky lived. I noticed a mail box in the window of one of the rooms situated so the name on it was visible. It was John Krier, a professor in the forestry school from whom I had taken a course the year before. I learned the name of the person with Krier's box from a girl who lived in New Hall. When the box-napper came by the checking station at the evening meal I talked with her about it, explaining that tampering with mail boxes was a serious offense and it was not very smart to display it in her window. She said someone else had taken it, but I pointed out that Krier would be coming after her if he knew she had it. Then she asked if I would return it. I reluctantly said I would try.

I went to see Dr. Krier. He was understandably irate over the loss of his mail box, and he was convinced somebody in the forestry school was responsible. I assured him that was not the case—a girl from New Hall had it. I also told him I could get it for him on the condition he would let the matter drop. He agreed and I retrieved the box for him. The next day Corky told me the house mother in New Hall questioned her about stealing a mail box, but Corky said she knew nothing about it. It didn't seem to particularly bother Corky, but when I found out about it I went to see Dr. Krier. I clearly let him know he had violated our agreement, but he again stated his belief that forestry students were involved and he was going to find out who—obviously meaning me. I tried to once again explain how I found out about the box and told him

I was only trying to help, but now regretted becoming involved in any way. Then I calmly said his actions were less than honest.

The incident was dropped, and the encounter wouldn't have been so significant if I wasn't already smarting from the sting of the harsh treatment in my forest engineering class. It all left me with the feeling that I just wanted to be out of school; perhaps I was suffering from depression.

As if this wasn't enough, the forest management course began to loom as a problem because I couldn't get on the wave length of the professor. The principles he was teaching could just as well have been some kind of voodoo, because I was unable to understand the logic of their application. I actually liked the teacher, and recognized it was my responsibility to figure out his teaching style and how to meet his expectations, but couldn't. Still, I thought an acceptable grade was within reach.

I put a lot of effort into acing the tests in forest engineering because otherwise I wouldn't graduate. I did, but my reward was only a "D," a bitter pill to swallow, particularly since I understood the material well and made "As" and "Bs" on all but the first test.

I failed to do well on the final in the forest management course and received another "D." It was a disappointment, but it was my fault. My only redeeming grade for the quarter was a "B" in psychology. There must be a message there somewhere.

The "Ds" were my first since the one I earned in military science in my first quarter of school. I was devastated; this was the only quarter my grade point average was less than a two-point. And to think I had hoped to maintain a three-point for my senior year.

The irony in all this is that the next quarter (the last of my college career) I again had courses in forest engineering and forest management from the same profs and earned "Bs." I also had a course from Dr. Krier and earned an "A." My only other course was in silviculture and I earned another "A." So I went from my lowest grades to my highest grades in back-to-back quarters. What a roller coaster ride!

But I'm getting ahead of myself. After winter quarter Ted and I decided to bring another bed into our room so Bill Taliaferro could bunk with us. I don't remember all the reasons for this change, but one consideration was that much of the quarter would be consumed by a 17-day field trip—first by those of us majoring in forestry with a timber option (Bill and I), and then a 17-day field trip for those engaged in the range option (Ted). So, for a substantial part of the quarter there wouldn't be three of us in the room.

The purpose of the trip was to visit tree farms, sawmills, paper mills, and various forest operations in the northwest. We started our 2,242 mile bus trip on Thursday, March 25, 1954 and returned April 11. It was great fun to travel together and to be able to learn and enjoy experiences outside the classroom. I wrote a letter to my mother part way through the trip:

Thursday, April 4, 1954

Dear Ma,

I hope I'm doing something now that I'll be able to do a lot more of—traveling and seeing things. This is really a fine tour. We took the ferry across Pudget Sound a few days ago, and although riding a ferry was nothing new to me, I enjoyed it.

We visited a paper mill yesterday and saw a veneer and fiber board plant the day before. Equally as interesting to me is the scenery between stops. It's different from Missoula and quite beautiful, but the country is a little too wet for me. We've had no snow except at Mt. Rainier, but, oh golly, the rain. We stood in a downpour two days ago watching a horse logging operation. Steam just rolled off the horses' backs—it was almost as if they were walking in clouds.

When we went to Mt. Rainier, we stopped at the entrance to the park to pay a fee. We got out and five deer came running up. Cameras were clicking faster than you could count. Everyone wanted to get a picture before they ran off, but it turned out they were tamer than expected. We held crackers out and they ate out of our hands. I tried holding a cracker between my teeth and I'll be darned if one didn't take it out of my mouth. I tried petting it, but no go.

We're in Portland now. I got your letter. Thanks. It's raining something awful, but Bill Taliaferro, John Lowell and I are going to church today. We located it yesterday. Maybe we'll go to Wesley tonight, too.

Most of the guys like what they're seeing, but we're all tired of living from a suitcase and traveling on a bus. We still have a week to go. The married men are anxious to get back to their families, and I'd like to get back and make some money.

Love to all, R.

P.S. Montana still gets top billing in my book.

When we returned we still had eight weeks of school left. The field trip was educational and a good break, allowing me to bring renewed vitality to my studies. Many of us also attended several no-credit sessions to prepare ourselves to take the Junior Forester's Examination given by the federal government. A grade of 70 was needed to be eligible for consideration for jobs in permanent positions with the federal government. It was impossible to predict who would pass and who wouldn't—grade standing certainly wasn't a reliable indicator. This was later borne out in the results. A few of the best students didn't pass, so I felt a great deal of relief when I did.

*   *   *

My siblings saw to it that my mother could afford the trip to Missoula for my graduation. She arrived about June 1, and I found her an apartment near the campus. We spent a lot of time together, but I still had some school chores needing attention. She understood and was happy to poke around on her own.

Graduation was on June 7. I didn't feel the same sense of excitement and expectation that graduating from high school brought. Perhaps part of it was due to my being four years older and no longer a teenager. It seemed that at the high school ceremony we all held hands tightly, not certain we wanted to leave the joys of youth.

College graduation was different. We were ready to step out into the world and anxious to put into practice the things we had learned. The graduation exercise seemed like a perfunctory step leading to that adventure. Some of my classmates must have viewed graduation with a certain ambivalence because a few didn't even bother to attend.

I felt relieved to survive my senior year, and a measure of uncertainty about the route leading to a job in forestry. For one thing it seemed likely the draft would get me just as it had Tom and Chuck after they graduated.

Nevertheless, I was pleased to take part in the graduation exercises and was honored to have my mother there. It was an immensely satisfying conclusion to my four-year college career.

*   *   *

After graduation, I had a week before reporting for work with the smokejumpers. Ted joined with us in an excursion to Glacier National Park. The weather was perfect and we had a festive time. It was much more fun with the three of us and my mother appreciated the opportunity to get to know Ted.

The Rocky Mountains were a sight mother had long dreamed of seeing and the rugged peaks of Glacier awed her. She frequently wrote about the things that inspired her and she drafted several versions of a poem about the mountains. This is the version I like best:

The Mountain's Message

I went to see the mountains
Out toward the Western sea . . .
Those great and glorious Rockies
In all their majesty.

I can't forget the lesson
Those mountains taught to me.
I can't forget how near
My Maker seemed to be.

I have found I love the mountains
As much as I love the sea.
They both tell the same story—
They speak of Eternity.

I'm glad I've seen the mountains—
I'm glad I've seen the sea.
I'm glad to get the message
God speaks through them to me.

—Helen Fowler

We also went to Flathead Lake and visited the Methodist Camp there. She had read so much about the area from my letters that it was particularly meaningful to her to finally visit the place. It wasn't until years later, long after her death, that I saw a short story she had written about her visit there. Following is the first page:

A Tree on Flathead's Shore

"There's your tree, mother."
We had just beached our rowboat on the rocky shore by the cottages. It was hard for me to realize that I was really in Montana. It was harder still to realize that I had really been for a row on beautiful Flathead Lake. I had sat in the stern

and dabbled my fingers in the water. I had looked at the Mission Range and said to myself, "You are looking at part of the Rockies. You are seeing snowcapped mountains. You are breathing air filled with the scent of northern pines. You are here where you have dreamed of being for so long."

It seemed that I was just about as happy as a person could be, but something better was ahead. That "something better" was when my attention was called to the tree. It stood by the edge of the lake looking as it did in the picture my son had taken three years before and sent to me. He had written on the back of the snapshot that he thought it would appeal to me as much as it had to him; that whenever he looked at it he felt the beauty of it even though it was dead. [The tree was a windswept, gnarly mountain ash.] *It had appealed to me so much that I put it in a little frame and hung it on the wall where I could see it often. Now I was looking at the real thing. While the two boys were securing the boat and getting out the lunch, I walked over to the tree. It was rough-going for the beach was covered with loose pebbles and a lot of driftwood that had been washed ashore by the storms of the winter that was not too far behind us.*

A long drive after an early start that morning, and the row on the lake in the noontime heat made me feel drowsy. Sitting down on a log near the tree and leaning back against a high rock, I thought again of the words that had come to me so often when I had looked at the picture at home. Majestic . . . brave . . . courageous . . . sheltering . . . .

Her writing continued, telling how she fell asleep and had a dream about speaking to the tree after which she is awakened by Ted and me calling her to lunch. The story ends with a melodramatic flare, *"Good-by, you wonderful tree. I will never forget you."*

My mother saw adventure in whatever she did and wherever she was, and she tried desperately to write about it so she could share it with others.

Her visit ended shortly after that trip. We were both grateful for having finally been able to venture into a part of the West together.

Mother and I in Glacier National Park.

CHAPTER 13

Big Prairie

I t was Monday, June 14 when we started refresher training at the new smokejumper base at the county airport. Training with a paved tarmac and runways instead of the dirt and gravel of Hale Field was strange. The training routine, however, was unchanged. We had three days of instruction and two days of jumping: first from the Ford and then from a DC-2, a smaller version of the DC-3.

On the last Friday of our training many of us witnessed a Twin Beech aircraft coming in for a landing. The flight wasn't associated with jumping activity even though it was often used for that purpose. The landing seemed smooth enough but the landing gear collapsed, resulting in a belly landing. Although no one was hurt and the damage was repairable, it served to remind us that we never knew when something could go wrong.

The following Monday we all left for project. Brauer tried to give those who had jumped the longest first choice for assignment, so I could be more selective than in the past. Since my summer work experience would no longer be used by the Dean to document my field development in forestry, I decided to do what seemed the most enjoyable rather than looking for a technical forestry job. Nothing seemed more inviting than working in the middle of the Bob Marshall Primitive Area doing whatever needed to be done.

No one expected to be on project very long because our thinking had been tempered by the extremely busy 1953 fire season. Little did we know the 1954 season would end up being on the opposite end of the spectrum. Those assigned uninteresting projects ended up with a frustrating summer because they stayed there.

Four of us were selected to go to Big Prairie Ranger Station: Bill Hale, Ed Henry, Connie Orr, and me. We were all old men although I had trained a year before the other three. I knew Bill from our experience patrolling the Tango Fire the year before, but had no previous encounters with either Connie or Ed.

Bill and Ed flew together to Big Prairie in a Cessna 180 piloted by Floyd Bowman. The plane wasn't big enough to carry all of us, so Connie and I waited for a second trip. I had been to Big Prairie in 1952 when Bill Demmons and I walked there from my first fire jump. It was such a beautiful place I was glad to be returning

Occasionally recreationists would venture by, but there were no roads and no other people except the few that worked on Big Prairie Ranger District. The only persons consistently at the station were the dispatcher and the ranger's wife. Everyone else was gone for days at a time maintaining trail, fixing telephone line, fighting fire, or doing other routine administrative duties.

The buildings were located next to the airstrip. A combination office/kitchen building stood immediately adjacent to the airstrip. It also had an upstairs used as sleeping quarters for the dispatcher.

In close proximity was a dwelling for the ranger, Oliver W. (Slim) Meyer and his wife, a bunk house, a small fuel house (for saws and a tractor), a 20 by 30 foot tool house, and several small out buildings containing warehousing and tack for stock.

The next day Bill was assigned to help one of the regular station workers maintain telephone line using horses.

Connie was assigned the job of cook. He didn't relish the prospect of spending his time in the kitchen, but there weren't many of us to feed, so it wasn't a difficult chore.

Ed and I were told to take down and coil a telephone line no longer needed. We used a small Farmall tractor and wagon in places where we could reach the line from the airstrip.

Slim was an old time ranger who appeared to be approaching retirement age, but you couldn't tell by his active schedule. He was frequently out on the trail with his horse inspecting the work of his summer help. As his name suggests, he was tall and thin. He was a nice enough guy, but he had a manner that clearly indicated he was a "no nonsense" boss. On the first day when Bill was getting ready to leave, he tied his horse to a hitching rail with the reins.

Slim instantly barked, "Don't tie that horse up by the reins. If he rears back the reins will snap. Use the halter rope." It wasn't that what he said was wrong, just heavy handed. We had to learn to work in a way that minimized raising his ire, and soon found that he was a good fellow to work for. His wife had a jolly personality and was easy to be around. She did some mighty fine baking and shared many delicious goodies with us.

The same job assignments continued through most of the week. Ed and I finished coiling three miles of telephone line and began cutting fire wood. We were a mile-and-a-half from the station and had loaded our wood on the wagon. The tractor's gears got messed up and somehow engaged in reverse and forward simultaneously, so we had to walk back to the station. Slim was on a trip to Basin Creek (where the Ford Trimotor had landed to rescue the injured Doug Morrison in 1952), so he couldn't help resolve our difficulty. The dispatcher told us that this was not the first time the tractor had locked up. A feeling of relief followed because it seemed less likely Slim would go on the war path.

We had a list of several other chores, so the next day we slashed the small trees encroaching both sides of the airstrip. After dropping the trees, we piled the slash for burning in the fall. It was enjoyable and we appreciated the local scene, the warm weather, and physical work. In the afternoon we tested linen hose for leaks by hooking it up to a marine pump. In the process we wet down a portion of the runway closest to the ranger station because the packer would frequently stop there with his pack string. The water helped rejuvenate the grass.

It was pleasant working with Ed and as we toiled at our chores, we would exchange smokejumping experiences. Ed had jumped on the Tango Fire with Bill in 1953. He said after the jump, he and three others had come together and saw the fire approach the tree where Bill had landed. They were sure he had been caught in the blaze.

I was able to locate Ed in August 2004 and talked with him on the telephone—a long overdue reunion. He remembered clearly my telling him about the Danaher Rescue, but he had no recollection that Bill was one of the jumpers he went with to the Tango Fire. We hadn't had contact for 51 years, but he remembered our Big Prairie days well. With lots of time on our hands we fished a little during the June 26-27 weekend. It was excellent, but there was a limit to how many fish we could eat, so we looked for another pasttime.

We saw a stand of lodgepole timber close by where elk had shed their antlers, and found several excellent specimens to make into cribbage boards. It took hours to work them down with a rasp and smooth them with a file. Drilling holes was time consuming because there were no power tools. We found that a file-sharpened nail could be used to etch a figure or words on the smoothed antler surface—the words "Big Prairie" were etched on mine. We rubbed graphite into our lettering before varnishing so they would be more visible. I have made many elk horn cribbage boards since then, and even though they are much more sophisticated, they are always given away—"Big Prairie" remains my favorite.

It was raining so hard Monday morning that we stayed inside checking the flashlight batteries in fire packs and sharpening tools. By afternoon the rain had stopped, so we dragged the fire hose we had worked with on Friday to the barn and draped it over the roof to drain and dry.

The horses and mules were pastured a mile-and-a half up river in Cayuse Meadows. We went there the next day to repair the fence that circled it. We thought it would have been better named Cayuse Swamp because much of it was under water. Although it was enjoyable work, having wet feet all day was uncomfortable.

Bill continued maintaining telephone line. Connie stayed at the station doing odd jobs and preparing dinner for those of us who worked away from the station, but returned in the evening.

My letters to my mother described my time at Big Prairie; however, she saved only one of them because they didn't relate directly to smokejumping or fire fighting. She probably thought those were the ones that might be of future interest. The one about Big Prairie follows:

Friday, July 9, 1954

Dear Ma,

Last Wednesday [June 30], *it was decided that I would go with Bruce Pyles, the packer, to Holbrook Cabin. I had gotten to know Bruce during my assignment on the Tango Fire, and knew that we would work well together. I got up at dawn to help him wrangle the stock in Cayuse Meadows. It was a cold, wet job and by the time we got two horses and four mules rounded up and saddled, I felt like we had already put in a half-day's work, but our day hadn't even started yet. I was glad to be able to work with livestock and learn more about packing mules, and Bruce was a willing teacher. We left right after breakfast for Holbrook with Bruce leading the string of four mules. Riding behind four flatulent mules wasn't the most pleasant at times, so I occasionally drifted back. The country was pretty and was especially enjoyable to view from a saddle instead of on foot. It was harder for me to judge the distance we traveled from a horse's back compared to walking, but I guessed it to be six-and-a-half miles.*

When we reached Holbrook, Bruce and I pulled the light packs off the mules and he hitched them to a roller. The roller had been made at the site with a two-foot diameter metal culvert and concrete. The mules were four abreast, but seemed to want to be in their pack string arrangement—that is, in a line. They danced and stammered around and Bruce kept talking to them, sometimes soothingly and sometimes yelling. It appeared to be an impossible task because they refused to pull in a straight line. What a mass of power he had to control. As much as I enjoyed working around stock, I didn't much cotton to the prospect of trying to control all that erratic energy, but eventually Bruce was able to settle them down and they went to work.

The cabin was small and made of lumber—adequate, but not substantial. They had been having some difficulty with bears trying to push in the door, so it was my job to give it the Houdini treatment. You guessed it, I pounded in heavy spikes from the inside of the door so that it looked like the mat the Great Houdini lay on in one of his magical acts. Then I took a file and sharpened the points to make them as inhospitable as possible. The windows had already been crisscrossed with barbed wire. Thus, Holbrook was deemed bear proof—or at least resistant. [In 2003 the cabin burned down and probably will not be replaced.]

By this time Bruce and the mules were briskly thundering their way up and down the strip, mashing the gopher hole mounds and compacting the soil. The strip wasn't used very often so it was only minimally maintained. [After the Bob Marshall was included in the wilderness system in 1964, none of the airstrips were shown on maps. Their use was conditional.]

I cleaned up the cabin, built a fire, and tried to bake some biscuits from a mix I found in the cabin. The stove was tricky, and the cook not very good, but they were edible.

We had a good time just messin' around the place that evening and Bruce gave me a few more pointers on how to pack a mule. The next morning I tried catching our horses. They gave me a hard time, but I finally got 'em. I never realized how much I liked working around stock until now.

We finished a few more chores around the cabin and returned to Big Prairie. What a nice way to spend a summer, but I have to admit I was saddle sore when we pulled back into the station.

[What a come-down. The next day, Friday, Ed and I worked on a new septic system for the ranger residence. The details have faded, but we dug a huge pit, or at least started it. It was tough work, but fortunately we had the three-day Fourth of July weekend ahead of us, so we got a break.]

Bill was at the station over the long weekend, so the four of us decided to climb Brown Sandstone Mountain on Saturday just for the fun of it. It was only two air miles east of Big Prairie, although it was a steep cross-country climb—at least most of the way. Big Prairie was at 4,640 feet of elevation and Brown Sandstone was at 7,560, so we had about a 2,920 foot climb.

On Sunday Connie and I walked over to the river and went swimming. The water was cold, but we still thought it felt good. After our swim, we caught a mess of fish for supper and headed back to the station, satisfied with our weekend diversion.

Monday was a "nothing" day—we just read and played cribbage until Bruce said he needed help pulling some quills out of one of the horse's mouth. He had her hitched to a rail by the tack shed where she nervously weaved from side to side. It doesn't take many quills to make it impossible for a horse to graze, and Bruce was insistent they come out right away. Luckily there weren't many or we would have needed a vet.

She seemed to know we were trying to help, but the pain of jerking them out sent her wild and it was all we could do to keep her in control, so there was a long interlude between extractions.

Dick, the dispatcher, started yelling over by the ranger station office, but we couldn't understand what it was he was saying. All of a sudden he whipped out his chrome plated .45 and started shooting toward the top of a lodgepole near the office. Bruce had his pliers on the last quill in the horse's mouth. He had been reluctant to pull because it was deeply implanted. When the shooting started the horse reared so violently we couldn't hold her, but the quill was out. Bruce didn't know whether to be mad or grateful, but in any case he went over to the place where Dick was standing.

"Why the hell are you firing that .45 here?" Bruce demanded.

"There's a porcupine up in that tree and I was trying to get him," he replied, showing no concern for how his shooting may have affected anyone else.

What happened next was confusing, but after more shooting the critter was killed. Several of us were skeptical that this porcupine was the one that quilled the horse since the incident occurred far away in Cayuse Meadows.

*　　*　　*

Ed and I were back digging the septic pit on Tuesday. We had the sewer line from the house set and were putting rock in the hole when we heard a rumbling in the pipe. It was understood the toilet would not be flushed until we were through. We scrambled out of the pit as effluent gushed from the pipe.

"Hey, Mrs. Meyer, you're not supposed to use that thing while we're working on it," Ed yelled.

We couldn't see her, but knew she was the culprit because Slim was away on an inspection trip.

"Oops. Sorry. I forgot. Lucky for you guys I smell like a rose," she said, in a way that meant she wasn't the least bit sorry.

We were annoyed with her lack of consideration, and her bad humor, but she was hard not to like despite her brassiness.

*   *   *

A plane delivered mail and groceries. We unloaded the cargo and carried it to the kitchen, noticing a box of oatmeal for Bruce. It seemed strange he had made a special order for breakfast cereal until we happened to see him open it—revealing a bottle of Jack Daniels packed in the oatmeal. It may have been more of a precaution to keep it from breaking than a clandestine maneuver, but alcohol was uniformly discouraged in all Forest Service stations. We didn't ask any questions. The large boxes of groceries included a generous supply of fresh fruit. Connie was delighted and decided a fruit salad would be in order. He asked Ed and me if we thought it would be a good idea. We agreed, thinking it would be a side dish with soup and a sandwich. When we went in for lunch the meal consisted of a huge bowl of chopped up fruit mixed with mayonnaise and nuts. He even mixed in some raisins. It tasted good to me even though it wasn't what I expected, but some of the fellows working at the station that day thought it was grossly inadequate—they were meat and potatoes guys. Slim was away from the station, but when he returned and heard about the fruit salad lunch he hit the ceiling; that ended Connie's cooking career.

It's puzzling to me that my July 9 letter to my mother did not include these happenings. The letter, however, continued . . .]

Ed and I worked on the new septic tank Tuesday and part of Wednesday. We finished up in the morning. At noon a fire on the Big Prairie District was reported and those of us at the station were put on standby. The patrol plane flew over the fire and decided that two men could handle it and that it wasn't in bad enough fuel to warrant a call for smokejumpers. That meant smoke chasers would man it—and they would come from Big Prairie. And since Bill was out on trail work, and all the other district fellows were out, the two would be picked from among Connie, Ed and me. We drew straws to see which two would go and Connie and I won (or lost, depending on how you looked at it—at the time we thought we'd won).

The fire was 20 miles from Big Prairie, but only eight miles from Black Bear. (I went through Black Bear coming off the Silver Tip Fire in October of 1952, remember?)

When the patrol plane landed, Ed helped us load our fire packs and said, "How's it feel to be a ground pounder?" We took off at 2:50 p.m. for Black Bear thinking about his remark. It was a strange feeling not to be jumping. The pilot flew over the fire on the way. It was a snag lightning had knocked over at the top of an old burn that was now green with brush and balsam root. There were a few trees about 40 feet above it, and the slope was extremely steep—maybe 45 degrees.

It was a new experience for us both to be circling that fire knowing we wouldn't be jumping on it. It didn't look all that far from the fire to the river, but I had learned from previous experiences not to be fooled by how easy the travel appeared from the air. We mentally mapped our cross-country route from the trail to the fire as we headed for Black Bear.

When we landed at 3:30 p.m. I saw two smokejumpers at the far end of the air strip working. I knew they were the only ones stationed at Black Bear now. They could just as well have gone to this fire except they were working on the Spotted Bear Ranger District and the fire was on the Big Prairie Ranger District. No doubt they would have been sent if the fire was threatening, but since it was just a nuisance, the approach was territorial.

We had a long way to walk so we cut out without seeing the boys. Our route followed the trail up the South Fork of the Flathead River for six miles, so it was good walking. I set a fast, steady pace which would have been a good clip even without fire packs. We had left our two-gallon water bag at Black Bear figuring the two canteens we had were enough—one was a gallon, and the other a half-gallon.

We waded Helen Creek and Damnation Creek and reined-up at Lewis Creek where we would leave the trail and hit the brush. We had gone an hour-and-a-half and had covered six miles. Now the hard part. We filled our canteens from the creek and headed up Lewis Creek.

We both expressed appreciation for having seen the fire from the air because it would have been difficult to find if we hadn't known exactly where it was. We climbed up on a bench above the creek to avoid the heavy brush and found an old abandoned trail. What a joy! I'm not exaggerating. By this time the packs were getting heavy and our stomachs said it was chow time, but we continued. We stumbled over the fallen trees across the trail and kept a sharp eye ahead so we wouldn't lose it. I'd rather walk three miles on a trail than one across country, particularly if the brush is heavy.

The handles from the shovels in our packs stuck up above our heads and kept catching tree branches, throwing us off our balance, but at least we were on a trail of sorts. The bears and other big game apparently used it often and their use kept it somewhat open. We could see grizzly claw marks on the larger trees across the way.

Directly across from us on the other side of the creek and at the top of the mountain stood Mud Lake Lookout. We knew the fire was almost directly across from it. Shortly we came to a clearing and before us stood the treeless mountain side. Boy, I was hungry! Connie had a Hershey bar that he split with me, and it seemed to give me a shot of energy. We couldn't see smoke, but we knew where it was, so we started up. It was hard going, especially with the fire pack, and I know there were times when I lost more ground than I gained with a single step. We stopped to rest often. Connie was hurting pretty bad at the shoulders from the pack straps of the Clack frame and my legs were beginning to feel it a little. Connie is a track man at the university, so he's very trim and in good shape. We took it at a slow pace and it seemed we would never get there. I felt faint several times, but couldn't figure out why. I'm in good shape. Maybe it was because I hadn't eaten much lunch and was mighty hungry, or maybe I was just fagged.

At last we saw the fire. It was ahead about five miles. Actually it was only about 100 yards—it just seemed like five miles getting there. We arrived at 7:30 p.m., and since the fire wasn't going anywhere, we ate right away, not exactly the way we approached a fire when we arrived via parachute, even on a slow burner. At that moment I came to fully appreciate how much the smokejumpers have it over the smoke chasers (or ground pounders as we call them). I was in no mood to fight fire. I wished I was as fresh as when I jumped on one.

We put a line around the fire and hit the hot spots—there were only a few. The snag had been killed in a burn many years ago and was pretty rotten. The fire had crept into the punky roots and burned deep in the ground—that was our only hard job. By 2:00 a.m. we had the whole fire pretty cold. I figured she was done except maybe a few roots and they would boil up in the morning when they could generate a little more heat, so we decided to try and sleep. Again we found another big disadvantage of the ground pounder—no sleeping bag. We each had a manty a piece, but they didn't provide much warmth. We couldn't sleep.

After the darkness had pulled the moon to the top of the sky, it set in the saddle of two snow-capped mountains. It was a sight that clearly defined the attractiveness of fighting fire at high elevations. When the moon went down the stars shone in full force. You can't imagine it! There was not a direction where man-made light could be seen, not even on the far horizons. The stars had absolutely no competition and they sang in numbers and with a vibrance that forced me to stand in awe. This scene alone was worth the cost of getting high on the mountain and working late into the night.

The spread between daytime and nighttime temperatures high in the mountains can be more than 50 degrees. It was obvious we needed a different approach to get warm. We tried laying back-to-back and building a small fire facing each of us. As cold as it was, this plan worked and we slept for an hour. Then our small fires burned out and we woke up cold and stiff.

Big Salmon Lake didn't look as pretty as it did earlier when the moon was shining on it. Last year I was looking east from the Tango Fire to Big Salmon Lake; now we were looking west at it.

With the cold grey morning, Big Salmon Lake looked cold and lonely, and our experience seemed deflated—like a ballroom after a big dance when everyone has left. We killed what was left of the fire and mopped her up good. The exertion was enough to keep us warm. When the sun rose it rapidly got hot and Connie said he worked up a sweat tying his shoe laces.

With no sign of smoke, we found it very hard to sit there in the sun and just wait, but we did—until 3:00 p.m., just to make sure she was dead out.

[We used some sticks and rocks to make a support for one of our manties to give us a little shade. I stretched out and thought about our time on the fire. This was our first fire for the season, and in a way it qualified as a high-mountain two-manner. Perhaps not in the classic sense of smokejumper fire, but it certainly qualified in every other way. It was rather ironic that my first fire in every one of my three smokejunping years was a high-mountain two-manner . . . and they all were on the Flathead National Forest (in or near the Bob Marshall Primitive Area). Of course, the one in 1953 didn't stay a two-manner very long—it quickly deteriorated into a nightmare.

It was nice to have two day's supply of food and know that it was more than enough. We could high-grade our food cache, eating only what we liked best.]

As expected, we found the way out to be much easier. We weren't carrying much grub or water, so our packs were lighter, and since we were not pressed for time, we took a relaxed pace. I measured a grizzly track in the trail and it was fourteen inches from the heel to the end of the claw mark. I'm glad we didn't see him.

We got back to Black Bear at 7:00 p.m.

It had taken us the same amount of time to walk from the fire as it had to walk to it. I really don't think it was so much that we poked on the return as it was that we put forth such effort going in.

Joe Roemer and Bob Chrismer were at the Black Bear Cabin when we arrived. I had trained with Joe in 1952, but never jumped with him. On his first jump in 1953 he cut off the end of one of his fingers crossing the Selway River on a cable tram. He somehow got his finger under the pulley that ran on the cable. I didn't know Bob—he was a new man. They cooked us some steaks to eat. We were hungry and they tasted delicious. It was fun sitting in the cabin comparing our summer experiences. Joe and Bob were very hospitable, and it was great to visit with them. It was also nice to have hot water to bathe with and to sleep on a soft cot in a warm building. I slept like a rock.

We cranked-up Big Prairie on the grounded line and they said the patrol plane would pick us up today. We are just waiting around. A plane came in a few minutes ago, but it was the Montana State Fish & Game.

I guess we are the first smokejumperes to go on a fire this year, even though we did ground pound it. The fire season should start in earnest soon.

Love, R.

P.S. I may call smoke chasers "ground pounders," but by golly I'll say it with respect from now on.

It was late in the afternoon when the patrol plane picked us up for the flight back to Big Prairie. Everyone was out working except the dispatcher. He told us how many would be coming for dinner, so we had it prepared when they arrived.

On the weekend we were content to take it easy. We fished a little, went swimming once, and visited with some trail riders who stopped by the station. Otherwise, it was pitching horse shoes or playing cribbage—a lazy respite.

Job assignments changed on Monday. Bill and Ed stayed close to Big Prairie and started building jackleg fence in Cayuse Meadows. Connie and I were sent to White River Parks—about the same distance away as Holbrook—only on the east side of the river instead of the west side. We were to inspect the telephone line from there back to Big Prairie and do whatever maintenance was needed. We started out on foot. Bruce was going somewhere down river with a string of mules over the same trail we were traveling, so he carried our equipment. Even though we were traveling light, Bruce and his string caught us a couple of miles from Big Prairie. I begged a ride, knowing it was generally against policy to ride a mule with a packsaddle, but he said, "Sure, you can climb up on Cascade, but a packsaddle isn't the most comfortable way to ride."

"I'll be okay. Thanks," I shouted as I mounted up.

Bruce also told Connie which other mule could be trusted to ride, and he climbed aboard.

Bruce was right, the ride was challenging. Cascade behaved well enough; it was the decker saddle that was hostile. When we clopped along in a smooth rhythm it was possible to shift my position often enough to avoid a pounding on the tender spots, but when the string moved in accordion fashion, the quick stops and rapid starts brought agony. Fortunately, most of the trek was smooth and I had survived pretty well as we approached White River Parks.

Then we came to a draw with a steep slope in and out of it—15 feet down and 15 feet up. Bruce, on his lead mare, didn't break stride as they crossed, nor did the first mule, but the second one rushed down so he would have momentum going up. The next mule with Connie aboard closely followed and consequently all the slack was taken out of the lead rope to the next mule.

The half-inch lead rope was attached to the halter at one end and was substantial, that is, would not break. The other end of the lead rope was attached to a loop, called a pigtail, on the back of the saddle of the mule in front. The pigtail rope was much smaller in diameter (quarter-inch), and would break under extreme tension, thus preventing a fallen mule from dragging the whole string over a cliff.

Once again the mules used the accordion maneuver and the one behind me tried to come up beside Cascade. I put out my leg in an effort to discourage him, but the lead rope got tangled around my boot. Afraid, Cascade would bolt ahead, I deftly slipped my fingers under her halter strap where it crossed the back of her neck and pulled back—at the same time yelling "Whoa!" Undaunted, she forced her way up to the brink of the draw, but the mule behind did stop; in fact, she set her brakes and wouldn't move.

My right leg was beginning to feel numb because it was still caught in the taut rope. Cascade was straining to go ahead because the animals in front of her were pulling mightily to continue along the trail. Her head was stretched forward, thus taking the slack out of the halter and pinning my fingers so tightly to her neck they couldn't be removed. It began to feel like an arm or a leg would be pulled from its socket. A torture rack couldn't have been more efficient. I would have dismounted, but was helplessly stretched out, unable to move.

Suddenly the pigtail broke between Cascade and the mule in front of her, freeing my left hand from the halter. I grabbed the iron ring at the top of the packsaddle with my freed hand, slid back on Cascade, and tried to free my right foot from the lead rope. It came loose just as Cascade and the three trailing mules all rushed forward, swerving off the trail and across White River Flats. The situation called for firmness, so I yelled at the top of my voice, "WHOA, YOU SON-OF-A-BITCH!" It was a very commanding exhortation, but undoubtedly the roar of thundering hoofs and the racing wind drowned out my voice, preventing Cascade from receiving my message.

Obviously the mules had an excellent communication system because they simultaneously executed the Ben Hur Maneuver, swinging into a flanking movement and lining up four abreast—then running like hell.

At that point in my career I had jumped 16 times from the Ford, six from the Travelair, three from the DC-3, and one each from the DC-2 and Twin Beech. I would soon be the first to jump from a mule, traveling at warp speed—or so it seemed.

Even though fire was not involved, it would definitely be done in the line of duty, and probably under more dangerous conditions than any fire jump—at least by me. Fortunately the other three mules were flanked on my right. The probabilities of survival, had there been animals on both sides of Cascade, were decidedly in favor of the Grim Reaper.

My tail bone, inner thighs, and groin area were taking a tremendous pounding, still, I was reluctant to jump. The din from hoofs, slapping leather, and heavily breathing mules was angry and foreboding. A quick glance ahead revealed we were rapidly approaching scattered lodgepole pine. That didn't bother the Ben Hur gang even though it was likely some of the trees would pass between them (and they were still tethered together). Procrastination was no longer an option and I jumped, skipping the "Geronimo" bit.

Usually a jump ended with an Allan roll. Mine ended with several, but because of the blurred atmosphere, there's no telling how many. My adrenaline-laden body came to rest after an involuntary addition to the rapid series of rolls. Connie, witnessing the event from afar, named it the Fowler Flop.

It was scarcely believable that no bones were broken. The mules were 100 yards away grazing, and at least one additional pigtail had snapped. Bruce rounded them up, dropped our pack and was on his way. So much for tea and sympathy.

It was our job to inspect the telephone line all the way back to Big Prairie, being certain it was hanging evenly from the tree insulators. Trees growing up to the line had to be cut, and branches drooping from larger trees pruned. Anything touching the line would diminish its transmitting effectiveness.

Somehow we managed to leave one of our canteens with Bruce, so we were short of water early in the afternoon, but we managed to complete several miles of line.

The next day we had to walk five miles in order to pick up where we had left off. The climbing was my job and Connie did the brushing. He continually sang a country western song with the lines, "Winchester Cathedral, you're getting me down . . ." He didn't know any more words, but those were sufficient for him. Over and over he would sing the same line, a necessary chant for him to work. No matter how severely I admonished him for his monotonous repetition, he'd slip back into it. Even today, 51 years later, I occasionally find myself singing that line as I work.

On the third day it was a short walk to our quitting point. It started to rain, but we were determined to finish. Although we could hear thunder in the distance, we didn't seem to be threatened with lightning close by, so we kept working. I reached for the galvanized telephone wire and got a good jolt of electricity.

In retrospect it was difficult to tell whether contact was actually made with the wire, or if I had just gotten close to it, but in either case, we deemed it unwise to continue working under those conditions. Fortunately, it wasn't long before the storm passed and we finished the job.

By noon we were back at Big Prairie so we went up to Cayuse Meadows to help Ed and Bill build jackleg fence. It was fun, the four of us working together—we made a good team. We had to cut lodgepole to length, notch the "X" pieces, and drive a couple of spikes at the intersection to keep them together. We used a single-jack—a cross between a hammer and a sledge hammer. It had a short handle like a hammer, and a heavy head like a sledge. A sledge hammer usually weighed eight to 12 pounds, and a single-jack four to six pounds, depending on the job to be done and the strength of the man using it. Ours were four pounders, but it still didn't take too many strokes before the arm tired, so we switched-off regularly.

We continued on Thursday until a storm came up. Bill knew a gentle mule close by and was able to catch him. We both mounted up bare back, using only a rope halter we had fashioned. A mule's back bone protrudes appreciably and is not comfortable to sit on, but it was only a quarter-of-a-mile to the end of the fence where we would dismount, so we toughed it out—laughing all the way. Of course, we still had a mile-and-a-half to walk to the ranger station.

On Friday we were close to finishing the jackleg fence when Bill missed with the single-jack and hit his thumb. The pain from a miss-hit with a hammer is one thing, but with a single-jack it's excruciating. Fortunately for him, the weekend was coming up, so he would have a two-day reprieve to nurse his injury. All weekend he walked around with his injured hand held on his chest—the throbbing and pain was too much for him when he let his arm hang. On Monday morning when we noticed numerous pieces of match sticks on the floor by Bill's bed. He had been awake most of the night chewing on them to fortify himself against pain and would periodically spit the masticated match sticks on the floor.

We finished the fence on Monday, likely without Bill, but it didn't matter because on Tuesday we flew to Condon Ranger Station. At that time the Condon Ranger District contained the Mission Mountain Primitive Area but none of the Bob Marshall. Unlike Big Prairie it also had considerable territory outside of the primitive area. We knew we were not being called for fire and had mixed feelings about leaving Big Prairie. We had been there a month—it had been a great place to work. Little did we know that we would end up spending another month at Condon. It was great having a cook and the option of traveling by car, but the road up the Swan Valley to Condon was gravel, so travel to town was difficult. However there were some girls at a camp on Holland Lake called the Kiwadens. Some of us went there several times to dance and sing.

Dick Austin and Roger Hearst were at Condon—and had been for two months. Dick, a second year jumper, was in the plane with his brother when I jumped alone on the Marion Meadows Fire in October 1953. Roger trained in 1950 but worked elsewhere during the intervening years to 1954.

Bob Fry was the ranger at Condon. He was easy to get to know and Dick and Roger spoke highly of him. It wasn't long before we felt like part of the crew. We worked around the ranger station doing whatever needed to be done—mending fences, painting buildings, and cleaning the warehouse.

It wasn't until July 28, 12 days after Bill's injury, that he decided to see a doctor. I went with him. The doctor drilled a hole in his nail and relieved the pressure. While he was receiving medical attention, I went to a dentist and had a tooth yanked, and afterwards made a telephone call to Butte to arrange to see Corky the coming weekend.

*   *   *

The mail was a long time coming, so when it arrived on August 5 we were all excited. It was noontime and we were lounging on our cots in the bunkhouse. Ed rushed to the screen door and hit it with the heel of his hand to knock it open. In his haste, he drove the head of a protruding nail into his palm then ripped it out—all in one motion. He ended up with a nasty gash and had to be transported to Missoula for treatment, 85 miles away. Fortunately it didn't knock him off the jump list.

Another week went by before we were called to Missoula for fire. When we got there many jumpers had gone out, but we were too late, at least for that day.

The next day, Saturday, August 14, 12 of us boarded a DC-2 for a fire on the Helena National Forest. Ed and I were the only crew members from the Condon group. Fred Barnowski was the foreman—we had jumped together on the Sheep Creek Fire in 1952. Chuck Dysart was also in our plane. He had jumped with Ed Henry and Bill Hale on the Tango Cabin Fire. It was named the Big Log Gulch Fire and was burning a scant six miles from the location of the tragic Mann Gulch Fire.

Thursday, August 19, 1954

Dear Ma,

Last Friday we all got called in for a fire bust. Thirty men went to jump out of McCall, Idaho and 12 went to California. They got back today and only a few had jumped. I went out with 19 others to a fire on the Helena National Forest. [There were only 12 in our plane, so there must also have been a Ford with 8 jumpers who went to the same fire.] *It was only a few miles from Mann Gulch. The foreman, Fred Barnowski, and I jumped together on the first stick. It was more fun being first, especially since we didn't have to fly in circles for so long. The fire was over-rated and we had her whipped in a few hours. Ground pounders came in and we left the same evening on a chartered bus back to Missoula.*

In spite of the conditions, it was good to jump again—it may be my last, ever. What a terrific experience to float . . . I guess I've talked about it enough . . .

Clouds and rain have kept the fire season down and I'm ready to call it quits.

Love, R.

Above: Big Prairie Ranger Station, 1954. The clearing on the
right is the airstrip.
Below: Some of the buildings at Big Prairie Ranger Station.

Condon Ranger Station, 1954.

CHAPTER 14

A New Adventure

When it became apparent an active fire season was not going to materialize, I began to think about returning home. My loans had been repaid with several hundred dollars to spare, so there was no financial reason to stay. I had passed the junior forestry examination and would be considered for a permanent position when the need arose for entry-level foresters. There was no way of knowing how long it would take before an offer might be made, but before making a commitment for permanent employment, a visit home was top priority. It was time.

On August 26 my summer employment with the smokejumpers ended and I left for home on the Milwaukee Road with my foot locker and suitcase—no more than when I arrived four years hence. I felt a strange mixture of elation and regret. Montana had become my home. My friends were there. Corky was there. And while I had disciplined myself to view the smokejumper program as summer employment and not a career opportunity, it was still difficult to accept that it was now a thing of my past.

Some day I would return to Montana, but the path was obscure at best. A chapter in my life had been completed—my four-year search for adventure had been fulfilled beyond anything imagined when I left Lanham in 1950. My "Love, R." letters had served their purpose to document that adventure and would now gather dust in a closet. I didn't know at the time that a two-year stint in the Army would send me to South Carolina, North Carolina, Louisiana, Kentucky and Germany where my exploration and search for adventure continued before finally "settling" down.

*   *   *

From August 26, when leaving the jumpers and heading home, it was exactly 10 years to the day that my mother died. Upon my return home in 1954, Ma and I had a good visit, but it didn't last long. On September 23, I accepted a Forest Service appointment with the Southeast Forest Experiment Station with headquarters in Asheville, North Carolina. Mr. Woolfolk had been transferred there, but his job was in range research. I was to work in the Division of Forest Economics Research doing timber inventory as part of a national effort to gather timber data on all lands in the United States.

There was no question Woolfolk had put in a good word for me, resulting in my getting the job, only I didn't work in the Asheville area. Instead, I sloshed around in the Dismal Swamp on the coastal plain for several months before being drafted in the Army—with a military leave of absence from the Forest Service.

After two years in the Army, serving with relative humility, I was able to obtain a transfer from the Southeast Forest Experiment Station to a ranger district in the Northern Region (R-1). After visiting family in the Washington, D.C. area, I once again embarked for the West. Corky and I were married and we made our home in an old CCC building on the Sullivan Lake Ranger District of the Colville National Forest in the northeast corner of Washington. My job was assistant ranger in charge of timber management. Corky taught grade school in the town of Metaline Falls, seven miles from the ranger station.

In 1958 Corky and I spent several weeks in Europe, and on the way back managed a visit home, but only briefly. In 1960 Ma came to visit us for several weeks. She had become acquainted with the Rocky Mountains when she was in Missoula for my graduation, but this trip allowed her to become more intimately familiar with them. She loved the Rockies. Our home overlooked Sullivan Lake, a beautiful body of water a half mile wide and three miles long. Towering immediately next to the lake was Hall Mountain. Ma spent many hours basking in the sun and staring at the lake and mountain. Her imagination would soar and she wrote her thoughts in a poem:

To the Friend of Our Imagination
Mr. Hall of Hall Mountain

I

Good-day, Mr. Hall of the mountain—
Let the day be stormy or fair,
We like to think we can see you
Milking your goats up there.

Are those trees in the back in your orchard?
Can you grow a good apple and pear?
Is there room down behind those bare ledges
To raise beans and potatoes somewhere?

We know that your days are all happy.
We're happy because of you.
There's lots of good fun and pleasure
Imagining what you do.

II

Good-night, Mr. Hall of the mountain—
The shadows are growing deep—
We folks that are down in the valley
Will soon find it's time to sleep.

Do you, way up there on your hillside
When the sun drops behind the crest,
Do you seek the quiet of slumber,
Do you, too, lie down and rest?

Or do you just keep up a vigil
'Neath clouds or the starlight's glow,
As dreamily, oft you look downward
Where the lake lies so still below?

Good-night, Mr. Hall,
Good-night.

Her stay was obviously an adventure for her, and one couldn't help but be impressed by her enthusiasm for every new encounter.

Corky and I went back East again in 1961. This visit was more extended than our last, but still not long enough to get acquainted with the vast changes rapidly occurring, or to overcome the feeling we were visitors from a distant place. It was long enough, however, to have a good visit with my mother. She was always interested in what we were doing and managed to make me feel it was only yesterday that we had an intimate conversation—and she let us go like she would see us tomorrow.

In 1963 we moved to Powell Ranger Station where I was assigned the district ranger position. It was a large district with a portion of the Selway/Bitterroot Wilderness within its boundaries. The Lochsa Highway had just been completed and provided good access within a quarter of a mile of the station, but the facilities were still rather primitive. The buildings were mostly log structures and there was no electricity or commercial telephone line. We did, however, have a grounded line (with a crank telephone) and a connection to the operator in Missoula—allowing us to be "patched-in" to commercial service.

Shortly after we arrived I wrote my mother an enthusiastic letter with considerable detail about the challenges of my new job. Once again I signed my letter in the college-day way—"Love, R."

My brother Earl called me in July of 1964. He said Ma was in the hospital and was not likely to last much longer. Her heart was troubling her and the doctor was doubtful she would improve. Earl advised an airplane flight right away if I wanted to see her before she died. He cautioned that some of our siblings didn't think we should "gather around" lest she sense the seriousness of her condition. Corky and I decided to go immediately with our two-year old son, Chris.

When we arrived at the hospital Ma's head and shoulders were covered by an oxygen tent. I opened it and leaned to kiss her. She said, "It's so good to see you, but what are you doing here?"

"I've been detailed to Washington to work on a special project," I lied.

"That's nice," she responded, in a way that let me know she still knew when I wasn't telling the truth.

I hesitated, then said, "Actually, Ma, I came for only one reason, to see you."

She smiled and said, "Thank you, I'm so tired of all the lies."

She obviously knew her situation and wasn't nearly as threatened as those who thought we needed to be careful not to let her know how sick she was.

She wanted to see our son, Chris, and asked that we bring him in to visit the next day.

"But they don't allow small children in the hospital," I explained.

"You let me worry about that," she said, "you just get him here."

She evidently had made arrangements with the doctor because in those days that kind of visitation was unusual. When we arrived the next day the oxygen tent had been removed. It was the only time we visited that she was not covered by it. Chris crawled around on the bed and Ma spoke with him and held him. You'd have thought it was her first grandchild, not her fourteenth. It was a terrific visit. The oxygen tent had not just been opened, or set aside close by, it had been taken from the room. I thought it rather remarkable that both my mother and her doctor were able to agree the unimpeded visit with Chris was a higher priority than the oxygen.

After a lengthy visit, Corky took Chris and left the room. I remained for a few moments to tell her how much I appreciated her unencumbered time with Chris.

"Oh, the pleasure was mine," she bubbled, "I'm so happy to have had the opportunity to meet him." Then she paused and smiled at me. After a few moments of silence she said, "You know, Frank, it won't be long before I will be seeing your father."

I thought, "How typical of her." She hadn't seen the only man she ever loved for 26 years, but she didn't say, "I will be seeing Wallace, or I will be seeing my loving husband." She said, "I will be seeing *your* father."

Then she added, "That will be a high-mountain two-manner."

EPILOGUE

When my mother said, "That will be a high-mountain two-manner," all I could do was smile. What a profound understanding of how to convey so much while saying so little. She had lived those days in the early 50s when I was smokejumping, and she remembered all the stories because they had become a part of her. In that brief moment our souls touched. It was not a time of sadness, and it was not emotional—it was bliss. She closed her eyes, but not just because she was tired or needed oxygen. She had stepped into another place. She had concluded our time together, for that day, anyway.

She had clearly communicated several things beyond what was contained in those two sentences. She had said all is well. She said she was looking forward to what was to come next. She said she loved me. Even though I visited her several more times before returning to Powell, I knew on that special day she had sent me on my way with her blessing, just as she had done so many times before.

We returned to Powell while my mother was still in the hospital. Earl called me a short time later. Mother had died. I shared the news with Corky, then felt the need to be alone. I began to walk down the heavily forested road leading to Elk Summit. My siblings had assured me they didn't expect me to make a second trip when she died. I was comfortable with the decision and didn't feel needed. They had each other and could adequately take care of all that needed to be done. But what I hadn't prepared myself for was the loss I would feel at not being there. I knew they were circling the wagons and I felt a great need to participate.

As I walked, surrounded by silence, I didn't think much, just felt. I knew her death was coming and thought I was prepared, but no one ever is. I'm sure my eyes were wet for a spell, but what I remember most was that I found myself smiling, and thinking of Ma and her new adventure—her high-mountain two-manner.

NOTES

Note 1, Chapter 3, Fort Keogh

A return to Fort Keogh.

Corky, and I took a tour of my old haunts at Fort Keogh in 1995. The Forest Service no longer had a presence at Fort Keogh because their studies were absorbed by the Agriculture Research Service, another branch of the Department of Agriculture. Most of the buildings at the station were new since the 1950s. The grand old military houses had been razed, except for two. One sat in a field, presumably en route to a new location, and another had recently been moved next to the Range Riders Museum where it would be preserved. It was nostalgic to look inside and feel the past.

Larry's house was very much the same, not surprising since it was probably the newest building when I worked there. It was referred to as the "Forest Service house," perhaps the only remnant of the agency's past presence.

Janice, the receptionist, introduced us to Byron, a researcher at the fort who spent a lot of time in the field. He took us on a tour of the rangeland. I had intended to peruse the place on our own, but in recent years all gates were kept locked because of vandalism.

The road location had changed since I worked there and no longer skirted Camel Hump or the row of cottonwood trees where I had creased the fender of my truck. It was not until we reached the trap at Hogback that I clearly recognized features.

The cabin was familiar, but the front porch was gone, giving me the feeling that its character had been diminished. It was used only as a storage shed. Electricity had been extended to Hogback, so the windmill had been removed and replaced with an electric pump. The arrangement of the watering tank and the fences delineating the six pastures was unchanged.

The cattle, however, were another matter. Gaping holes (about eight inches square) had been cut in their sides by veterinarians as part of a study. It was appalling to see, but the cattle didn't seem uncomfortable. If the sight wouldn't turn you off, the stench certainly would. The smell of partially digested food was pervasive. I was convinced I wouldn't want to live there under those conditions.

Corky and I walked up the sloping ground to the east that was the namesake of the area—Hogback Ridge. The general landscape was the most enduring unchanged aspect of the visit. The ridge in the distance I called Identification Point unexpectedly affected me. I wouldn't have been able to describe its appearance, but every detail was intimately familiar. Its sight instantly brought back a mixture of feelings difficult to label, but nonetheless intensely real. Standing there on Hogback Ridge seemed like looking down at the cabin and myself 44 years ago, and I was swept with a feeling of adventure, anticipation, and loneliness.

Many people say, "never go back," but I found it rewarding.

Note 2, Chapter 9, A Record Fire Season

Smokejumper Reunions

I missed several smokejumper reunions, but Corky and I attended the ones in 1995 and 2004. They were especially enjoyable because Ted and his wife, Arlys, were there to share in the celebrations.

Before each reunion, I steeped myself in the research I had done at the jumper base and in the letters I had written to my mother. I'm afraid I allowed several old friends to think I had a much better memory than I actually possess, but it was fun to spill out minute detail, like it all happened just last week.

Corky had mentioned several times that she thought jumpers were hurt more often than they related in general conversation. She decided to run a survey on her own. After a few minutes of conversation with an ex-jumper, she would say, ". . . and how were you hurt?" It was amazing how many told of their mishaps, and many were not of the Band-Aid variety. It became evident that while most of us thought of ourselves as injury-free, when we thought about it, we had all experienced some bad scrapes—and many could easily have been more serious. But at the time, we were young and oblivious.

At both reunions I spoke with several fellows who told stories about one guy or another in the 1953 season trying to hide so he could get a little rest before going out again. The anecdotes were humorous, but there was an implied recognition that conditions were bad and we were all standing on a threshold of work overload.

I remember one fellow in particular because we worked together for awhile after our jumping days were over. I respected him and knew he was a hard working, dedicated person. When I asked if he thought we tended to exaggerate the stress we felt when the season was at its peak, he unhesitatingly said, "Not a bit. I was so out of it that I just couldn't go on, but I should have."

"What do you mean, you should have," I asked?

"I quit, and it's something I have regretted ever since," he candidly replied. "I felt like I let everyone down, and to this day it haunts me. I was just so tired and sick I couldn't continue."

"What do you mean, sick?" I queried.

"I had had a miserable cold for over a week and felt I couldn't get on top of it without more rest. I had no way of knowing at the time, but if I had just toughed it out another week, the fire season would have been over. As it was, Brauer was more than a little unhappy with my early departure," he lamented.

"But you jumped the next year, didn't you?"

"Yes, but it took a lot of begging before Brauer let me come back. I was truly grateful for an opportunity to redeem myself, but I still feel bad about leaving early in the 1953 season."

I thought he was rough on himself. He was carrying a lot of baggage that he should have put down a long time ago, and I told him so. Besides, Brauer knew he was a good man or he wouldn't have let him come back.

Note 3, Chapter 9, A Record Fire Season

Jerry Soaps

In the course of writing *High-mountain Two-manner*, I contacted many jumpers I hadn't spoken with since those days when we jumped together. In every instance, the contact was richly rewarding, and they were all special. One, however, lingered in my thoughts.

With considerable difficulty I finally contacted Jerry Soaps in 2005. He was surprised to hear from me, and it seemed apparent he hadn't spoken with many of his jumping buddies since he jumped in 1953. After that one summer, he entered the Navy and something ironic happened. A special assignment was available for a sailor who had parachute experience. Jerry applied, but when an interviewer asked how he happened to parachute, Jerry told him about the smokejumpers. The interrogator figured out that for his story to be true, Jerry would only have been 17 years old. It was obvious that the Forest Service would not hire smokejumpers that young, and he was dropped from further consideration in the special assignment.

Jerry said he felt that some of his friends were skeptical that he ever spent a summer jumping on forest fires. I suggested to him that if my account of those years was ever put in book form, perhaps it would add to the veracity of his claim. He seemed pleased with the prospect.

Jerry, I hope this does it!

Edwards Brothers Malloy
Thorofare, NJ USA
November 18, 2013